# Fodor's 91 Bermuda

W9-DJI-049

Fodor's Travel Publications, Inc.
New York and London

**Copyright © 1991**
**by Fodor's Travel Publications, Inc.**

Fodor's is a trademark of Fodor's Travel Publications, Inc.

All rights reserved under International and Pan-American Copyright Conventions. Published in the United States by Fodor's Travel Publications, Inc., a subsidiary of Random House, Inc., New York, and simultaneously in Canada by Random House of Canada Limited, Toronto. Distributed by Random House, Inc., New York.

*No maps, illustrations, or other portions of this book may be reproduced in any form without written permission from the publishers.*

ISBN 0-679-01883-2

"America's Rebel Colonies and Bermuda: Getting a Bang for Their Buckwheat" is excerpted from *Bermuda Journey,* by William Zuill. Copyright © 1946 by William Edward Sears Zuill. Reprinted by permission of the Estate of William Edward Sears Zuill.

"Following in the Tracks of the Bermuda Railway," by Ben Davidson, was originally published as "Off Bermuda's Beaten Track." Reprinted with permission from *Travel & Leisure,* November 1987. Copyright © 1987 by American Express Publishing Corporation. All rights reserved.

**Fodor's Bermuda**

**Editor:** Andrew Barbour
**Contributors:** Suzanne Brown, John DeMers, Honey Naylor, Peter Oliver
**Art Director:** Fabrizio LaRocca
**Cartographer:** David Lindroth
**Illustrator:** Karl Tanner
**Cover Photograph:** Andrew McKim/Masterfile

**Design:** Vignelli Associates

## Special Sales

Fodor's Travel Publications are available at special discounts for bulk purchases (100 copies or more) for sales promotions or premiums. Special editions, including personalized covers, excerpts of existing guides, and corporate imprints, can be created in large quantities for special needs. For more information, write to Special Marketing, Fodor's Travel Publications, 201 East 50th St., New York, NY 10022. Inquiries from the United Kingdom should be sent to Fodor's Travel Publications, 20 Vauxhall Bridge Rd., London SW1V 2SA.

MANUFACTURED IN THE UNITED STATES OF AMERICA
10 9 8 7 6 5 4 3 2 1

# Contents

**Maps**

# Foreword

For their help in preparing this guide, we would like to thank the Bermuda National Trust; Connie Dey; Elsbeth Gibson; Stephen Martin of Bermuda Small Properties; David Mitchell for the Bermuda Collection; Jacqueline Pash of Porter/Novelli; Judy Blatman of Princess Hotels; Vivian Guerrero of Trust House Forte; Charles Webbe and Pam Wissing of the Bermuda Department of Tourism; Lisa Weisbord of Hill & Knowlton; and Jim Zuill of the Bermuda Book Store.

While every care has been taken to assure the accuracy of the information in this guide, the passage of time will always bring change, and consequently, the publisher cannot accept responsibility for errors that may occur.

All prices and opening times quoted here are based on information supplied to us at press time. Hours and admission fees may change, however, and the prudent traveler will avoid inconvenience by calling ahead.

Fodor's wants to hear about your travel experiences, both pleasant and unpleasant. When a hotel or restaurant fails to live up to its billing, let us know and we will investigate the complaint and revise our entries where the facts warrant it.

Send your letters to the editors of Fodor's Travel Publications, 201 E. 50th St., New York, NY 10022.

# Highlights '91 and Fodor's Choice

# Highlights '91

In January 1990, troubled **Eastern Airlines** cancelled its flights to Bermuda, but service has suffered little because **USAir** and **Continental Airlines** both initiated service to the island in June 1989. **American Airlines** has doubled its carrying capacity with DC10 service from JFK in New York and Boeing 727 service from both Boston and Raleigh/Durham. **Delta Airlines** has also increased service to Bermuda with the addition of Tri-Star flights from Atlanta.

On the hotel scene, the luxury **Bermudiana,** near downtown Hamilton, has been closed since 1988 and its future remains unclear. The hilltop **Hamiltonian Hotel** has been demolished; a residential development that includes some time-share units will be built in its place. The **Banana Beach** and **Flamingo,** adjoining hotels on the south shore, have both been sold and are now closed. The new owner plans to build a luxury resort on the site, which boasts 1,500 feet of oceanfront. Slated to open in 1992, the resort has been leased to **Ritz Carlton.** The **Inverurie Hotel** reopened in early 1990 as the **Palm Reef Hotel.** Now classified as a small hotel, the Palm Reef has 94 guest rooms, including 60 rooms in the main building and 34 rooms in the pool wing.

In 1990, the government restricted the number of cruise-ship visits to Bermuda to four per week, none on weekends. Bermuda has always been a popular cruise destination, so the demand for cabins is likely to be high, and prices can be expected to rise. Despite the new policy, one of the cargo sheds in St. George's is being renovated for use as a **cruise ship terminal.** Scheduled for completion in April 1991, the new terminal is expected to resemble the cruise facilities in Hamilton. The multimillion-dollar revitalization of **Dockyard,** Bermuda's third cruise-ship terminal, also continues. On Ireland Island in the West End, Dockyard was area headquarters for the British Royal Navy until 1951. The old naval base is now home to the Maritime Museum, a new Visitors Information Centre, arts and crafts centers, and a luxury mall. Reaching Dockyard by road is considerably easier now, too, thanks to the inauguration of **express bus service** in 1990. Buses leave Hamilton every 15 minutes for Dockyard, and the nonstop trip takes about a half hour—half the time of regular bus service.

Visitors can gather information about various restaurants and attractions on the island at the new **CompuGuide Video Guide Kiosks,** available in Visitors Information Centres and in some hotels. A free map and index of subscribing restaurants and attractions are also available. For more information, call 809/292–5816.

**Ocean View Golf & Country Club,** taken over by the Bermudian government in 1988, is gradually making improvements to the course, which had fallen into disrepair. Several holes have been lengthened or redesigned, and a new clubhouse is scheduled to be built in 1991. Also new on the sports scene are two competitions: the **Diadora Youth Soccer Cup** and the **Bermuda Triathlon.** Held in March, the soccer tournament will bring together teams from the United States, Canada, Britain, and the Caribbean. The triathlon, held in late September, is open to all and relatively soft as triathlons go: a 1-mile swim, a 15-mile cycling leg, and a 6-mile run. (For more information, *see* Chapter 6, Sports and Fitness.)

In 1988, the United States and Bermuda signed a tax treaty, giving meetings held in Bermuda the same tax privileges as those held in the United States. Less than a year after the signing of the treaty, Bermudian officials noted a significant rise in the amount of group travel to the island from the United States.

# Fodor's Choice

No two people will agree on what makes a perfect vacation, but it's fun and helpful to know what others think. We hope you'll have a chance to experience some of Fodor's Choices yourself in Bermuda. For detailed information about each entry, refer to the appropriate chapter.

## Beaches

Chaplin Bay

Horseshoe Bay

Somerset Long Bay

Warwick Long Bay

## Favorite Outdoor Activities

Offshore wreck diving

Snorkeling at Church Bay

Golfing at Port Royal Golf & Country Club

Running or riding through the dunes at South Shore Park

## Favorite Sights

Pink-and-white cottages dotting the island

Pipers going at full kilt on the green at Ft. Hamilton

The children's room at Verdmont

The astonishing blues and greens of the sea

Statues by Desmond Fountain

Pastel Hamilton from the deck of a ferry

The narrow alleys in St. George's

The view from Gibb's Hill Lighthouse

## Lodging

Cambridge Beaches *(Very Expensive)*

Horizons & Cottages *(Very Expensive)*

The Reefs *(Very Expensive)*

The Princess *(Expensive)*

Rosedon *(Expensive)*

Waterloo House *(Expensive)*

Oxford House *(Moderate)*

Pretty Penny *(Moderate)*

Little Pomander Guest House *(Inexpensive)*

Salt Kettle House *(Inexpensive)*

## Restaurants

Waterlot Inn *(Very Expensive)*

Plantation *(Expensive)*

Black Horse Tavern *(Moderate)*

Colony Pub *(Moderate)*

Once Upon a Table *(Moderate)*

Dennis's Hideaway *(Inexpensive)*

## Special Moments

The ferry ride from Hamilton to Somerset

Driving around the island in a London cab

Browsing through the Bermuda Book Store

Watching the Gombey Dancers

Swimming and sunning at Horseshoe Bay

## Taste Treats

A Dark and Stormy (or two or three) at Casey's Bar

Diet destroyers at Fourways Pastry shops

Burgers at the Ice Queen at 3 AM

A rum swizzle at the Swizzle Inn

Shark hash at Dennis's Hideaway

## Bermuda

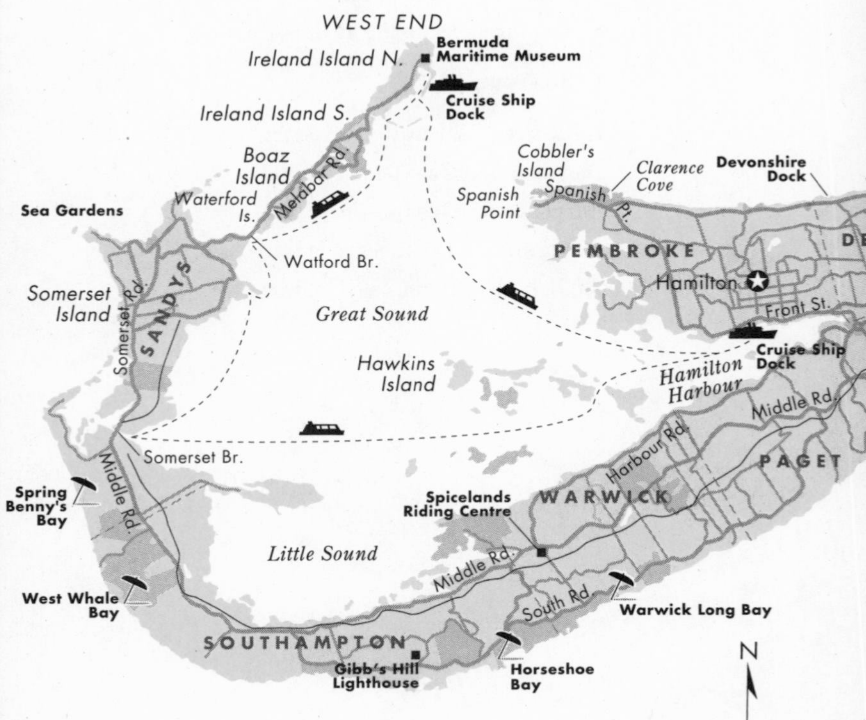
ATLANTIC OCEAN
WEST END
Ireland Island N.
Bermuda Maritime Museum
Cruise Ship Dock
Ireland Island S.
Boaz Island
Melabar Rd.
Waterford Is.
Sea Gardens
Watford Br.
Cobbler's Island
Clarence Cove
Devonshire Dock
Spanish Point
Spanish Pt.
PEMBROKE
DE
Hamilton
Front St.
Somerset Island
Somerset Rd.
SANDYS
Great Sound
Hawkins Island
Cruise Ship Dock
Hamilton Harbour
Middle Rd.
Somerset Br.
Harbour Rd.
PAGET
Spring Benny's Bay
Middle Rd.
Spicelands Riding Centre
WARWICK
Little Sound
Middle Rd.
West Whale Bay
South Rd.
Warwick Long Bay
SOUTHAMPTON
Gibb's Hill Lighthouse
Horseshoe Bay
N

Fort St. Catherine
Tobacco Bay
St. Catherine Beach
ST. GEORGE'S
St. George's Island
Mullet Bay Rd.
St. George's
Cruise Ship Dock
St. George's Harbour
Ferry Rd.
St. David's Rd.
Bermuda Airport
St. David's Lighthouse
St. David's Island
The Causeway
Bermuda Perfumery
Bermuda Pottery
Crystal Caves
HAMILTON
Castle Harbour
Leamington Caves
Church Bay
Harrington Sound Rd.
TUCKER'S TOWN
Harrington Sound
Aquarium, Museum, and Zoo
Harrington Sound Rd.
John Smith's Bay
North Shore Rd.
SMITH'S
VONSHIRE
South Rd.
KEY
Cruise Ship
Ferry
Beach
Railway Trail
0
2 miles
0
3 km

## World Time Zones

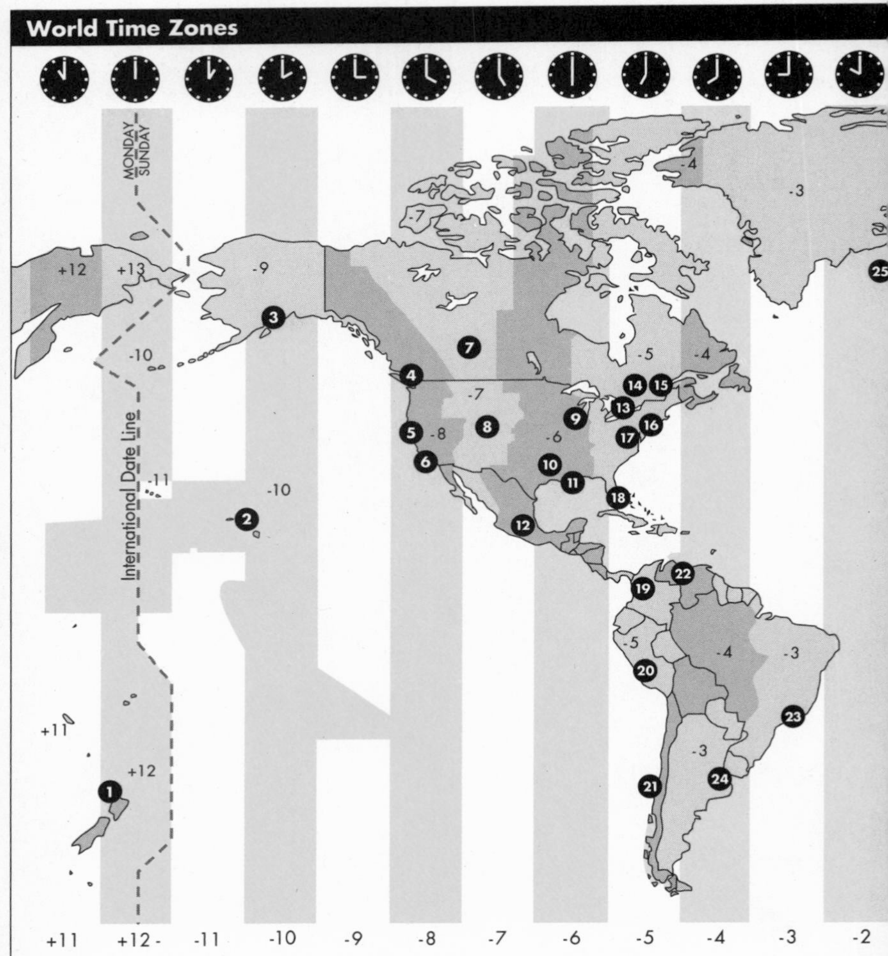


Numbers below vertical bands relate each zone to Greenwich Mean Time (0 hrs.). Local times frequently differ from these general indications, as indicated by light-face numbers on map.

Algiers, **29**
Anchorage, **3**
Athens, **41**
Auckland, **1**
Baghdad, **46**
Bangkok, **50**
Beijing, **54**
Berlin, **34**
Bogotá, **19**
Budapest, **37**
Buenos Aires, **24**
Caracas, **22**
Chicago, **9**
Copenhagen, **33**
Dallas, **10**
Delhi, **48**
Denver, **8**
Djakarta, **53**
Dublin, **26**
Edmonton, **7**
Hong Kong, **56**
Honolulu, **2**
Istanbul, **40**
Jerusalem, **42**
Johannesburg, **44**
Lima, **20**
Lisbon, **28**
London (Greenwich), **27**
Los Angeles, **6**
Madrid, **38**
Manila, **57**

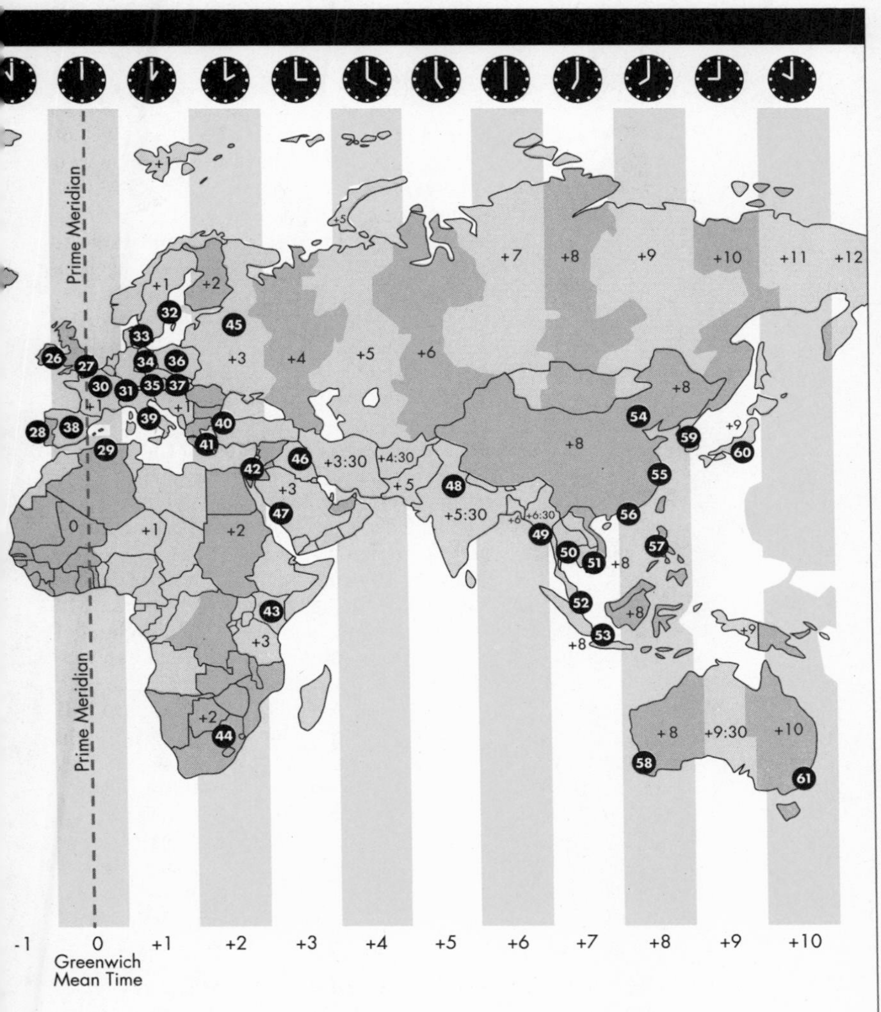


Mecca, **47**
Mexico City, **12**
Miami, **18**
Montreal, **15**
Moscow, **45**
Nairobi, **43**
New Orleans, **11**
New York City, **16**

Ottawa, **14**
Paris, **30**
Perth, **58**
Reykjavík, **25**
Rio de Janeiro, **23**
Rome, **39**
Saigon, **51**

San Francisco, **5**
Santiago, **21**
Seoul, **59**
Shanghai, **55**
Singapore, **52**
Stockholm, **32**
Sydney, **61**
Tokyo, **60**

Toronto, **13**
Vancouver, **4**
Vienna, **35**
Warsaw, **36**
Washington, DC, **17**
Yangon, **49**
Zürich, **31**

# Introduction

Basking in the Atlantic 508 miles due east of Cape Hatteras, Bermuda is one of the wealthiest countries in the world—average per capita income is $20,000. Bermuda has no income tax, no sales tax, no slums, no unemployment, and no major crime problem. Don't come to Bermuda expecting a tropical paradise where laid-back locals wander around barefoot drinking piña coladas. On Bermuda's 20 square miles, you will find neither towering mountains, glorious rain forests, nor exotic volcanos. Instead, pastel cottages, quaint shops, and manicured gardens are indicative of a more staid, suburban way of life. As a British diplomat once said, "Bermuda is terribly middle-age"—and in many ways he was right. Most of the island is residential; the speed limit is 20 mph; golf and tennis are popular pastimes; the majority of visitors are over 40 years old; restaurants and shops are expensive; and casual attire in public is frowned upon. The population of 54,000 is 61% black and 39% white, but Bermudians speak the Queen's English in the Queen's own accent. White Bermudians, in particular, have strived to create a middle-class England of their own. And like almost all colonies, the Bermudian version is more insular, more conservative, and more English than the original. Pubs, fish-and-chips, and cricket are just outward manifestations of a fierce loyalty to Britain and everything it represents (or used to represent). A self-governing British colony, with a Parliament that dates to 1620, Bermudians love pomp and circumstance, British tradition, and Bermudian history. Great ceremony attends the convening of Parliament; marching bands parade through the capital in honor of the Queen's official birthday; regimental bands and bagpipers reenact centuries-old ceremonies; and tea is served each afternoon.

Bermuda wears its history like a comfortable old coat—land is too valuable to permit the island's legacy to be cordoned off for mere display. A visitor need only wander through the 17th-century buildings of St. George's, now home to shops and private residences, to realize that Bermudian history remains part of the fabric of life, with each successive generation adding its own thread of achievement and color. Indeed, the island's isolation and diminutive size have forged a continuity of place and tradition almost totally missing in the United States. Walk into Trimingham's or A. S. Cooper & Son department stores, and you are likely to be helped by a descendant of the original founders. The same names from history keep cropping up—Tucker, Carter, Trott—and a single lane in St. George's can conjure up centuries of memories and events. Even today, the brief love affair in 1804 between Irish poet Thomas Moore and the married Hester Tucker—the "Nea" of his odes—is gossiped about with a zeal usually reserved for the transgressions of a neighbor. Bermuda's attachment to its history is more than a product of its size, however. Through its past, Bermuda invokes its own sense of identity and reinforces its relationship with Britain. Otherwise, cast off in the Atlantic more than 3,445 miles from London (yet only 508 miles from the United States), Bermuda would probably have succumbed to American cultural influences long ago.

Since the very beginning, the fate of this small colony in the Atlantic has been linked to that of the United States. The crew of the *Sea Venture*, whose wreck on Bermuda during a hurricane in 1609 began the settlement of the island, was actually on its way to Jamestown in Virginia. Indeed, the passenger list of the *Sea Venture* reads like a veritable *Who's Who* of early American history. Aboard were Sir Thomas Gates, Deputy Governor of Jamestown; Christopher Newport, who had led the first expedition to Jamestown; and John Rolfe, whose second wife was Princess Pocahontas. In succeeding centuries, Bermuda has been a remarkable barometer of the evolving relationship between the United States and Britain. In 1775, Bermuda was secretly forced to give gunpowder to George Washington in return for the lifting of a trade blockade that threatened the island with starvation. In the War of 1812, Bermuda was the staging post for the British fleet's attack on Washington, DC. And with Britain facing a national crisis in 1940, the United States was given land on Bermuda to build a Naval Air Station in exchange for ships and supplies. As recently as 1990, Prime Minister Thatcher and President Bush held talks on the island.

The fact that Bermuda—just two hours by air from New York—has maintained its English character through the years is obviously part of its appeal for the more than half-million Americans (89% of all tourists) who flock here each year. More importantly, however, Bermuda means sun, sea, and sand. This bastion of Britain boasts a mild climate year-round, pink beaches, turquoise waters, coral reefs, 17th-century villages, and splendid golf courses (Bermuda has more golf courses per square mile than anywhere else in the world).

Bermuda did not always seem so attractive. After all, more than 300 wrecks lie submerged on those same reefs where divers now frolic. William Strachey, Secretary-elect for Virginia and a passenger on the *Sea Venture* in 1609, wrote that Bermuda was "a place so terrible to all that ever touched on them—such tempests, thunders and other fearful objects are seen and heard about those islands that they are called The Devills Islands, feared and avoided by all sea travellers above any place in the world." For the crew of the *Sea Venture*, however, the 181 small islands that comprise Bermuda meant salvation. Contrary to rumor, the islands proved to be unusually fertile and hospitable, supporting the crew during the construction of two new ships, in which they departed for Jamestown on May 10th, 1610.

Shakespeare drew on the accounts of the survivors in *The Tempest*, written in 1611. The wreck of the *Sea Venture* on harsh yet benificent Bermuda—"these infortunate (yet fortunate) islands," as one survivor described them—contained all the elements of Shakespearean tragicomedy: That out of loss something greater is often born. Just as Prospero loses the duchy of Milan only to regain it and secure the kingdom of Naples for his daughter, Admiral Sir George Somers lost a ship but gained an island. Today, Bermuda's motto is "Quo Fata Ferunt" (Whither the Fates Carry Us), an expression of sublime confidence in the same providence that carried the *Sea Venture* safely to shore.

That confidence has largely been justified over the years, but concerns have recently been raised about congestion, overfishing, reef damage, and a declining quality of life. Nearly 600,000 visitors a year are the golden eggs that many Bermudians feel are now killing the goose. In the face of such an influx of tourists, the behavior of some service employees, particularly bus drivers and young store clerks, has become sullen and rude. Traffic jams leading into Hamilton, the island's capital, are no longer a rarity, despite the fact that families can only have one car and car rentals are prohibited. In 1990, the government restricted the number of cruise-ship visits to four per week, citing the large numbers of passengers who add to the congestion but contribute little to the island's coffers. Instead, the Bermuda Department of Tourism hopes to attract a wealthier clientele (Bermuda's tourists are already among the most affluent anywhere), preferably during the less-frequented winter season, when golf and tennis are the island's major attractions.

When all is said and done, however, Bermuda's problems stem from a surfeit of advantages rather than a dearth, and almost every island nation would gladly inherit them. The "still-vexed Bermoothes" is how Shakespeare described this Atlantic pearl, but the author of *The Tempest* may have changed his tune if he had had a chance to swim at Horseshoe Bay, or hit a mashie-niblick to the 15th green at Port Royal. Who knows, instead of referring to a storm-wracked island, *The Tempest* might have been Shakespeare's reaction to a missed putt on the 18th.

# 1 Essential Information

# Before You Go

## Government Tourist Offices

The **Bermuda Department of Tourism** has offices in the following locations:

**In Bermuda** Global House, 43 Church Street, Hamilton HM BX, Bermuda, tel. 809/292–0023, fax 809/292–7537.

**In the United States** 310 Madison Avenue, New York, NY 10017, tel. 800/223–6106, in NY 800/223–6107, or 212/818–9800 in New York City, fax 212/983–5289; 235 Peachtree Street NE, Suite 2008, Atlanta, GA 30303, tel. 404/524–1541, fax 404/586–9933; 44 School St., Suite 1010, Boston, MA 02108, tel. 617/742–0405, fax 617/723–7786; Randolph-Wacker Building, Suite 1070, 150 North Wacker Drive, Chicago, IL 60606, tel. 312/782–5486, fax 312/704–6996; John A. Tetley Co. Inc., 3075 Wilshire Blvd., Suite 601, Los Angeles, CA 90010–1293, tel. 800/421–0000 or 800/252–0211 in CA, fax 213/487–5467.

**In Canada** 1200 Bay Street, Suite 1004, Toronto, Ont. M5R 2A5, tel. 800/387–1304, fax 416/923–4840.

**In the United Kingdom** Bermuda Tourism, BCB Ltd., 1 Battersea Church Road, London SW11 3LY, tel. 071/734–8813, fax 071/352–6501.

## Tour Groups

The majority of visitors to Bermuda opt for independent travel packages. Group tours are scarce for good reason: Because the island is just 20 square miles in size (slightly smaller than Manhattan), it's easy to get around on your own via taxi or moped. Furthermore, Bermuda is a resort destination, offering sun-and-sea vacations that require little organization. An incredible number of packages is available from tour operators, airlines, and travel agencies. Some are land only; others include round-trip airfare. Which package you choose will depend mostly on your pocketbook. Accommodations range from small guest houses to super-deluxe resorts. As usual, you get what you pay for.

When evaluating any tour, be sure to find out: (1) exactly what expenses are included, particularly side trips, meals, entertainment, taxes, and tips; (2) the ratings of all hotels on the itinerary and the facilities they offer; (3) the additional cost of single, rather than double, accommodations if you are traveling alone; and (4) the number of travelers in your group. Note whether the tour operator reserves the right to change hotels, routes, or even prices after you've booked, and check the operator's policy regarding cancellations, complaints, and trip-interruption insurance. Many tour operators request that packages be booked through a travel agent; there is no additional charge for doing so.

Listed below is a sampling of operators and packages to give you an idea of what is available. For additional resources, contact your travel agent or the Bermuda Department of Tourism.

## Package Deals for Independent Travelers

**In the United States**

**Bermuda Travel Planners** (420 Lexington Ave., Suite 401, New York, NY 10170, tel. 212/867–2718 or 800/323–2020) offers a wide selection of four- to seven-night air/hotel packages that include a sightseeing cruise, meal plan of your choice, discount coupons, and other perks.

**Globetrotters** (124 Mt. Auburn St., Cambridge, MA 02138, tel. 617/661–4555 or 800/999–9696), **Travel Impressions** (465 Smith St., Farmingdale, NY 11735, tel. 516/845–8000 or 800/284–0044), and **Pan Am Holidays** (124 Mt. Auburn St., Cambridge, MA 02138, tel. 800/THE–TOUR) offer a dozen hotels and a range of departure dates from which you can choose. Packages are available for three to seven nights and include round-trip airfare.

**Delta Dream Vacations** (110 Broward Blvd., Ft. Lauderdale, FL 33301, tel. 305/522–1440 or 800/872–7786) has four-night air/hotel packages in small and large hotels, guest houses, housekeeping cottages and apartments, and cottage colonies.

**American Express Vacations** (Box 5014, Atlanta GA 30302, tel. 800/241–1700, or 800/282–0800 in GA) offers three- and seven-night stays at several hotels; extra nights are available. Airfare is not included.

**GoGo Tours** (69 Spring St., Ramsey, NJ 07446, tel. 201/934–3500 or 800/821–3731), a veritable supermarket of hotel packages, offers a range of accommodations for a minimum three-night stay; airfare is not included.

Other experienced operators include **Friendly Holidays** (1983 Marcus Ave., Lake Success, NY 11042, tel. 516/358–1200 or 800/221–9748) and **Martin Empire Tours** (1865 Palmer Ave., Larchmont, NY 10538, tel. 914/834–2805 or 800/232–8747).

**In the United Kingdom**

**Cadogan Travel** (Cadogan House, 9–10 Portland St., Southampton SO9 1ZP, tel. 0703/332661) offers the widest range of holidays in Bermuda, with 10 hotels and nine houses all situated by the sea. Some of the houses also have pools.

**Elegant Resorts** (Lion House, 23 Watergate Row, Chester CH1 2LE, tel. 0244/329671) is a group of seven first-class cottage colonies and small hotels. Prices are high, but so are the quality of the facilities and the level of comfort.

**Silkcut Faraway Holidays** (Meon House, Petersfield, Hants. GU32 3JN, tel. 0730/65211) offers a variety of beach-based vacations, some in small hotels with no more than 15 rooms, and other more expensive packages in resorts.

**Tradewinds Faraway Holidays** (Station House, 81–83 Fulham High St., London SW6 3JP, tel. 071/731–8000) sells vacations in four Bermuda properties, three of them large international resorts, the other a cottage-style hotel.

## When to Go

Bermuda has a remarkably mild climate that seldom sees extremes of either heat or cold. During the winter (December–March), temperatures range from around 55°F at night to 70°F in the early afternoon. High, blustery winds can make the temperature feel cooler, however, as can Bermuda's high humidity. The hottest part of the year is between May and mid-October, when temperatures range from 75°F to 85°F, but 90°F is not uncommon in July and August. The summer months are somewhat drier, but rainfall is spread fairly evenly throughout the year. Bermuda depends solely on rain for its supply of fresh water, so residents usually welcome the brief storms that interrupt the pleasant weather. In August and September, hurricanes moving northward from the Caribbean sometimes batter the island.

During the summer season, the island teems with activities. Hotel barbecues and evening dances complement daytime sightseeing excursions, and the public beaches are always open. The one drawback, however, is the high cost of staying in a hotel. The pace during the off-season slows considerably. A few of the hotels and restaurants close, some of the sightseeing boats are dry-docked, and only the taxis and the St. George's minibus operate tours of the island. The majority of hotels remain open, however, slashing their rates by as much as 40%—similar rates apply during shoulder seasons (March–April and October–November). The weather at this time of year is perfect for golf and tennis, and visitors can still rent boats, tour the island, and take advantage of the myriad special events and walking tours offered (*see* Festivals and Seasonal Events, below).

**Climate** What follows are average daily maximum and minimum temperatures for Bermuda.

| | | | | | | | | |
|---|---|---|---|---|---|---|---|---|
| **Jan.** | 68F | 20C | **May** | 76F | 24C | **Sept.** | 85F | 29C |
| | 58 | 14 | | 65 | 18 | | 72 | 22 |
| **Feb.** | 68F | 20C | **June** | 81F | 27C | **Oct.** | 79F | 26C |
| | 58 | 14 | | 70 | 21 | | 70 | 21 |
| **Mar.** | 68F | 20C | **July** | 85F | 29C | **Nov.** | 74F | 23C |
| | 58 | 14 | | 74 | 23 | | 63 | 17 |
| **Apr.** | 72F | 22C | **Aug.** | 86F | 30C | **Dec.** | 70F | 21C |
| | 59 | 15 | | 74 | 23 | | 61 | 16 |

**Weather Trak** provides information on more than 750 cities around the world—450 of them in the United States. Dialing 900/370–8725 will connect you to a computer, with which you can communicate by touch tone at a cost of 75¢ for the first minute and 50¢ a minute thereafter. The computer plays a taped message, which tells you to dial a three-digit access code for information on your destination. The code is either the area code (for cities in the United States) or the first three letters of the name of the foreign city. For a list of all access codes, send a self-addressed stamped envelope to Cities, Box 7000, Dallas, TX 75209, or call 214/869–3035 or 800/247–3282.

## Festivals and Seasonal Events

Precise dates and information about any of the events listed below are available from the Bermuda Department of Tourism (*see* Government Tourist Offices, above).

**January** **Jan. 1: New Year's Day** is a public holiday.
**Jan. 18: Regimental Musical Display** is held at 8 PM on Front Street in Hamilton.

**January–February** **Jan. 11–Feb. 23: The Bermuda Festival** attracts internationally known artists for a series of concerts, dances, and theatrical performances (*see* Chapter 9, The Arts and Nightlife).

**February** **Feb. 1–3: Bermuda International Open Chess Tournament,** open to all visitors and residents, is an annual tournament at the Elbow Beach Hotel. Contact Anthony Simpson (Elbow Beach Hotel, Box HM 455, Hamilton HM BX, tel. 809/293–8077).

**Feb. 2–9: The Annual Regional Bridge Tournament** is held in the Southampton Princess Hotel.

**Feb. 8–13: Bermuda Round Dance Convention** is an annual meeting held at the Sonesta Beach Hotel.

**Feb. 13: Regimental Musical Display** is given at 8 PM on Front Street in Hamilton.

**Feb. 20–24: Bermuda Cloggers Festival** is held at the Sonesta Beach Hotel in Southampton.

**February–March** **The Bermuda Golf Festival**, a two-week event held at six courses, includes tournaments for men, women, juniors, and seniors of all abilities. Contact the Bermuda Golf Festival (GD/T Sports Marketing, 5520 Park Ave., Trumbull, CT 06611, tel. toll-free 800/282–7656 or 203/373–7146 in CT).

**March** **Mar. 6–10: Bermuda All Breed Championship Dog Shows & Obedience Trials** draws dog lovers from far and wide to the Botanical Gardens in Paget.

**Mar. 10–17: Bermuda Super Senior Invitational Tennis Championship** is an annual tournament held at the posh Coral Beach & Tennis Club in Paget.

**Mid-Mar.: Bermuda Horse and Pony Association Spring Show** features driving, jumping, and Western and flat classes at the Botanical Gardens in Paget.

**Mar. 19–23: Bermuda Amateur Golf Championship for Men** is played at the Mid Ocean Club in Tucker's Town.

**Mar. 20: Regimental Musical Display** is held at 8 PM on Front Street in Hamilton.

**March–April** **The Bermuda College Weeks**, an annual fling for American college students on spring break, offers a program of free events. Included are beach parties, dances, free lunches, boat cruises, calypso, rock bands, limbo shows, and a steel-band concert. Admission to each event is free with a complimentary "College Week Courtesy Card," which is issued to all college students with student identification. Dates vary to coincide with U.S. college vacation periods (*see* Student and Youth Travel, below).

**Hasty Pudding Theatricals,** by the satirical Hasty Pudding Club of Harvard University, are staged at the Hamilton City Hall Theatre. Tickets are sold at the Visitors Service Bureau in Hamilton (*see* Chapter 9, The Arts and Nightlife).

**Diadora Youth Soccer Cup** attracts teams from a variety of Atlantic nations, including the United Kingdom, the United States, Canada, and several Caribbean nations.

**April** **Bermuda Kite Festival** at Horseshoe Bay is a party for the whole family that includes games, races, and prizes for the winners.

**The Agricultural Exhibition,** held annually at the Botanical Gardens in Paget, has horse and pony shows, culinary exhibits, and displays of Bermuda crafts.

**The Peppercorn Ceremony,** an annual event undertaken amid great pomp and circumstance, celebrates the payment of one peppercorn in rent to the government by the Lodge of St.

George No. 200 of the Grand Lodge of Scotland for their headquarters in the Old State House in St. George's.

**April–May** **Open Houses & Garden Tours**, sponsored by the Garden Club of Bermuda, give visitors the chance to walk through many of Bermuda's historic homes each Wednesday afternoon. Most of these houses are closed to the public during the rest of the year.

**International Race Week** pits sailors from the United States, the United Kingdom, Canada, and other countries against Bermudians in a series of races on the Great Sound. Sunfish and sail-board races are held in Shelly Bay.

**April–October** **The Beat Retreat Ceremony** is performed twice monthly by the Bermuda Regiment Band, the Bermuda Isles Pipe Band with Dancers, and members of the Bermuda Pipe Band. The historic ceremony is performed alternately on Front Street in Hamilton, King's Square in St. George's, and Dockyard in the West End. No performances are given in August.

**May** **Bermuda Heritage Month** features a host of cultural, commemorative, and sporting activities. The highlight is Bermuda Day, a public holiday that includes a parade at Bernard Park, a half-marathon (13 miles) for Bermuda residents only, and a Bermuda dinghy race in St. George's Harbour.

**The Pathmark Tennis Classic,** played in Bermuda since 1978, is an annual preview to the U.S. Open, bringing to the island such top-flight women players as Steffi Graf, Jennifer Capriati, and Zina Garrison. The event is held at one of the major hotels.

**June** **Newport–Bermuda Ocean Yacht Race,** sponsored by the Cruising Club of America and the Royal Bermuda Yacht Club, is a five-day race between Newport, Rhode Island, and Bermuda.

**Queen Elizabeth II's birthday** is celebrated in mid-June with marching bands parading down Front Street in Hamilton.

**July** **Marine Science Day** at the Bermuda Biological Station for Research (11 Biological La., Ferry Reach, St. George's, tel. 809/297–1880) gives visitors a rare opportunity to learn about marine research from the special perspective of a midocean island.

**August** **The Cup Match Cricket Festival** is a two-day match between East and West End cricket clubs. Held at the Somerset Cricket Club (Broome St., Sandys) or the St. George's Cricket Club (Wellington Slip Rd., St. George's), the match is one of the most festive occasions of the year and attracts thousands of fans who gather to picnic, chat, and dance.

**September** **Labour Day** is a public holiday featuring a wide range of activities, including a march from Union Square in Hamilton to Bernard Park.

**The Bermuda Fitted Dinghy Races,** hosted by the St. George's Dinghy & Sports Club, consist of three cup races in St. George's Harbour.

**October–November** **The Convening of Parliament** is preceded by the arrival of His Excellency the Governor, in plumed hat and full regalia, at the Cabinet Building on Front Street in Hamilton.

**The King Edward VII Gold Cup International Match Racing Tournament** is an exciting series of one-on-one yacht races between international and Bermudian competitors in the Great Sound.

**November** **Nov. 5: Guy Fawkes Night**, which originated from a plot to blow up the Houses of Parliament in Great Britain, is celebrated in

Bermuda with music by the Bermuda Regiment Band and the Bermuda Isles Pipe Band, the traditional burning of the Guy Fawkes effigy, food, and a half-hour fireworks display. All the festivities take place in the Keepyard of the Bermuda Maritime Museum at Dockyard.

**The World Rugby Classic** pits former international rugby players against the best players from Bermuda in a match at the National Sports Club (Middle Rd., Devonshire).

**Nov. 11: Remembrance Day** is a public holiday in memory of Bermuda's fallen soldiers and those of its allies. A parade, with Bermudian, British, and U.S. military units, the Bermuda Police, and veterans' organizations, begins at Front Street in Hamilton.

**December** **The West End Junior Chamber Santa Claus Parade** brings St. Nick to Somerset on a sleigh, along with bands, majorettes, floats, and other seasonal festivities. St. Nicholas will also be present at the Hamilton Jaycees Santa Claus Parade and the St. George's Junior Chamber Silver Bells Santa Comes to Town parade.

**Dec. 24: Christmas Eve** is celebrated at midnight candlelight services in churches of all denominations.

**Dec. 25: Christmas** is a public holiday.

**Dec. 26: Boxing Day** is a public holiday when Bermudians traditionally visit their friends and family. A variety of sporting events are also held, and the Gombey Dancers may put in an unexpected appearance.

## What to Pack

**Clothing** Bermudians are more formal than most Americans when it comes to dress. Although attire tends to be casual during the day—Bermuda shorts are acceptable, even for businessmen—cutoffs, short shorts, and halter tops are inappropriate. Swimsuits should not be worn outside pool areas or off the beach; you'll need a cover-up in the public areas of your hotel. Joggers may wear standard jogging shorts but should avoid appearing on public streets without a shirt. Bare feet and hair curlers in public are also frowned upon. In the evening, almost all restaurants and hotel dining rooms require that men wear a jacket and tie and that women dress comparably. For women, tailored slacks with a dressy blouse or sweater are fine, although most Bermudian women wear dresses or skirts and blouses. Bermudian men often wear Bermuda shorts (and proper knee socks) with a jacket and tie.

During the cooler months, you should bring lightweight woolens or cottons that you can wear in layers, depending on the vagaries of the weather; a few sweaters and a lightweight jacket are always a good idea, too. Regardless of the season, you should pack a swimsuit, a cover-up, sunscreen, and sunglasses, as well as an umbrella and raincoat. Comfortable walking shoes and a tote bag for carrying maps and cameras are a must. If you plan to play tennis, be aware that many courts require proper whites and that tennis balls in Bermuda are extremely expensive—bring your own balls if possible.

**Miscellaneous** An extra pair of glasses, contact lenses, or prescription sunglasses is always a good idea; it is important to pack any prescription medicines you use regularly, as well as any allergy medication you may need. Bermuda uses 110-volt, 60-cycle alternating current, so travelers from the United States won't need converters or adaptors for electrical appliances. Most cruise ships that use different voltages carry adaptors for electric razors. Pack light, because porters and luggage trolleys can be hard to find at New York airports, the main departure point for flights to Bermuda.

**Carry-on Luggage** Airlines generally allow each passenger one piece of carry-on luggage on international flights from the United States. The bag cannot exceed 45 inches (length × width × height) and must fit under the seat or in the overhead luggage compartment.

**Checked Luggage** Passengers are generally permitted to check two pieces of luggage, neither of which can exceed 62 inches (length × width × height) or weigh more than 70 pounds. Baggage allowances vary slightly among airlines, so check with the carrier or your travel agent before departure.

## Taking Money Abroad

The Bermudian dollar is on a par with the U.S. dollar, and the two currencies are used interchangeably. American money can be used anywhere, but change is often given in Bermudian currency. Try to avoid accumulating large amounts of this money, which is difficult to exchange for U.S. dollars in Bermuda and expensive to exchange in the United States. Loose change can be placed in marked boxes in the departure lounge at the airport—all donations go toward charity.

Most shops and some restaurants accept credit cards, but most hotels on the island insist on other forms of payment. Some take personal checks by prior arrangement (a letter from your bank is sometimes requested). U.S. traveler's checks are accepted almost everywhere. The most recognized traveler's checks are **American Express, Barclay's, Thomas Cook,** and those issued through major commercial banks such as **Citibank** and **Bank of America.** Some banks issue checks free to established customers, but most charge a 1% commission fee. Remember to take the addresses of offices where you can get refunds for lost or stolen traveler's checks. In Bermuda, the American Express representative is L. P. Gutteridge Ltd. (L. P. Gutteridge Bldg., Bermudiana Rd., Hamilton, tel. 809/295–4545). Thomas Cook is represented by Butterfield Travel Ltd. (75 Front St., Hamilton, tel. 809/292–1510).

## Getting Money from Home

There are at least three ways to get money from home:

1) Have it sent through a large commercial bank that has a branch where you are staying. The only drawback is that you must have an account with the bank; if not, you'll have to go through your own bank, and the process will be slower and more expensive.

2) Have it sent through American Express. If you are a cardholder, you can cash a personal check or a counter check at an American Express office for up to $1,000; $200 will be in cash and $800 in traveler's checks. A 1% commission is charged on the traveler's checks. You can also receive money through an American Express MoneyGram, which enables you to obtain

up to $10,000 in cash. It works this way: You call home and ask someone to go to an American Express office—or an American Express MoneyGram agent in a retail outlet—and fill out an American Express MoneyGram. It can be paid for with cash or with any major credit card. The person making the payment is given a reference number and telephones you with that number. The American Express MoneyGram agent calls an 800 number and authorizes the transfer of funds to the American Express office or participating agency in the city where you are staying. In most cases, the money is available immediately on a 24-hour basis upon presentation of identification and the reference number. Fees vary with the amount of money sent. For $300, the fee is $30; for $5,000, the fee is $195. For the American Express MoneyGram location nearest your home and locations in Bermuda, call 800/543–4080. You do not have to be a cardholder to use this service.

3) Have money sent through Western Union (tel. 800/325–6000 in the United States). If you have a MasterCard or Visa, money can be sent for any amount up to your credit limit. If not, have someone take cash or a certified cashier's check to a Western Union office. The money will be delivered to a bank where you are staying. Fees vary with the amount of money sent: For $1,000, the fee is $47; for $500, the fee is $37.

**Cash Machines** The Bank of Bermuda's 10 branches have automatic teller machines (ATMs). Using a Visa card with your personal identification number (PIN), you can withdraw up to $500 a day in Bermudian currency for a fee. The service is available 24 hours a day. Virtually all U.S. banks belong to a network of ATMs, and some banks belong to more than one. The Plus network plans to extend its automatic teller service to Bermuda within the next two years. Call 800/THE–PLUS to locate machines in a given city. Check with your bank for information on fees and the amount of cash you can withdraw on any given day.

## What It Will Cost

Bermuda imports everything from cars to cardigans, so prices are high. In fact, the most common complaint of visitors to Bermuda is the high cost of a vacation on the island. At an upscale restaurant, for example, be prepared to pay as much for a meal as you would in New York, London, or Paris. The average cost of dinner in a chic restaurant is $50–$70 per person—$100 with drinks and wine. Upscale restaurants, however, are not your only option. The island abounds with little coffee shops, where locals and thrift-minded tourists can eat hamburgers and french fries for about $4. The same meal at a restaurant costs about $12.

Hotels add a 6% government tax to the bill and, instead of tips, a 10% service charge or a per diem dollar equivalent. Other supplemental charges include a 5% "energy surcharge"at small guest houses, and a 15% service charge at most restaurants.

**Sample Costs** A cup of coffee costs between 80¢ and $2.50; a mixed drink $3–$5; a bottle of beer $1.75–$5; and a can of Coke about $1. A 15-minute cab ride will set you back about $15 including the tip, and a pack of Kodak 110 cartridge film, with 12 exposures, costs about $3.95.

## Passports and Visas

**U.S. Residents** You do not need a passport or visa to enter Bermuda if you plan to stay less than six months, although you must have onward or return tickets and proof of identity (original birth certificate with raised seal, voter's registration card with photo; a driver's license is unacceptable). If you have a passport, bring it to ensure quick passage through immigration and customs. For further information, check with the **British Embassy** in Washington (tel. 202/462–1340).

**Canadian Residents** Canadians need a passport to enter Bermuda. To obtain a passport, send your completed application (available at any post office or passport office) to the **Bureau of Passports, External Affairs** (Ottawa, Ont. K1A OG3). Include $25, two photographs, a guarantor, and proof of Canadian citizenship. Application can be made in person at the regional passport offices in Edmonton, Halifax, Montreal, Calgary, St. John's (Newfoundland), Victoria, Toronto, Vancouver, and Winnipeg. Passports are valid for five years and are nonrenewable. A visa is not required to enter Bermuda.

**U.K. Residents** British citizens require a valid passport or a British Visitor's Passport to enter Bermuda. Passport application forms are available from most travel agents and major post offices, or contact the **Passport Office** (Clive House, 70 Petty France, London SW1H 9HD, tel. 071/279–3434). The cost is £15 for a standard 32-page passport, £30 for a 94-page passport. British Visitor's Passports, valid for one year only and nonrenewable, cost £7.50. All applications must be countersigned by your bank manager or a solicitor, barrister, doctor, clergyman, or justice of the peace and must be accompanied by two photographs.

## Customs and Duties

**On Arrival** In addition to personal effects, visitors entering Bermuda may bring in duty-free up to 50 cigars, 200 cigarettes, and one pound of tobacco; one quart of wine and one quart of liquor; 20 pounds of meat; and other goods to the value of $30. You should not import plants, fruits, vegetables, and animals without an import permit from the **Department of Agriculture, Fisheries and Parks** (Botanical Gardens, Point Finger Rd., Paget, tel. 809/296–4201). Any amount of foreign or Bermudian currency may be imported. Remember, though, that merchandise and sales materials for use by conventions must be cleared with the hotel concerned before you arrive.

**On Departure**
*U.S. Residents* If you are bringing any foreign-made equipment from home, such as cameras, carry the original receipt with you or register it with U.S. Customs before you leave (Form 4457). Otherwise, you may end up paying duty on the equipment when you return. U.S. citizens go through U.S. Customs at the Bermuda airport before departing from the island. A $15 departure tax ($5 for children between 2 and 11) is also levied at the airport; a $60 port tax is included in cruise-ship fares.

You may import up to $400 worth of foreign goods duty-free, as long as you have been out of the country for at least 48 hours and you haven't made an international trip in 30 days. Each member of the family is entitled to the same exemption, regardless of age, and exemptions may be pooled. For the next $1,000 worth of goods, a flat 10% rate is assessed; above $1,400, duties vary with the merchandise. Travelers 21 or older are entitled to bring in one liter of alcohol, 100 cigars (non-Cuban), and 200 cigarettes. Only one bottle of perfume trademarked in the United States may be imported. However, no duty is charged on antiques or works of art more than 100 years old. Anything exceeding these limits will be taxed at the port of entry and may be taxed additionally in the traveler's home state. Gifts valued at under $50 may be mailed to friends or relatives at home duty-free, but you may not send more than one package per day to any one addressee; in addition, packages may not include tobacco, liquor, or perfumes costing more than $5.

*Canadian Residents* Canadian residents have a $300 exemption and may also import duty-free up to 50 cigars, 200 cigarettes, 2.2 pounds of tobacco, and 40 ounces of liquor, provided these items are declared in writing to customs on arrival and accompany the traveler in carry-on luggage or checked-through baggage. These restrictions apply for absences of at least seven days and a maximum of one year. If you are out of Canada for less than seven days, but for a minimum of 48 hours, there is a $100 exemption, with the same restrictions on alcohol and tobacco products. Personal gifts should be mailed as "Unsolicited gift—value under $40." Request a copy of *I Declare,* the Canadian Customs brochure, for further details. Copies are available at local customs offices.

*U.K. Residents* British residents may import duty-free: (1) 200 cigarettes or 100 cigarillos or 50 cigars or 250 grams of tobacco (if you live outside Europe these allowances are doubled); (2) one liter of alcohol over 22% volume or two liters of alcohol under 22% volume—fortified or sparkling wine; (3) two liters of still table wine; (4) 60 milliliters of perfume and 250 milliliters of toilet water; and (5) other goods to the value of £32. Although it is not classified an alcoholic drink for customs' purposes—and is thus part of the "other goods" allowance—you may not import more than 50 liters of beer. For further information, contact **HM Customs and Excise** (Dorset House, Stamford St., London SE1 9PS, tel. 071/928–0533).

## Traveling with Film

The cost of film on Bermuda is exorbitant, so bring all the film you need with you from home. If your camera is new, shoot and develop a few rolls before leaving home. Pack some lens tissue and an extra battery for your built-in light meter. Invest about $10 in a skylight filter: It will protect the lens and reduce haze.

On a plane trip, never pack unprocessed film in luggage you plan to check; if your bags get X-rayed, say good-bye to your pictures. Always carry undeveloped film with you through security and ask to have it inspected by hand. (It helps to keep your film in a plastic bag, ready for quick inspection.) The old airport scanning machines, still in use in some countries, use heavy doses of radiation that can make a family portrait look like an early morning fog. The newer models used in all U.S. airports are safe for anything from five to 500 scans, depending on the speed of your film. The effects are cumulative, however. You can put the same roll of film through several scans without worry, but you're asking for trouble after five scans. If your film gets fogged and you want an explanation, send it to the **National Association of Photographic Manufacturers** (550 Mamaroneck Ave., Harrison, NY 10528). The association will try to determine what went wrong. The service is free.

## Staying Healthy

Sunburn and sunstroke are chronic problems for summer visitors to Bermuda. On a hot, sunny day, even people who are not normally bothered by strong sun should cover themselves with a long-sleeve shirt, a hat, and long pants or a beach wrap. These are essential for a day on a boat, but are also advisable for midday at the beach. Also carry some sunscreen for nose, ears, and other sensitive areas such as eyelids and ankles. Keep drinking liquids but, above all, limit the amount of time you spend in the sun until you become acclimatized.

No special vaccinations are required for a visit to Bermuda. If you have a health problem for which you might have to purchase prescription drugs while in Bermuda, have your doctor write a prescription using the drug's generic name—brand names can vary widely.

The **International Association for Medical Assistance to Travelers (IAMAT)** is a worldwide organization offering a list of approved English-speaking doctors whose training meets British and U.S. standards. Contact IAMAT for a list of physicians and clinics in Bermuda that belong to this network. **In the United States:** 417 Center St., Lewiston, NY 14092, tel. 716/754–4883. **In Canada:** 40 Regal Road, Guelph, Ontario N1K 1B5. **In Europe:** 57 Voirets, 1212 Grand-Lancy, Geneva, Switzerland. Membership is free.

## Insurance

Travelers may seek insurance coverage in three areas: health and accident, lost luggage, and trip cancellation. Your first step should be to review your existing health and home-owner policies; some health-insurance plans cover health expenses incurred while traveling, some major medical plans cover emergency transportation, and some home-owner policies cover the theft of luggage.

**Health and Accident**

Several companies offer coverage designed to supplement existing health insurance for travelers:

**Association of British Insurers** (Aldermary House, Queen St., London EC4N 1TT, U.K., tel. 071/248–4477) gives free general advice on holiday insurance.

**Carefree Travel Insurance** (Box 310, 120 Mineola Blvd., Mineola, NY 11501, tel. 516/294–0220 or 800/343–3553) provides coverage for emergency medical evacuation. It also offers 24-hour medical phone advice.

**Europ Assistance** (252 High St., Croyden, Surrey CRO 1NF, U.K., tel. 081/680–1234) is a proven leader in the holiday-insurance field.

**International SOS Assistance** (Box 11568, Philadelphia, PA 19116, tel. 215/244–1500 or 800/523–8930) provides medical evacuation services to its clients, many of whom are international corporations.

**Travel Assistance International** (1133 15th St., NW, Suite 400, Washington, DC 20005, tel. 202/347–2025 or 800/821–2828) provides emergency evacuation services and medical referrals 24 hours a day.

**Travel Guard International,** underwritten by Transamerica Occidental Life Companies (1100 Centerpoint Dr., Stevens Point, WI 54481, tel. 715/345-0505 or 800/782-5151), offers reimbursement for medical expenses with no deductibles or daily limits and emergency evacuation services.

**Wallach and Company, Inc.** (243 Church St. NW, Suite 100D, Vienna, VA 22180, tel. 703/281-9500 or 800/237-6615) offers comprehensive medical coverage, including emergency evacuation, for trips of 10–90 days.

**WorldCare Travel Assistance Association** (605 Market St., Suite 1300, San Francisco, CA 94105, tel. 415/541-4991 or 800/666-4993) provides unlimited emergency evacuation, 24-hour medical referral, and an emergency message center.

**Lost Luggage**

On international flights, airlines are responsible for lost or damaged property at rates up to $9.07 per pound (or $20 per kilogram) for checked baggage, and up to $400 per passenger for unchecked baggage. If you're carrying valuables, either take them with you on the plane or purchase additional insurance for lost luggage. Some airlines will issue extra luggage insurance when you check in, but many do not. Insurance for lost, damaged, or stolen luggage is available through travel agents or directly through various insurance companies. Luggage-loss coverage is usually part of a comprehensive travel-insurance package that includes personal, accident, trip-cancellation, and sometimes default and bankruptcy coverage. Two companies that issue luggage insurance are **Tele-Trip** (Box 31685, 3201 Farnam St., Omaha, NE 68131, tel. 800/228-9792), a subsidiary of Mutual of Omaha, and the **Travelers Insurance Co.** (Ticket and Travel Dept., 1 Tower Sq., Hartford, CT 06183, tel. 203/277-0111 or 800/243-3174). Tele-Trip, which operates sales booths at airports and also issues insurance through travel agents, will insure checked luggage for up to 180 days for $500–$3,000 valuation. For one to three days, the rate for a $500 valuation is $8.25; for 180 days, $100. The Travelers Insurance Co. will insure checked or hand luggage for $500–$2,000 valuation per person, also for a maximum of 180 days. The rates for one to five days for $500 valuation is $10; for 180 days, $85. Other companies with comprehensive policies include **Access America, Inc.**, a subsidiary of Blue Cross-Blue Shield (Box 807, New York, NY 10163, tel. 212/490-5345 or 800/284-8300); **Near Services** (450 Prairie Ave., Suite 101, Calumet, IL 60409, tel. 708/868-6700 or 800/654-6700); and **Travel Guard International** and **Carefree Travel Insurance** (*see* Health and Accident, above).

Before you go, itemize the contents of each bag in case you need to file an insurance claim. Be certain to put your home or business address on each piece of luggage, including carry-on bags. If your luggage is lost or stolen and later recovered, the airline will deliver the luggage to your home free of charge.

**Trip Cancellation**

Flight insurance is often included in the price of a ticket paid for with American Express, Visa, or other major credit card. It is also usually included in combination travel-insurance packages available from most tour operators, travel agents, and insurance agents.

## Student and Youth Travel

Like everyone else, students arriving in Bermuda must have confirmation of hotel reservations, a return plane ticket, a photo ID, and proof of citizenship, such as a passport, birth certificate, or a signed voter's registration card. There are no youth hostels, YMCAs, or YWCAs on the island. During Bermuda College Weeks (*see* Festivals and Seasonal Events, above), however, special student rates are offered at hotels and guest houses, restaurants, pubs, and nightclubs.

The **International Student Identity Card (ISIC)** entitles full-time students to reduced fares on local transportation; discounts at museums, theaters, and sports events; student charter flights; and many other attractions. If purchased in the United States, the $10 cost of the ISIC card also includes $2,000 in emergency medical coverage, $100 a day for up to 60 days of hospital coverage, as well as a collect phone number to call in case of emergency. Apply to the **Council on International Educational Exchange** (CIEE, 205 E. 42nd St., New York, NY 10017, tel. 212/661–1414). In Canada, the ISIC is available for $10 from the **Association of Student Councils** (187 College St., Toronto, Ont. M5T 1P7).

Travelers under age 26 can apply for a **Youth International Educational Exchange Card (YIEE)** issued by the **Federation of International Youth Travel Organizations** (81 Islands Brugge, DK-2300 Copenhagen S, Denmark). The services and benefits provided by the YIEE card are similar to those offered by the ISIC card. The YIEE card is available in the United States from CIEE (*see* above) and in Canada from the **Canadian Hostelling Association** (333 River Rd., Vanier, Ottawa, Ont. K1L 8H9, tel. 613/476–3844).

**Council Travel**, a CIEE subsidiary, is the foremost U.S. student travel agency specializing in low-cost charters, and the exclusive U.S. agent for many student airfare bargains and student tours. CIEE's 80-page *Student Travel* catalogue and *Council Charter* brochures are available free from any Council Travel office in the United States (enclose $1 postage if ordering by mail). Contact the CIEE headquarters in New York (*see* above) to locate the nearest Council Travel office.

The **Educational Travel Center** (438 N. Frances St., Madison, WI 53703, tel. 608/256–5551) is another student-travel specialist worth contacting for information on student tours, bargain fares, and bookings.

## Traveling with Children

**Publications** *Family Travel Times* is a newsletter published 10 times a year by Travel with Your Children (TWYCH, 80 Eighth Ave., New York, NY 10011, tel. 212/206–0688). A one-year subscription ($35) includes access to back issues and twice-weekly opportunities to call in for specific advice.

**Getting There** On international flights, children under age 2 not occupying a seat pay 10% of the adult fare. Various discounts apply to children from ages 2 to 12, so check with your airline when booking. If possible, reserve a seat behind one of the plane's bulkheads, where there's usually more legroom and enough space to fit a bassinet, available from the airlines. At the same time, ask about special children's meals or snacks—most airlines offer them. See TWYCH's "Airline Guide," published in the February 1990 issue of *Family Travel Times* (and due to be updated in February 1992), for more information about children's services offered by 46 airlines.

If you want your child to travel in a safety seat, you must buy a separate ticket and bring your own infant car seat. (Check with the airline in advance; certain seats aren't allowed.) Some airlines allow infants to travel in their own car seats free if there's a spare seat; otherwise, safety seats must be stored and the child held by a parent. At press time, the FAA was considering two alternatives to the present regulations governing child-restraint systems aboard aircraft. The first alternative would require that air carriers supply children under 40 pounds or 3 years of age with a safety seat; the second alternative would require that air carriers allow the use of safety seats brought on board by a parent, guardian, or attendant. In both cases, a ticket would have to be purchased for the child. For the booklet **"Child/Infant Safety Seats Acceptable for Use in Aircraft,"** write to the Federal Aviation Admininstration (APA-200, 800 Independence Ave., SW, Washington, DC 20591, tel. 202/267–3479).

**Baby-sitting Services** In Bermuda, few hotels cater to children (*see* Chapter 8, Lodging), and others actively discourage parents from bringing them. Nevertheless, baby-sitting can usually be arranged through the hotel or guest house upon advance request. The charge is $4–$8 per hour, and sitters expect paid transportation. Check with your hotel for specifics.

## Home Exchange

Exchanging homes is a surprisingly low-cost way to enjoy a vacation abroad, especially a long one. The largest home-exchange service, **International Home Exchange Service** (Box 3975, San Francisco, CA 94119, tel. 415/435–3497), publishes three directories a year. Membership, which costs $35, entitles you to one listing and all three directories. Photos of your property cost an additional $8.50; listing a second home costs $10. **Loan-a-Home** (2 Park La., Mount Vernon, NY 10552, tel. 914/664–7640) is popular with academics on sabbatical and businesspeople on temporary assignment. There's no annual membership fee or charge for listing your home, but one directory and a supplement cost $30. Loan-a-Home publishes two directories (in December and June) and two supplements (in March and September) each year. The set of four books costs $40 per year.

## Hints for Disabled Travelers

The Bermuda Chapter of the **Society for the Advancement of Travel for the Handicapped** (SATH, 26 Court St., Brooklyn, NY 11242, tel. 718/858–5483) publishes the *Access Guide to Bermuda for the Handicapped Traveler*, available free of charge.

The **Information Center for Individuals with Disabilities** (Ft. Point Pl., 1st floor, 27–43 Wormwood St., Boston, MA 02210, tel. 617/727–5540) offers useful problem-solving assistance, including lists of travel agents who specialize in tours for the disabled.

**Moss Rehabilitation Hospital Travel Information Service** (12th St. and Tabor Rd., Philadelphia, PA 19141, tel. 215/329–5715) for a small fee provides information on tourist sights, transportation, and accommodations in destinations around the world.

**Mobility International USA** (Box 3551, Eugene, OR 97403, tel. 503/343–1284) is an internationally affiliated organization with 500 members. For a $20 annual fee, it coordinates exchange programs for disabled people around the world and offers information on accommodations and organized study programs.

**Travel Industry and Disabled Exchange** (5435 Donna Ave., Tarzana, CA 91356, tel. 818/368–5648) publishes a quarterly newsletter and a directory of travel agencies and tours to Europe, Canada, Great Britain, New Zealand, and Australia, all specializing in travel for the disabled. Annual subscription fee is $15.

## Hints for Older Travelers

The **American Association of Retired Persons** (AARP, 1909 K St., NW, Washington, DC 20049, tel. 202/662–4850) has two programs for independent travelers: (1) the **Purchase Privilege Program,** which comes with membership, offers discounts on hotels, airfares, car rentals, RV rentals, and sightseeing; (2) the **AARP Motoring Plan** furnishes emergency road service and trip-routing information for an annual fee of $33.95 per person or couple. (Both programs include the member and member's spouse, or the member and another person who shares the household.) The AARP also arranges group tours through **American Express Vacations** (Box 5014, Atlanta, GA 30302, tel. 800/241–1700). AARP members must be 50 or older; annual dues are $5 per person or per couple.

When using an AARP or other discount identification card, ask for reduced hotel rates at the time you make your reservation, not when you check out. At restaurants, show your card to the maître d' before you're seated, because discounts may be limited to set menus, days, or hours. When renting a car, remember that economy cars priced at promotional rates may cost less than cars available with your discount ID card.

**Elderhostel** (80 Boylston St., Suite 400, Boston, MA 02116, tel. 617/426–7788) is an innovative 16-year-old educational program for people 60 and older. Participants live in dorms on any of 1,200 campuses around the world. Mornings are devoted to lectures and seminars; afternoons to sightseeing and field trips. Fees for two- to three-week trips, including room, board, tuition, and round-trip transportation, range from $1,700 to $3,200.

**Mature Outlook** (6001 N. Clark St., Chicago, IL 60660, tel. 800/336–6330), a subsidiary of Sears Roebuck & Co., is a travel club for people over age 50. It offers hotel and motel discounts and a bimonthly newsletter. Annual membership is $9.95; there are currently 800,000 members. Instant membership is available at participating Holiday Inns.

The **National Council of Senior Citizens** (925 15th St., NW, Washington, DC 20005, tel. 202/347–8800) is a nonprofit advocacy group with about 5,000 local clubs across the country. Annual membership is $12 per person or per couple. Members receive a monthly newspaper with travel information and an ID card for reduced hotel and car-rental rates.

**Saga International Holidays** (120 Boylston St., Boston, MA 02116, tel. 800/343–0273), an affiliate of Elderhostel, specializes in group travel for people over age 60. A selection of variously priced tours allows you to choose the package that meets your needs.

### Further Reading

The late William Zuill, a well-respected historian, wrote extensively about the island. Published in 1945 and now somewhat outdated, Zuill's 426-page *Bermuda Journey: A Leisurely Guide Book* provides a fascinating look at the island and its people, with historical notes and anecdotes. The book was scheduled to go out of print in 1990, so check with the Bermuda Book Store in Hamilton (tel. 809/295–3698) to see if it's available. (Proprietor Jim Zuill is the author's son.) William Zuill's other books include *The Wreck of the Sea Venture*, which details the 1609 wreck of Admiral Sir George Somers's flagship and the subsequent settlement of the island, and *Tom Moore's Bermuda Poems*, a collection of odes by the Irish poet who spent four months on Bermuda in 1804.

W. S. Zuill, the son of the noted historian, wrote *The Story of Bermuda and Her People*, a recently updated volume tracing the history of the island from the *Sea Venture* wreck to the present. *Bermuda*, by John J. Jackson, contains an abundance of facts on Bermudian business, economics, law, ecology, history, as well as tourist information. John Weatherill's *Faces of Bermuda* is a marvelous collection of photographs, and those curious about the legendary Bermuda Triangle can read about its history in *The Bermuda Triangle Mystery Solved*, by Larry David Kusche.

For a charming account of growing up in Bermuda during the 1930s and 1940s, refer to *The Backyard*, by William Zuill's daughter Ann Zuill Williams. Two books for a younger audience are Willoughby Patton's *Sea Venture*, about the adventures of a young boy on the crew of the ill-fated ship in 1609, and E. M. Rice's *A Child's History of Bermuda*, which tells the story of the island in terms children can understand.

# Arriving and Departing

### From North America by Plane

**Airport and Airlines**

The **Civil Air Terminal** (Kindley Field Rd., St. George's) is on the east end of the island, approximately 9 miles from the center of Hamilton and 17 miles from Somerset.

Airlines with direct flights to Bermuda include **American Airlines** (tel. 800/433–7300) from New York (JFK and LaGuardia), Boston, and Raleigh/Durham; **Continental** (tel. 800/525–0280) from Newark; **Delta Airlines** (tel. 800/221–1212) from Boston and Atlanta; **Pan Am** (tel. 800/221–1111) from New York's JFK airport; **USAir** (tel. 800/428–4322) from Baltimore; and **Air**

**Canada** (tel. 800/776–3000) from Toronto, with connections from all over Canada.

**Flying Time** From New York, Boston, Raleigh/Durham, and Baltimore, the flight to Bermuda takes about two hours; from Atlanta, 2½ hours; and from Toronto, 2¾ hours.

**Enjoying the Flight** Unless you're flying from the West Coast or Britain, jet lag won't be a problem. If you're lucky enough to be able to sleep on an aircraft, request a window seat to curl up against; those who like to move about the cabin should request aisle seats. Bulkhead seats (located in the front row of each cabin) have more legroom, but seat trays are attached rather awkwardly to the arms of the seat rather than to the back of the seat ahead. Generally, bulkhead seats are reserved for the disabled, the elderly, or parents traveling with babies.

**Discount Flights** The major airlines offer a range of tickets that can lower the price of any given seat by nearly 70%, depending on the day of purchase. As a rule, the further in advance you buy the ticket, the less expensive it is and the greater the penalty (up to 100%) for canceling. Check with the airlines for details. The best buy is not necessarily an APEX (advance purchase) ticket on one of the major airlines, because these tickets carry certain restrictions: They must be bought in advance (usually 21 days); they restrict your travel, usually requiring a minimum stay of seven days and a maximum of 90; and they penalize you for changes—voluntary or not—in your travel plans. But if you can work around these drawbacks (and most travelers can), they are among the best fares available.

Charter flights offer the lowest fares, although departure days are usually limited. It can be especially difficult to find a charter going to Bermuda, but if you do manage to secure a seat, be prepared for late departures. Travel agents can make bookings, although they won't encourage you to take a charter, because charter commissions are lower than on scheduled flights. As a rule, checks should be made out to the bank and the specific escrow account for your flight. Don't sign up for a charter flight unless you've asked a travel agency about the reputation of the packager. It's particularly important to know the packager's policy on refunds in the event of a canceled flight; some agents advise travelers to purchase trip-cancellation insurance if they are booked on a charter flight. Check the Sunday travel sections of newspapers for the advertisements of charter operators.

Other discounted fares—up to 50% lower than the cost of APEX tickets—can be found through consolidators, companies that buy blocks of tickets on scheduled airlines and sell them at wholesale prices. Tickets are subject to availability, so passengers should have reasonably flexible travel schedules. Here again, you may lose all or most of your money if you change plans, but you will be on a regularly scheduled flight with less risk of cancellation than on a charter. As an added precaution, consider buying trip-cancellation insurance. Once you've made a reservation, call the airline to confirm it. Many consolidators advertise in newspaper Sunday travel sections.

Travelers willing to put up with some inconveniences in return for substantially reduced airfares may be interested in flying as air couriers. An air courier is someone who accompanies shipments (documents or packages) between designated points.

There are two sources of information on courier deals: (1) A telephone directory, which lists courier companies by the cities to which they fly, is available for $5 (plus a stamped, self-addressed business envelope) from **Pacific Data Sales Publishing** (2554 Lincoln Blvd., Suite 275-F, Marina Del Ray, CA 92091); (2) *A Simple Guide to Courier Travel* can be purchased for $12.45 (includes postage and handling) from the **Carriage Group** (Box 2394, Lake Oswego, OR 97035, tel. 800/344–9375).

Another option is to join a travel club that offers special discounts to its members. Among such organizations are **Discount Travel International** (114 Forrest Ave., Narberth, PA 19072, tel. 215/668–2182), **Moment's Notice** (40 E. 49th St., New York, NY 10017, tel. 212/486–0503), **Traveler's Advantage** (CUC Travel Service, 40 Oakview Dr., Trumbull, CT 06611, tel. 800/648–4037), and **Worldwide Discount Travel Club** (1674 Meridien Ave., Miami Beach, FL 33139, tel. 305/534–2082). Always compare the cut-rate tickets offered by these organizations with APEX tickets on the major airlines.

**Smoking** As of February 1990, smoking is banned on all routes within the 48 contiguous states; within the states of Hawaii and Alaska; to and from the U.S. Virgin Islands and Puerto Rico; and on flights of under six hours to and from Hawaii and Alaska. The rule applies to both domestic and foreign carriers. On a flight where smoking is permitted, you can request a nonsmoking seat during check-in or when you book your ticket. If the airline tells you no seats are available in the nonsmoking section, insist on one: Department of Transportation regulations require carriers to find seats for all nonsmokers, provided they meet check-in time restrictions. These regulations apply to all international flights on domestic carriers, but the Department of Transportation has no jurisdiction over foreign carriers.

**Between the Airport and Hotels**

*By Taxi* Taxis meet all flights in Bermuda and are readily available at the airport. The approximate fare (not including tip) to Hamilton is $15; to St. George's, $7; to south-shore hotels, $19; and to the West End, $26. A surcharge of 25¢ is added for each piece of luggage stored in the trunk or on the roof. Between 10 PM and 6 AM, and on Sundays and public holidays, fares are 25% higher. Depending on traffic, the driving time to Hamilton is about 20 minutes, and about 45 minutes to the West End.

*By Bus* **Bermuda Aviation Services Ltd.** (tel. 809/293–2500) operates an eight-passenger Volkswagen minibus to the smaller hotels and a 26-passenger bus to the large resorts. You must make reservations two weeks prior to your arrival. At the airport, look for the BAS sign after you leave customs. Fares and driving times are as follows: Zone 1—a 15-minute trip to the Grotto Bay Beach Hotel—costs $4; Zone 2—a 20-minute trip stopping at St. George's and Flatts Village—is $6; Zone 3—a 35-minute ride to hotels in Smith's, Devonshire, Pembroke, Hamilton, and Paget parishes—costs $12; Zone 4—a 45-minute journey to Warwick and half of Southampton Parish—is $16; and Zone 5—a 90-minute trip to hotels in the other half of Southampton and in Sandys Parish—costs $21.

## From the U.K. by Plane

The options for flying to Bermuda from Great Britain are limited. Only **British Airways** (tel. 071/897–4000) flies direct, with six flights a week from Gatwick. Flying time is approximately seven hours. No charter flights are available, but travel packages offer reduced fares on the British Airways flights. Peak-season round-trip economy fares range from £589 to £914; in first class, tickets are as much as £2,464. Flying to New York, and then taking a connecting flight to Bermuda, takes longer and costs as much—even with the cheapest fares—as the scheduled British Airways flight direct to Bermuda.

## From the U.S. by Cruise Ship

Bermuda has long been a favorite destination of cruise lines, and (except for a few cruises that continue down to the Caribbean) it is usually a ship's only port of call. Most ships make seven-day loops from New York, with four days spent at sea and three days in port; other cruises leave from Baltimore, Philadelphia, Boston, and Charleston. The cruise season in Bermuda runs from March to October. Concerned about overcrowding, the Bermudian government recently limited the number of regularly scheduled visits by cruise ships to four per week, none on weekends. The restrictions will probably make it more difficult to find cabins on cruises to Bermuda, and prices are likely to rise. At the same time, however, passengers will be able to enjoy the island without being jostled by other tourists, and many of the island's attractions are relatively empty during the week.

Ships tie up at one of three harbors on Bermuda: Hamilton, St. George's, or the West End. The traditional port is Hamilton, the capital and the most commercial area on the island. If you want to shop until you drop, choose a cruise that anchors here. Passengers whose ship ties up at St. George's walk off the vessel into Bermuda's equivalent of Colonial Williamsburg. Located at the east end of the island, St. George's is a charming town of 17th-century buildings, narrow lanes, and small boutiques. West End is the farthest cruise port from Bermuda's main attractions. A new tourist complex is under construction in the West End, however, including a shopping mall, museums, and crafts stores. (For more information about Bermuda's ports and attractions, *see* Chapter 3, Exploring Bermuda.)

**Cruise Lines and Ships**

**Royal Viking Line** (Kloster Cruise Limited, 2 Alahambra Plaza, Coral Gables, FL 33134, tel. 800/422–8000) offers one-week, upscale cruises to Bermuda from New York aboard the ***Royal Viking Star.*** The 900-passenger ship calls at both St. George's and Hamilton. Cabin rates range from $133 to $650 per diem.

**Royal Caribbean Cruise Line** (903 South America Way, Miami, FL 33132, tel. 800/327–2055) offers mainstream, party-oriented cruises to Bermuda from New York aboard the ***Nordic Prince.*** The 1,012-passenger ship spends three days in the port of Hamilton and four days at sea. Cabin rates range from $106 to $384 per diem.

**Chandris Celebrity Cruises** (900 Third Ave., New York, NY 10017, tel. 800/621–3446) has two ships that sail to Bermuda during the summer months, offering a mainstream cruising experience. One-week cruises leave from New York between early July and mid-September, but trips in May, June, and late September leave from such ports as Boston, Philadelphia, Baltimore, Wilmington (NC), Charleston, and Fort Lauderdale. The ***Horizon*** is a brand-new vessel that moors at St. George's, while the ***Meridian*** is a refitted old liner that docks in the West End. Cabin rates range from $138 to $314 per diem.

**Shore Excursions**

Shore excursions are usually group tours arranged for passengers by their cruise ship. Almost all ships sell these tours, which tend to follow well-established formulas. Information about the shore excursions offered by a ship is sent to passengers before the cruise. Depending upon availability, shore excursions can be booked from the time you first reserve your cruise until right before the excursion begins. Listed below are the shore excursions offered by cruise lines in Bermuda, although not all excursions are offered by all cruise lines. (For more information about the attractions listed below, *see* Chapter 3, Exploring Bermuda.) Times quoted are approximate, and passengers should check with their travel agent or cruise director for tour prices.

*Boats and Beaches*

**Bermuda Glass-Bottom Boat Cruise:** A tame but pleasant cruise through the harbor and over reefs that includes feeding the fish from the boat. *2 hrs.*

**Coral Reef and Calypso Cruise:** Rum swizzles and island music set the tone for a cruise aboard a glass-bottom party boat. *2½ hrs.*

**Reef Roamer Island Party:** A beach party that includes snorkeling, dancing, and rum swizzles. *3½ hrs.*

**Sailing Cruise:** A relaxing, romantic, and quiet sailing trip, with a short stop to allow guests to swim. *3 hrs.*

**Snorkeling Tour:** Equipment, lessons, and underwater guided tour are included. Underwater cameras are available for an extra charge. *3¾ hrs.*

**South Shore Beaches:** This is a sightseeing tour along scenic South Road, with an hour for swimming at Horseshoe Bay Beach. Wet bathing suits are not allowed on the bus, but changing facilities are available. *4 hrs.*

*Cultural and Scenic*

**West End Highlight Tour:** Visit the Island Pottery, Art Centre, Crafts Market, Maritime Museum, Heydon Trust Chapel, and Gibb's Hill Lighthouse during a drive through Sandys Parish. This tour is recommended for passengers whose ships dock in Hamilton or St. George's and who are unlikely to travel to the West End on their own. *4 hrs.*

**St. George's Highlight Tour:** A quick overview of the area around St. George's includes Fort St. Catherine, Fort William, Gates Fort, the Unfinished Church, Somers Garden, Tobacco Bay, and the government housing complex. The guide is informative and will point out the popular shopping areas. *2 hrs.*

**Bermuda's Attractions Tour:** Visit Leamington or Crystal caves and the Aquarium, Museum and Zoo. The tour ends at the Bermuda Perfumery, where the essence of flowers is made into perfume. *4 hrs.*

*Entertainment*

**Coca-Cola Steel Band at the New Clayhouse Inn:** An evening of island music played on homemade instruments, limbo, and fire dancing. Two free drinks are included.

**Hamilton Princess "Big, Bad and Beautiful" Revue:** A salute to famous female performers such as Ella Fitzgerald and Anita Baker. Two free drinks are included. *4 hrs.*

# Staying in Bermuda

## Important Addresses and Numbers

**Tourist Information** **Visitors Service Bureaus,** which provide tourist information and assist with reservations and ticketing, can be found at the following locations:

**Hamilton.** *Ferry Terminal Bldg., Front St., tel. 809/295–1480. Open weekdays 9–4:45.*

**Civil Air Terminal–Airport.** *Tel. 809/293–0030. Open daily 9–5.*

**Vistors Information Centres,** which offer tourist information but no other services, are at the following locations:

**St. George's.** *King's Sq., next to Town Hall, tel. 809/297–1642. Open Mon.–Wed., Fri, and Sat. 10–3; closed Thurs. and Sun.*

**Somerset.** *Nr. St. James's Church, tel. 809/234–1388. Open April–November, weekdays 10–4.*

**Consulates** Neither the Canadian nor the British government has a consulate in Bermuda.

**American Consulate General.** *Crown Hill, 16 Middle Rd., Devonshire, tel. 809/294–1342. Open weekdays 9–noon and 1:30–4.*

**Emergencies** Dial 911 for the **police, fire brigade**, or an **ambulance. Air/Sea Rescue** (tel. 809/297–1010).

*Hospitals* The **King Edward VII Memorial Hospital** (Point Finger Rd., outside Hamilton near the Botanical Gardens, tel. 809/236–2345) is a fully equipped medical facility with a 24-hour emergency room.

*Doctors and Dentists* Contact the hospital or the **Government Health Clinic** (Victoria St., Hamilton, tel. 809/236–0224) for referrals to a doctor or dentist.

*Late-Night Pharmacies* **Hamilton Pharmacy.** *Church and Parliament Sts., Hamilton, tel. 809/295–7004. Open weekdays and Sat. 8AM–9PM.*
**Phoenix Store.** *Marriott's Castle Harbour Resort, tel. 809/293–8119. Open weekdays and Sat. 9–10.*
**Collector's Hill Apothecary**. *Collector's Hill, Smith's, tel. 809/236–8664. Open weekdays and Sat. 8–8, Sun. 7:30–9 PM.*

**Travel Agencies** The American Express agent is **L. P. Gutteridge Ltd.** (L. P. Gutteridge Bldg., Bermudiana Rd., Hamilton, tel. 809/295–4545). Thomas Cook is represented by **Butterfield Travel Ltd.** (75 Front St., Hamilton, tel. 809/292–1510).

## Telephones

**Local Calls** Pay phones, identical to those found in the United States, can be found on the streets of Hamilton, St. George's, and Somerset, as well as at ferry landings and some bus stops. Deposit 20¢ (U.S. or Bermudian) in the meter as soon as your party answers. Most hotels charge 20¢–75¢ for local calls.

**International Calls** Direct dialing is possible from anywhere on the island. Most hotels impose a surcharge for long-distance calls, even those made collect. Many of the small guest houses and apartments have no central switchboard; if you have a phone in your room, it's a private line from which you can make only collect or credit-card calls (and local calls, of course). Some of the small hotels have a telephone room or kiosk where you can make long-distance calls. Specially marked **AT&T USA Direct** phones can be found at the airport, the cruise-ship dock in Hamilton, and at King's Square and Ordnance Island in St. George's. International calls can also be made from the **main post office** (Church and Parliament Sts., Hamilton, tel. 809/295–5151) and from the **Cable & Wireless Office** (20 Church St., opposite City Hall, Hamilton, tel. 809/295–1815), which makes its overseas telephone, telex, cable, and fax facilities available to the public weekdays and Saturdays from 9 to 5.

To call the United States, Canada, Hawaii, and most Caribbean countries, dial 1 (or 0 if you need an operator's assistance), plus the area code and the number. For all other countries, dial 011 (or 01 for an operator), the country code, the area code, and the number. Using an operator for an overseas call is more expensive than dialing direct. For calls to the United States, rates are highest between 10 AM and 7 PM, and discounted between 7 PM and 11 PM; the lowest rates are from 11 PM to 7 AM. (No rate reductions are given for calls to Alaska and Hawaii.) Calls to Canada are cheapest from 9 PM to 7 AM, and to the United Kingdom from 6 PM to 7 AM.

**Operators and Information** To find a local number or to request information, dial 902. For information about international calls, dial 01.

## Mail

**Postal Rates** Airmail letters and postcards to the United States and Canada require 50¢ postage per half ounce, and 60¢ per half ounce to the United Kingdom.

**Receiving Mail** If you have no address in Bermuda, you can have mail sent care of General Delivery (General Post Office, Hamilton HM GD, Bermuda).

## Tipping

A service charge of 10% (or an equivalent per diem amount), which covers everything from baggage handling to maid service, is added to your hotel bill. Most restaurants, too, tack on a 15% service charge; otherwise a 15% tip is customary (more for exceptional service). Porters at the airport expect about a dollar, while taxi drivers usually receive 15% of the fare.

## Opening and Closing Times

**Banks** All branches of the **Bank of Bermuda** are open Monday–Thursday 9:30–3, and Friday 9:30–4:30. The exception is the airport branch, which is open Monday–Thursday 11–4 and Friday 11–4:30. The airport branch of the **Bermuda Commercial Bank** is open weekdays 11–4. All other banks on the island operate from Monday to Thursday 9:30–3, and Friday 9:30–3 and 4:30–5:30. All branches of the Bank of Bermuda have automatic teller machines, where travelers can obtain Visa cash advances up to $500 (in Bermudian currency) at any time of day.

**Museums** Hours vary greatly, but generally museums are open weekdays and Saturday from 9 or 9:30 until 4:30 or 5; some museums close on Wednesday or Saturday. Check with the Visitors Information Centre or with the museum itself for exact hours.

**Stores** Most stores are open weekdays and Saturday from around 9 until 5 or 5:30. Some Hamilton stores keep evening and Sunday hours when cruise ships are in port.

## Convention and Business Services

Its proximity to U.S. East Coast cities and its diverse range of attractions—from sea and sun to shopping, sightseeing, tennis, and golf—have made Bermuda a popular center for conventions and conferences. In fact, meetings and incentives account for 33% of the island's tourism. Many hotels and resorts offer comprehensive meeting facilities and help expedite customs procedures for business and convention materials. The **Bermuda Chamber of Commerce** (tel. 809/295–4201) will help group organizers plan a variety of activities for group participants and/or spouses, including lectures, shopping tours, fashion shows, and sightseeing excursions. In 1988, Bermuda and the United States signed a tax treaty, giving business meetings in Bermuda the same tax privileges as those held in the United States. For more information about convention facilities and services in Bermuda, obtain a copy of *Bermuda: A Meeting and Incentive Travel Planner's Guide*, available free from the Bermuda Department of Tourism. Listed below are some of the business services available on the island.

**Dry Cleaners** Full-service hotels and cottage colonies have laundry and dry-cleaning services, but guest houses and housekeeping apartments do not. **Hamilton Valcleaners Ltd.** (Bermudiana Rd., Hamilton, tel. 809/292–3063) and **Paget Dry Cleaners Ltd.** (Lovers La., Paget, tel. 809/293–5142) both provide free pick-up and delivery, and express service on request.

**Flowers and Gift Baskets** Concierges in the major hotels can arrange delivery of flowers and gift baskets. **The Flower Shop** (14 Reid St., Hamilton, tel. 809/295–2903) is an FTD florist. Fruit baskets, gift baskets, and flowers are also available at **House of Flowers** (Washington Mall, Hamilton, tel. 809/292–4750). **Designer Flowers** (Market Place Plaza, Heron Bay, tel. 809/238–1490) creates special floral designs for any occasion.

**Formal Wear** Formal wear by After Six, for both men and women, can be rented at **Karl's/Guys 'n Dolls** (Church St., Hamilton, tel. 809/292–5948).

**Group Tours** Comprehensive group tours of the island are available through **L. P. Gutteridge Ltd.** (tel. 809/295–4545), **Butterfield Travel** (tel. 809/292–1510), **Penboss Associates** (tel. 809/295–3927), and **Meyer's Holiday Tours** (tel. 809/295–4176).

The **Bermuda National Trust** (tel. 809/236–6483) offers a variety of events for groups, including private house and garden tours, a champagne reception at the Verdmont house, walking tours, and slide shows and lectures.

**Group Transportation** From March to November, **Bermuda Aviation Services** (tel. 809/293–2500) provides group transport from the airport in eight-passenger minibuses and 26-passenger motorcoaches. From December through February, only taxis are available on the island. Taxi companies offering group service include **Bermuda Taxi Operators Company Ltd.** (tel. 809/292–4175), **Trott Travel**

**Ltd.** (tel. 809/295–0041), and **B.I.U. Taxi Co-op Transportation** (tel. 809/292–4476).

**Messenger Services** Radio-dispatched messengers of **International Bonded Couriers** (Mechanics Bldg., Hamilton, tel. 809/295–2467) offer guaranteed pick-up and delivery of packages island-wide within 90 minutes. Overnight international deliveries are available through **Federal Express** (Washington Mall, Hamilton, tel. 809/292–9094) and **DHL Worldwide Express** (Express Centre, 22 Washington Mall, tel. 809/295–3300).

**Photocopying** **The Copy Shop** (The Walkway, Reid St., Hamilton, tel. 809/292–5355) makes photocopies. The store is open weekdays 8:30–5, and Saturday 8:30–1.

**Secretarial Services** **Business Services of Bermuda** (tel. 809/295–5175) provides secretarial services, as well as photocopying and translation services.

**Cranleigh Limited** (tel. 809/292–3458) specializes in secretarial, translation, and messenger/telephone-answering services.

**ExecuTemps** (tel. 809/295–8608, fax 809/292–7783) offers secretarial services, meeting transcripts, conference-recording equipment, and word-processing and color photocopying services.

**Video and Film Services** **Electronic Services** (tel. 809/295–3885) has audiovisual equipment and operators for hire. **Panatel VDS Ltd.** (tel. 809/292–1600) is a full-service film and video production house.

## Getting Around Bermuda

Despite its small size (20 square miles), Bermuda does pose some transport problems. Most important, rental cars are not allowed, so visitors must travel by bus, taxi, ferry, moped, bike, or on foot. Furthermore, narrow, winding roads—more than 120 miles of them—and a 20-mph speed limit (15 mph in town) that is strictly enforced make moving around the island a time-consuming process. Traveling the length of this long, skinny island takes particularly long: The trip from St. George's to Hamilton takes an hour by bus, and the onward journey to the West End takes another hour, although a new express bus service from Hamilton to the West End takes only 30 minutes. Hiring a taxi can cut down the amount of time you spend on the road, but the cost may discourage you. Fortunately, Hamilton, St. George's, and Somerset are all manageable on foot. Anyone who plans to do a lot of traveling around the island should pick up a copy of the ***Bermuda Islands Guide,*** an atlas of every road, alley, lane, and landmark on the island. Available at the Bermuda Book Store (Queen and Front Sts., Hamilton, tel. 809/295–3698), it is well worth the $4.95 price tag.

**By Bus** Bermuda's modern pink-and-blue buses tour the island from east to west, grinding up hills and squeezing through alleys. Hamilton buses arrive and depart from the **Central Bus Terminal** (Washington and Church Sts., Hamilton, tel. 809/292–5854), a small kiosk that is open daily 7:30–5:30. Finding a bus stop outside Hamilton can be difficult. Some are easily identifiable stone shelters, but others are marked only by striped poles by the road. These poles can be short or tall, green and white, or black and white, but the net effect is confusing. Remember to wait on the proper side of the road—driving in Ber-

## Bus and Ferry Routes

ATLANTIC OCEAN

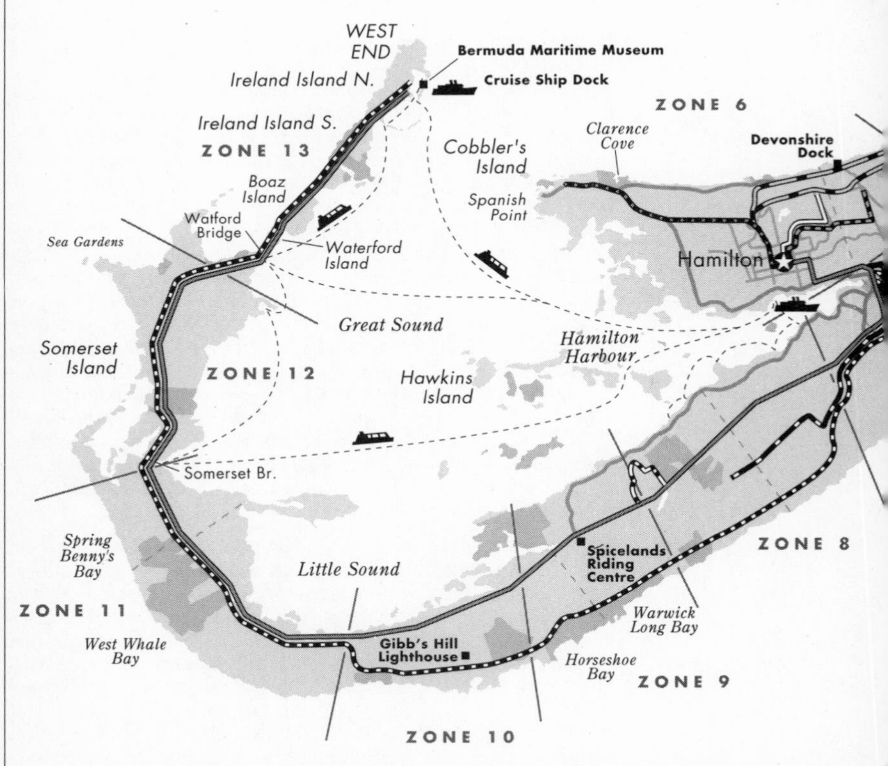

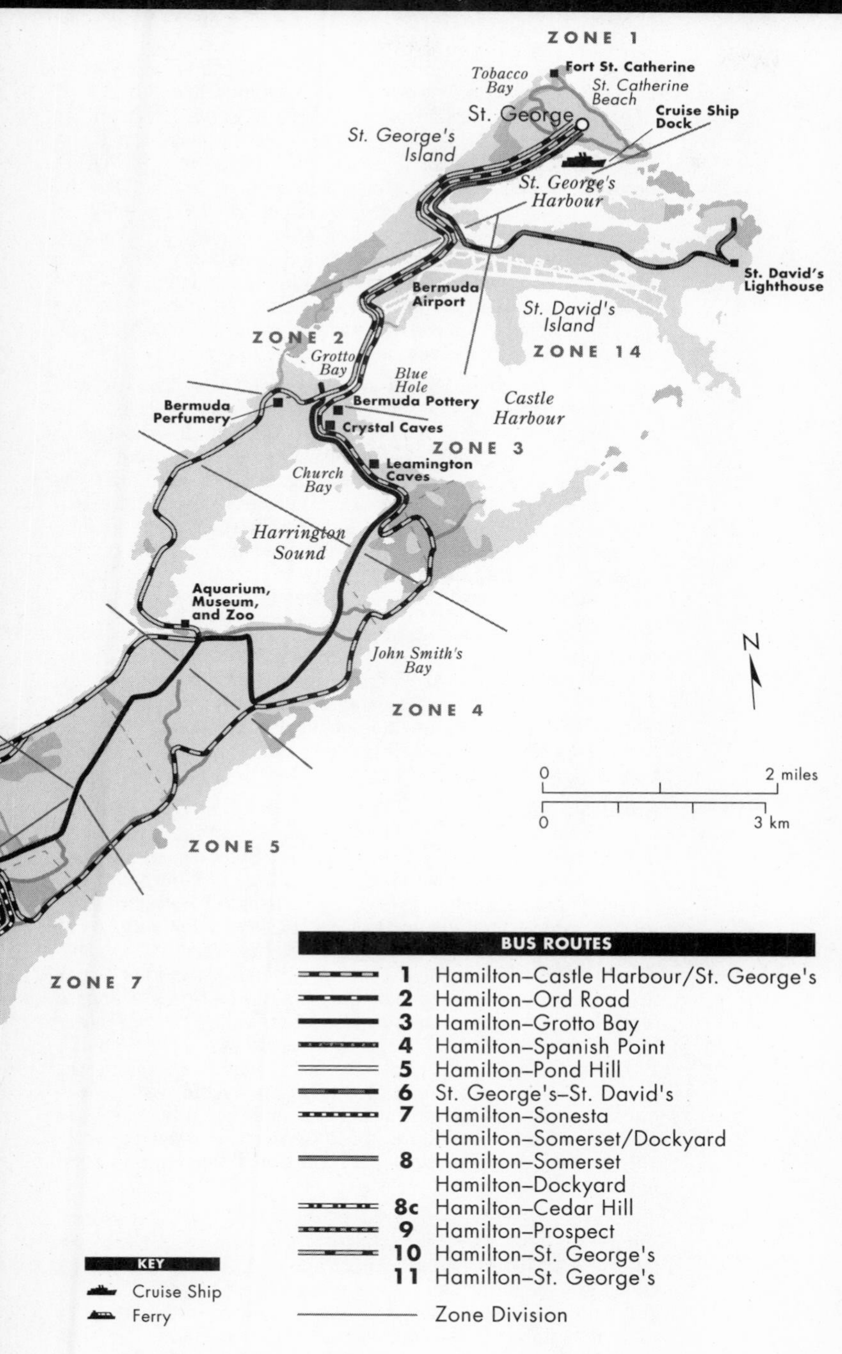
ZONE 1
Tobacco Bay
Fort St. Catherine
St. Catherine Beach
St. George
Cruise Ship Dock
St. George's Island
St. George's Harbour
St. David's Lighthouse
Bermuda Airport
St. David's Island
ZONE 2
Grotto Bay
ZONE 14
Blue Hole
Bermuda Perfumery
Bermuda Pottery
Castle Harbour
Crystal Caves
ZONE 3
Leamington Caves
Church Bay
Harrington Sound
Aquarium, Museum, and Zoo
John Smith's Bay
N
ZONE 4
0
2 miles
0
3 km
ZONE 5
ZONE 7
BUS ROUTES
1 Hamilton–Castle Harbour/St. George's
2 Hamilton–Ord Road
3 Hamilton–Grotto Bay
4 Hamilton–Spanish Point
5 Hamilton–Pond Hill
6 St. George's–St. David's
7 Hamilton–Sonesta
Hamilton–Somerset/Dockyard
8 Hamilton–Somerset
Hamilton–Dockyard
8c Hamilton–Cedar Hill
9 Hamilton–Prospect
10 Hamilton–St. George's
11 Hamilton–St. George's
Zone Division
KEY
Cruise Ship
Ferry

muda is on the left. Exact change is necessary when boarding a bus and, to make matters worse, the fare depends on your destination. Bermuda is divided into 14 bus zones, each about 2 miles in length. Within the first three zones, adults pay $1.25 (coins, tickets, or tokens only; no dollar bills) and children 3–12 pay 55¢. For greater distances, the fare is $2.50. If you plan to do much bus travel, it makes sense to buy a booklet of 15 14-zone tickets for $16 (or 15 three-zone tickets for $9). Ticket booklets and packets of discounted tokens are available at the Hamilton bus terminal and at post offices. Buses run about every 15 minutes, except on Sunday when they usually come every hour. Bus schedules, which also contain ferry timetables, are available at the bus terminal in Hamilton and at many of the hotels. Bermudian bus drivers are rude, but they do answer questions about fares and destinations; upon request, they will also tell you when you've reached your stop.

In addition to the public buses to and from Hamilton, private minibuses serve the eastern and western ends of the island. In the West End, **Sandys Taxi Service** (tel. 809/234–2344) operates a minibus service hourly between Somerset Bridge and Dockyard. The fare depends upon the destination, although you won't have to pay more than $3 (half price for senior citizens). Minibuses, which you can flag down on the road or summon by phone, drop passengers wherever they want to go. The service operates from 7:20 AM until 7 PM between December and March, and from 7:20 AM until 10:20 PM between May and mid-October.

**St. George's Transportation** (tel. 809/297–8199) has a similar minibus service around St. George's and St. David's in the east. The minimum fare is $1.35 for adults, 85¢ for senior citizens, and 75¢ for children. Buses are available in King's Square in St. George's's, or they can be flagged down from the roadside. The service operates between 7 AM and 11 PM from March to November, and between 7 AM and 7 PM from December to February.

**By Ferry** Quick and enjoyable, ferries sail every day from the **Ferry Terminal** (tel. 809/295–4506) in Hamilton, with routes to Paget, Warwick, and across the Great Sound to Somerset in the West End. On weekdays, most ferries run until 11 PM, although the last ferry from Hamilton to Somerset leaves at 6 PM; on Sunday, ferry service is limited and ends around 7 PM. A one-way fare to Paget or Warwick is $1, $2 to Somerset; children 3–13 pay 50¢. The turnstiles leading to the ferries accept only tokens, which are available at the terminal. Bicycles can be brought aboard free, but passengers must pay $2 extra to take a motor scooter to Somerset; motorized cycles are not allowed on the smaller Paget and Warwick ferries. The ferry operators, among the friendliest and most helpful people on the island, will answer questions about routes and schedules, and they'll even help get your bike aboard. Schedules, posted at each landing, are available at the Ferry Terminal, Central Bus Terminal, and most hotels.

**By Taxi** Taxis are metered and offer the fastest and easiest way around the island—and also the costliest. Taxis charge $4 for the first mile, and $1.40 for each subsequent mile. A half-hour trip costs about $20, including tip. Between 10 PM and 6 AM, or on Sunday and public holidays, a 25% surcharge is added to the fare. For radio-dispatched taxis, contact **Radio Cabs Bermuda** (tel. 809/295–4141) and **Bermuda Taxi Operators** (tel. 809/292–5600).

**By Moped** Mopeds, or motor-assisted vehicles as Bermudians call them, offer visitors the most flexibility for moving about the island. Riding a moped, however, is not without hazards—especially for first-time riders. The roads are narrow, winding, and full of blind curves, and accidents occur frequently. The best way to avoid a mishap is to obey the 20-mph speed limit and to remember to stay on the left-hand side of the road, especially at traffic circles (or roundabouts as they're known in Bermuda). In addition, avoid riding in the rain and at night. The law requires all riders to wear a crash helmet with the chin strap fastened. Single- or double-seat mopeds and scooters can be rented from cycle liveries by the hour, the day, or the week. The cycle liveries will show first-time riders how to operate the mopeds. Rates vary from livery to livery, but single-seat mopeds cost about $20 per day, or $74 per week (plus a mandatory $12 repair waiver). The fee includes helmet, lock, key, third-party insurance, breakdown service, pick-up and delivery, and a tank of gas. A $20–$50 deposit is required for the lock, key, and helmet, and you must be at least 16 to rent. Recommended liveries are **Oleander Cycles** (Valley Rd., Paget, tel. 809/236–5235, and Gorham Rd., Hamilton, tel. 809/295–0919); **Eve's Cycle Livery** (Middle Rd., Paget, tel. 809/236–6247); **Devil's Hole Cycles** (Harrington Sound Rd., Smith's, tel. 809/293–1240); and **St. George's Cycles** (Water St., St. George's, tel. 809/297–1463). Major hotels have their own cycle liveries, and all hotels and guest houses will make rental arrangements. Gas stations are open weekdays and Saturday from 7 AM to 7 PM; you will be lucky to find one open on Sunday.

**By Bicycle** Push bikes, as Bermudians call bicycles, are a pleasant way to travel around the island, provided you don't mind the hilly terrain (*see* Chapter 6, Sports and Fitness). Bikes can be rented at **Eve's Cycle Livery** (Middle Rd., Paget, tel. 809/236–6247), **St. George's Cycles** (Water St., St. George's, tel. 809/297–1463), and **Georgiana Cycles** (Cambridge Rd., Somerset, tel. 809/234–2404). Rentals cost $10 for the first day and $5 for each subsequent day.

**By Limousine** A limousine isn't the cheapest way to tour the island, but it is the most luxurious. If you reserve 24 hours in advance, **London Taxi Limousine Service** (tel. 809/292–3691) will provide a London-type cab, replete with liveried chauffeur, to drive you around for $60 per hour; corporate rates are available.

## Guided Tours

**Orientation Tours** **Butterfield Travel Ltd.** (tel. 809/292-1510), the local Gray Line representative, runs custom-designed tours for groups and individual tours for cruise passengers seeking an alternative to prearranged shore excursions. Among the tours are a glass-bottom boat trip ($20 per person), a three-hour taxi tour around Harrington Sound ($30), and a five-hour island cruise with stops at Dockyard and St. George's ($45).

**L. P. Gutteridge Ltd.** (tel. 809/295–4545), the American Express representative on the island, specializes in group tours, but individual packages can also be arranged.

*Taxi Tours* A blue flag on the hood of a cab indicates that the driver is a qualified tour guide. These cabs can be difficult to find, but most of their drivers are friendly, entertaining, and well informed about the island and its history. Ask your hotel to arrange a tour with a knowledgeable driver. Tours are a minimum of three hours long. The legal rate is $20 per hour for one to four passengers, and $30 per hour for five or six passengers. A 25% surcharge is added between 10 PM and 6 AM, and on Sunday and public holidays.

*Bus and Minibus Tours*

**Penboss Associates Ltd.** (tel. 809/295–3927) conducts narrated motorcoach tours of both St. George's and Hamilton. The five-hour St. George's tour ($28), which circles Harrington Sound, includes admission to the Aquarium, Museum and Zoo, and Leamington Caves. The three-hour tour of Hamilton ($18) covers Verdmont, the Botanical Gardens, and sights in the capital city.

**St. George's Transportation** (tel. 809/297-8199) runs minibus tours of St. George's and St. David's, leaving from King's Square in St. George's. A one-hour tour costs $12 per person, and the two-hour tour is $17.50.

*Carriage Tours*

There are only a few horse-drawn carriages on the island, but they are still a romantic way to see the sights. The raconteurs at the reins dispense a wealth of local lore and information—or misinformation. Regardless of the veracity of their tales, you'll enjoy the telling. Carriages can be hired on Front Street in Hamilton; for tours of the West End and Dockyard, contact **Bermuda Carriages** (tel. 809/238–2640). Rates for a one-horse carriage are $15 for a half hour, and $10 for each additional half hour. For a two-horse carriage, the fee is $20 for the first half hour, and $15 for each half hour thereafter.

**Special-Interest Tours**

*Open Houses and Garden Tours*

For six weeks each spring, several Bermudian homes and gardens are open for public tours, offering visitors a delightful glimpse of how the locals live. Most of the homes date from the 17th century, and all have lovely lawns and gardens. Arranged by the **Garden Club of Bermuda** (tel. 809/295–1301), tours visit three different houses each Wednesday between 2 and 5. A $7.50 admission fee helps sponsor the club's conservation projects and horticultural scholarships.

Free guided tours of the **Botanical Gardens** leave at 10:30 AM from the parking lot of Tavern on the Green, a restaurant on the grounds. These 90-minute tours are conducted year-round on Tuesday and Wednesday (Tuesday and Friday between November 15 and March 31).

**Boat Trips**

A host of boats offers sightseeing, snorkeling, and swimming excursions. Major attractions include the Sea Gardens, with their splendid underwater scenes, and the coral-wrapped wreck of HMS *Vixen*, both of which lie off the West End. Many of the boats operate only during high season, so call in advance for schedules.

The ***Looking Glass*** (tel. 809/236–8000), an 85-passenger glass-bottom boat owned by Beau Evans, heads out to the Sea Gardens twice daily from Hamilton on a two-hour cruise known as the "Reef and Wreck Adventure." En route, Evans offers an entertaining commentary on the islands of Hamilton Harbour and the Great Sound. Tours depart from Front Street and cost $20 for adults and $10 for children under 12; senior citizens receive a 20% discount. A four-hour dinner cruise ($49.50 adults, $24.75 for children, 20% discount for senior citizens) includes complimentary cocktails on board the *Looking Glass* and a four-course meal—accompanied by a calypso guitarist—at the Somerset Village Inn. The "Cruise of Lights" ($23.50 adults, $11.75 children, 20% discount for seniors) is a late-night outing with views of reefs, sea creatures, and constellations.

**Bermuda Island Cruises** (tel. 809/292–8652) operates the 120-passenger *Reef Explorer*, which leaves Hamilton on Tuesday, Thursday, and Saturday night for a "Shipwreck Dinner Cruise" ($50 adults, $25 children under 12). The boat travels along the reefs, stopping at Hawkins Island for dinner, dancing, and a show featuring limbo dancers and calypso music. Two-hour glass-bottom-boat tours of the Sea Gardens ($20 adults, $10 children) leave twice daily from the Ferry Terminal in Hamilton. And departing weekdays at 10 AM from Albuoy's Point in Hamilton, a five-hour Somerset cruise ($40 adults, $20 children) features shopping in Somerset Village and a rum-swizzle party on the return trip. A six-hour tour to St. George's ($50 adults, $25 children), including sightseeing, shopping, and rum swizzles, also operates from Albuoy's Point, Tuesday–Sunday.

**Bermuda Water Tours** (tel. 809/295–3727) offers a wide range of tours, including swimming and snorkeling outings. One tour takes passengers in a glass-bottom boat for a look at the reefs, a wreck, and fish. The $20 tour departs twice daily from Front Street, next to the Ferry Terminal in Hamilton. The six-hour "East Ender" tour ($42 per person) includes a trip to St. George's, complete with swimming, snorkeling, rum swizzles, and calypso music. The "West Ender" tour ($30) features a visit to the Maritime Museum, lunch at the Country Squire Restaurant (Mangrove Bay, Somerset, tel. 809/234–0105), shopping in Somerset Village, and a return trip to Hamilton by ferry. Dinner cruises are also occasionally offered.

**Whistler Charters** (tel. 809/234–7038) offers sailing parties and charters aboard the *Whistler of Paget*, a 10-passenger, 38-foot sloop. Half-day sailing parties and two-hour sunset sails cost $30 per person; private charters are $325 for a full day and $180 for a half day. Snorkeling gear is provided.

**Williams Marine Ltd.** (tel. 809/238–0774) operates half-day tours ($27.50) and sunset sails ($17.50) on the *Alibi*, a 40-foot ketch that can carry 15 passengers, and the *Sundancer*, a 50-foot ketch that carries 24. Rum swizzles, soda, and beer are complimentary.

**Salt Kettle Boat Rentals Ltd.** (tel. 809/236–4863) offers sailing parties aboard the 55-foot sloop *Brightstar* for $25 per person.

**Butterfield Travel Ltd.** and **L. P. Gutteridge Ltd.** (*see* Orientation Tours, above) also arrange boat trips.

**Walking Tours**

The Bermuda Department of Tourism publishes brochures for self-guided tours of Hamilton, St. George's, the West End, and the Railway Trail. Available free at all Visitors Information Centres and at hotels and guest houses, these brochures contain detailed directions for walkers and cyclists, historical notes, and anecdotes.

From November 15 to March 31, the **Bermuda National Trust** (tel. 809/236–6483) conducts one-hour walking tours of Hamilton, St. George's, and Somerset. The tours of Hamilton and St. George's take in the large number of 17th- and 18th-century buildings in the two towns, while the tour in Somerset focuses more on the island's flora. Hamilton tours begin from the Visitors Information Centre in the Ferry Terminal on Front Street every Monday at 10 AM; tours of St. George's are conducted on Wednesday and Saturday, starting at 10:30 AM in King's Square; the Somerset walk departs from the Country Squire Restaurant (Mangrove Bay, Somerset, tel. 809/234–0105) on Thursday at 10 AM.

Other free guided walks during the low season include a 2-mile walk through woodlands and scenic areas, leaving from the Clock Tower Building at Dockyard at 11 AM; and a tour around Dockyard, departing from the Craft Market on Sunday at 2 PM.

# 2 Portraits of Bermuda

# Bermuda at a Glance: A Chronology

**1503** Juan de Bermudez discovers the islands while searching for the New World. The islands are eventually named after him.

**1603** Diego Ramirez, a Spanish captain, spends several weeks on Bermuda making ship repairs.

**1609** An English fleet of nine ships, under the command of Admiral Sir George Somers, sets sail for Jamestown, Virginia, with supplies for the starving colony. Struck by a hurricane, the fleet is scattered, and the admiral's ship, the *Sea Venture*, runs aground on the reefs of Bermuda. The colonization of Bermuda begins.

**1610** After building two ships, *Deliverance* and *Patience*, from the island's cedar trees, the survivors depart for Jamestown, leaving behind a small party of men. Admiral Sir George Somers returns to Bermuda a few weeks later but dies soon afterward. He requests that his heart be buried on the island.

**1612** Asserting ownership of the islands, the Virginia Company sends 60 settlers to Bermuda under the command of Richard Moore, the colony's first governor. The Virginia Company sells its rights to the islands to the newly formed Bermuda Company for £2,000.

**1616** The islands are surveyed and divided into shares (25 acres) and tribes (50 shares per tribe). The tribes, or parishes, are named after investors in the Bermuda Company. The first slaves are brought to Bermuda to dive for pearls.

**1620** The Bermuda Parliament meets for the first time, in St. Peter's Church in St. George's, making it the third oldest parliament in the world after Iceland and Great Britain.

**1684** The Crown takes over control of the colony from the Bermuda Company. Sir Robert Robinson is appointed the Crown's first Governor.

**1775** The American Continental Congress announces a trade embargo against all colonies remaining loyal to the Crown. Dependent on America for food, Bermuda negotiates to give the rebellious colonies salt if they will lift the embargo. The colonies refuse, but state that they will end sanctions in exchange for gunpowder. Without the knowledge of Governor George Bruere, a group of Bermudians breaks into the magazine at St. George's and steals the island's supply of gunpowder. The gunpowder is delivered to the Americans, who lift the embargo.

**1780** The "Great Hurricane" hits Bermuda, driving ships ashore and leveling houses and trees.

**1784** Bermuda's first newspaper, *The Bermuda Gazette & Weekly Advertiser*, is started by Joseph Stockdale in St. George's.

**1804** Irish poet Thomas Moore arrives in Bermuda for a four-month stint as registrar of the admiralty court. His affair with the married Hester Tucker was the inspiration for his steamy love poems to her (the "Nea" in his odes), which have attained legendary status in Bermuda.

**1810** The Royal Navy begins work on Dockyard, a new naval base on Ireland Island.

**1812** In response to American raids on York (now Toronto) during the War of 1812, the British fleet attacks Washington, DC, from its base in Bermuda.

**1815** Hamilton becomes the new capital of Bermuda, superseding St. George's.

**1834** Slavery is abolished.

**1846** The first lighthouse in the colony, the 133-foot Gibb's Hill Lighthouse, is built at the western end of the island in an effort to reduce the number of shipwrecks in the area.

**1861** Bermuda enters a period of enormous prosperity with the outbreak of the American Civil War. Sympathetic to the South, Bermudians take up the lucrative and dangerous task of running the Union blockade of southern ports. Sailing in small, fast ships, Bermudians ferry munitions and supplies to the Confederates and return with bales of cotton bound for London.

**1883** Princess Louise, daughter of Queen Victoria, visits Bermuda. In honor of her visit, the new Pembroke Hotel changes its name to The Princess.

**1901** Afrikaner prisoners from the Boer War are incarcerated in Bermuda. By the end of the war, approximately 4,000 prisoners are housed on the islands.

**1915** A 120-man contingent of the Bermuda Volunteer Rifle Corps (B.V.R.C.) departs for service in France during World War I. In action at the battles of the Somme, Arras, and the Third Battle of Ypres, the unit loses more than 30% of its men. In 1916, the Bermuda Militia Artillery also heads for France.

**1931** Constructed at a cost of £1 million, the Bermuda Railway opens years behind schedule. Maintenance problems during World War II cripple train service, and the whole system is sold to British Guiana in 1948.

**1937** Imperial Airways begins the first scheduled air service to Bermuda from Port Washington in the United States.

**1940** During World War II, mail bound for Europe from the Americas is off-loaded in Bermuda and taken to the basement of The Princess hotel, where it is opened by British civil servants trying to locate German spies. Several spies in the United States are unmasked. As part of the Lend-Lease Act between Prime Minister Churchill and President Roosevelt, the United States is awarded a 99-year lease for a military base on St. David's Island. Construction of the base begins in 1941.

**1944** Women landowners are given the vote.

**1946** For the first time, automobiles are permitted by law on Bermuda.

**1951** The Royal Navy withdraws from Dockyard and closes the base.

**1953** Winston Churchill, Dwight D. Eisenhower, and Prime Minister Joseph Laniel of France meet on Bermuda for the "Big Three Conference."

**1959** NASA opens a space tracking station on Coopers Island, which is part of the American base.

**1971** Edward Richards becomes Bermuda's first black government leader (a title later changed to premier).

**1973** Governor Sir Richard Sharples and his aide, Captain Hugh Sayers, are shot dead. In 1976, Erskine "Buck" Burrows is convicted of the murder, as well as several other murders and armed robberies. He is hanged in 1977.

**1979** Gina Swainson, Miss Bermuda, wins the Miss World Contest. An official half holiday is announced and Gina Swainson postage stamps are released in 1980.

**1987** Hurricane Emily hits Bermuda, injuring more than 70 people and causing millions of dollars in damage.

**1990** President Bush and Prime Minister Thatcher meet on Bermuda.

# America's Rebel Colonies and Bermuda: Getting a Bang for Their Buckwheat

*by William Zuill*

*A native Bermudian and a member of the Bermuda House of Assembly, William Zuill is the author of several historical works about the island. This excerpt about the role of Bermuda in the American War of Independence is taken from his book,* Bermuda Journey. *William Zuill died in July 1989.*

When the War of American Independence began, Bermudians at first felt little personal concern. There was some sympathy for the colonists; quarrels between arbitrary executive power and people, which in America had now led to real trouble, had also been part of Bermuda's history, and besides this there were ties of blood and friendship to make for a common understanding. But for all that, Bermudians, while expressing discreet sympathy, were chiefly concerned for their ships and carrying trade, and realizing their helpless position, they believed their wisest course lay in continued loyalty to the Crown. The wisdom of this policy was suddenly brought into question when the Continental Congress placed an embargo on all trade with Britain and the loyal colonies, for as nearly all essential food supplies came from the Continent, the island faced starvation unless the decree was relaxed. Thus there was a swift realization that Bermuda's fate was deeply involved in the war.

The drama now began to unfold and soon developed into a struggle between the governor, George Bruere, and the dominant Bermuda clique led by the Tuckers of the West End. Bruere's chief characteristic was unswerving, unquestioning loyalty, and the fact that two of his sons were fighting with the royalist forces in America—one of them was killed at Bunker Hill—made the ambiguous behavior of Bermudians intolerable to him, both as a father and as an Englishman.

Of the Tuckers, the most prominent member of the family at this time was Colonel Henry, of the Grove, Southampton. His eldest son, Henry, colonial treasure and councillor, had married the governor's daughter, Frances Bruere, and lived at St. George's. There were also two sons in America, Thomas Tudor, a doctor settled in Charleston, and St. George, the youngest, a lawyer in Virginia. The two boys in America, caught up in the events around them and far removed from the delicacies of the Bermuda situation, openly took the side of the colonists.

Up to the time of the outbreak of the war there had been warm friendship between the Tuckers and the Brueres, a relationship made closer by the marriage of Henry Tucker to Frances Bruere. But when it became known in Bermuda that the Tuckers abroad were backing the Americans, Bruere publicly denounced them as rebels and broke off relations with every member of the family except his son-in-law. But Colonel Henry was more concerned with the situation in Bermuda than he was with the rights and wrongs of the conflict itself, and he believed that unless someone acted, the island was facing serious disaster. So, privately, through his sons in America, he began to sound out some of the delegates to the Continental Congress as to whether the embargo would be relaxed in exchange for salt. This move, never in any way official, had the backing of a powerful group, and before long it was decided to send the colonel with two or three others to Philadelphia to see what could be arranged. Meanwhile another but less powerful faction took form and likewise held meetings, the object of which was to oppose in every way these overtures to rebels.

Colonel Henry and his colleagues reached Philadelphia in July 1775 and on the 11th delivered their appeal to Congress. Though larded with unctuous flattery, the address met a stony reception, but a hint was thrown out that although salt was not wanted, any vessel bringing arms or powder would find herself free from the embargo. The fact that there was a useful store of powder at St. George's was by now common knowledge in America, for the Tucker boys had told their friends about it and the information had reached General Washington. Thus, before long, the question of seizing this powder for the Americans was in the forefront of the discussions.

Colonel Henry was in a tight corner. Never for an instant feeling that his own loyalty was in question, he had believed himself fully justified in coming to Philadelphia to offer salt in exchange for food. But these new suggestions which were now being put to him went far beyond anything he had contemplated, and he was dismayed at the ugly situation that confronted him. It is evident that the forces at work were too strong for him. The desperate situation in Bermuda, verging on starvation, could only be relieved by supplies from America, and an adamant Congress held the whip hand. In the end, after some agonizing heart-searching, he gave in and agreed with Benjamin Franklin to trade the powder at St. George's for an exemption of Bermuda ships from the embargo.

Colonel Henry returned home at once, arriving on July 25. His son St. George, coming from Virginia, arrived about the same time, while two other ships from America, sent especially to fetch the powder, were already on their way.

On August 14, 1775, there was secret but feverish activity among the conspirators as whaleboats from various parts of the island assembled at Somerset. As soon as it was dark, the party, under the command, it is believed, of son-in-law Henry and a Captain Morgan, set off for St. George's. St. George, lately from Virginia and sure to be suspect, spent the night at St. George's, possibly at the home of his brother Henry, and at midnight was seen ostentatiously walking up and down the Parade with Chief Justice Burch, thus establishing a watertight alibi. Meanwhile the landing party, leaving the boats at Tobacco Bay on the north side of St. George's, reached the unguarded magazine. The door was quickly forced, and before long, kegs of powder were rolling over the grass of the Governor's Park toward the bay, where they were speedily stowed in the boats. The work went on steadily until the first streaks of dawn drove the party from the scene. By that time 100 barrels of powder were on the way to guns that would discharge the powder against the king's men.

When Bruere heard the news he was frantic. A vessel which he rightly believed had the stolen powder on board was still in sight from Retreat Hill, and he determined to give chase. Rushing into town, the distraught man issued a hysterical proclamation:

*POWDER STEAL*

*Advt*

Save your Country from Ruin, which may hereafter happen. The Powder stole out of the Magazine late last night cannot be carried far as the wind is so light.

A GREAT REWARD

will be given to any person that can make a proper discovery before the Magistrates.

News of the outrage and copies of the proclamation were hurried through the colony as fast as rider could travel. The legislature was summoned to meet the following day. Many members of the Assembly doubtless knew a good deal, but officially all was dark and the legislature did its duty by voting a reward and sending a wordy message expressing its abhorrence of the crime.

But no practical help was forthcoming, and after several days of helpless frustration Bruere determined to send a vessel to Boston to inform Admiral Howe what had happened. At first no vessels were to be had anywhere in the island; then, when one was found, the owner was threatened with sabotage, so he withdrew his offer. Another vessel was found, but there was no crew, and for three whole weeks, in an island teeming with mariners, no one could be found to go to sea. At last, on September 3, the governor's ship put to sea, but not without a final incident, for she was boarded offshore by a group of men who searched the captain and crew for letters. These had been prudently hidden away in the ballast with the governor's slave, who remained undiscovered. The captain hotly denied having any confidential papers, so the disappointed boarders beat him up and then left.

In due course the ship reached Boston, and Admiral Howe at once sent the *Scorpion* to Bermuda to help Bruere keep order. Thereafter for several years His Majesty's ships kept a watchful eye on the activities of Bermudians, and in 1778 these were replaced by a garrison. It has always seemed extraordinary that no rumor of this bargain with the Americans reached the ears of Bruere before the actual robbery took place. It is even more amazing that within a stone's throw of Government House such a desperate undertaking could have continued steadily throughout the night without discovery.

The loss of the powder coincided with the disappearance of a French officer, a prisoner on parole. At the time it was thought that he had been in league with the Americans and had made his escape with them. But 100 years later when the foundation for the Unfinished Church was being excavated, the skeleton of a man dressed in French uniform was disclosed. It is now believed that he must have come on the scene while the robbery was in progress and, in the dark, been mistaken for a British officer. Before he could utter a sound he must have been killed outright by these desperate men and quickly buried on the governor's doorstep.

# Following in the Tracks of the Bermuda Railway

*by Ben Davidson*

*A former travel editor for* Sunset Travel *magazine, Ben Davidson specializes in travel writing and photography.*

Bermuda is lovely, but a walk along its narrow roads can involve close encounters with countless madcap moped drivers and a stream of cars. A more serene way to sample Bermuda's lush terrain, stunning seascapes, and colorful colonies of island homes is to follow the route of the railroad that once crossed this isolated archipelago. The Bermuda Railway Trail goes along the old train right-of-way for 18 miles, winding through three of the several interconnected islands that make up Bermuda.

Opened in 1931, the railway provided smooth-running transportation between the quiet village of Somerset at the west end and the former colonial capital of St. George's to the east. But by 1948 it had fallen a victim to excessive military use during World War II, soaring maintenance costs, and the automobile. The railroad was closed down, and all its rolling stock was sold to Guyana (then called British Guiana). In 1984, Bermuda's 375th anniversary, the government dedicated the lands of the old railway for public use and began to clear, pave, and add signs to sections of its route.

The trail's most enchanting aspect is that it reveals a parade of island views hidden from the public for nearly 30 years, scenes similar to what the first colonists must have found here in the early 1600s. In a few places the trail joins the main roads, but mostly it follows a tranquil, car-free route from parish to parish, past quiet bays, limestone cliffs, small farms, and groves of cedar, allspice, mangrove, and fiddlewood trees. Short jaunts on side trails and intersecting tribe roads (paths that were built in the early 1600s as boundaries between the parishes, or "tribes") bring you to historic forts and a lofty lighthouse, coral-tinted beaches, parks, and preserves.

I explored the Railway Trail on foot, moped, and horseback, using an 18-page guide available free at the Visitors Service Bureau in Hamilton. (You can also find the guide at some of the big hotels.) The booklet contains historical photos, a brief history of the railroad, maps, and descriptions of seven sections of trail, which range from 1¾ to 3¾ miles.

Sporting a pair of proper Bermuda shorts, I revved up my rented moped and headed out to the Somerset Bus Terminal, one of eight former railroad stations and the westernmost end of the trail. From there I followed the paved path to Springfield—an 18th-century plantation house used by the Springfield Library. A leisurely stroll in the adjoining five-acre Springfield & Gilbert Nature Reserve took me through thick forests of fiddlewood. I also saw stands of Bermuda cedars that once blanketed the island but were nearly wiped out by blight in the 1940s.

Back on the trail I spotted oleander, hibiscus, bougainvillea, and poinsettia bursting through the greenery at every turn. In backyards I could see bananas, grapefruit, oranges, lemons, and limes growing in profusion, thanks to Bermuda's consistent year-round subtropical climate.

I parked the moped at the trailhead to Fort Scaur—a 19th-century fortress built by the Duke of Wellington, conqueror of Napoleon at Waterloo—and strolled up to its mighty walls and deep moat. Through a dark passage I reached the grassy grounds with their massive gun mounts and bunkers. A telescope atop the fort's walls provided close-up views of the Great Sound and Ely's Harbor, once a smuggler's haven. A caretaker showed me around the fort, one of the three largest in Bermuda.

On my moped again, I motored past Skroggins Bay to the Lantana Colony Club, a group of beachside cottages. I stopped to sip a Dark and Stormy—a classic Bermudian rum drink—and to enjoy the view of the sail-filled Great Sound. My post-swizzle destination: Somerset Bridge. Only 32 inches wide, this tiny bridge was built in 1620 and looks more like a plank in the road than the world's smallest drawbridge—its opening is just wide enough for a sailboat's mast to pass through.

I ended my first Railway Trail ride at the ferry terminal near the bridge, where I boarded the next ferry back to Hamilton. Had I continued, the trail would have taken me through what was once the agricultural heartland of Bermuda. The colony's 20 square miles of gently rolling landscape, graced by rich volcanic soil and a mild climate, once yielded crops of sweet, succulent Bermuda onions, potatoes, and other produce. But tourism has become bigger business here, and today only some 500 acres are devoted to vegetable crops.

Just west of Sandys Parish the trail runs for some 3¾ miles through Warwick Parish. The path, now dirt, overlooks Little Sound and Southampton, where fishing boats are moored. Here the Railway Trail begins to intersect many of Bermuda's tribe roads, which make interesting diversions. Tribe Road No. 2 brings you to the Gibb's Hill Lighthouse, built around 1846. This 133-foot structure is one of the few lighthouses in the world made of cast iron. You pay $2 for the dubious privilege of climbing 185 steps to the lens house, where you're rewarded with far-reaching views of the island and Great Sound. The 1,500-watt electric lamp can be seen as far away as 40 miles.

Spicelands, a riding center in Warwick, schedules early-morning rides along sections of the Railway Trail and South Shore beaches. I joined a ride to follow part of the trail where it cuts deep into the rolling limestone terrain—so deep that at one point we passed through the 450-foot Paget Tunnel, whose walls are lined with roots of rubber trees.

We rode through woodlands and fields, past stands of Surinam cherry trees and houses equipped with domed water tanks and stepped, pyramid-shaped roofs designed to catch rainwater. As we trotted through the cool darkness beneath a dense canopy of trees it was hard to imagine a time when noisy rolling stock rattled along the same route, carrying some of the 14 million passengers who rode the railway while it was in operation. Finally, a tribe road led us through tropical vegetation to the clean, coral-pink beaches of Bermuda's beautiful South Shore.

East of Hamilton, the Railway Trail follows the North Shore, beginning in Palmetto Park in the lush, hilly parish of Devonshire. It hugs the coastline past Palmetto House (a cross-shaped, 18th-century mansion belonging to the Bermuda National Trust) and thick stands of Bermuda cedar to Penhurst Park, where there are walking trails, agricultural plots, and good swimming beaches.

Farther east the trail hits a wilder stretch of coast. The Shelley Bay Park and Nature Reserve along here has native mangroves and one of the few beaches on the North Shore. After a short walk on North Shore Road, the trail picks up again at Bailey's Bay and follows the coast to Coney Island. The park here has an old lime kiln and a former horse-ferry landing.

The remaining sections of the trail are in St. George's. Start at the old Terminal Building (now called Tiger Bay Gardens) and stroll through this historic town. The trail passes by Mullet Bay and Rocky Hill Parks, then heads to Lover's Lake Nature Reserve, where nesting longtails can be seen amid the mangroves. The end of the trail is at Ferry Point Park, directly across from Coney Island. In the park there's a historic fort and a cemetery.

Evenings are perhaps the most enchanting time to walk along the Railway Trail. As the light grows dim, the moist air fills with songs from tiny tree frogs hidden in hedges of oleander and hibiscus. The sound sets a tranquil, tropical mood that, for nearly a half century, has been undisturbed by the piercing whistle and clickety-clack of Bermuda's bygone railroad.

# 3 Exploring Bermuda

## Orientation

*by Honey Naylor*

*The major contributor to* Fodor's New Orleans *and* Caribbean, *Honey Naylor has worked on various other Fodor's guides. Her featured articles have appeared in* Travel & Leisure, USA Today, New Orleans Magazine, Travel-Holiday, *and other national publications.*

Bermuda is nothing if not colorful. The streets are lined with hedges of hibiscus and oleander, and rolling green hills are shaded by tall palms and casuarina trees. The limestone buildings are painted in pretty pastels (pink and white seem to be most popular), and their gleaming white roofs are steeply pitched to channel the rain upon which Bermudians depend—the island has no freshwater lakes or streams. In addition, many houses have quaint butteries, miniature cottages that were once used as ice houses. House numbers are a relatively new phenomenon on the island, although most houses have names, such as Tranquillity, Struggle, and Last Penny. Another architectural feature indigenous to Bermuda is moon gates. These free-standing stone arches can be found in gardens all over the island, and Bermudians favor them as backdrops for wedding pictures.

For exploring purposes, we've divided Bermuda into four separate tours. The first tour is of Hamilton, the island's capital. Hamilton is of primary interest for its harbor, its shops—housed in small pastel-colored buildings—and the government buildings, where visitors can watch sessions of Parliament. In addition, the town is the major departure point for sightseeing boats, ferries, and the pink-and-blue buses that ramble all over the island. Don't confuse Hamilton town with the parish of the same name—Hamilton town is in Pembroke Parish. The second tour is of St. George's town on the eastern end of the island, near the site of Bermuda's first settlement. History mavens will find much of interest in St. George's, which boasts several noteworthy 17th-century buildings. The third tour explores the West End, the site of the sleepy hamlet of Somerset and Dockyard, a former naval shipyard that is home to the Maritime Museum and a brand-new tourist center. The West End is in Sandys Parish, which can be pronounced either "Sandies" or "Sands."

The fourth tour is a rambling journey through the island's other parishes that is best done by moped, bicycle, or car. The parishes date back to 1616, when Bermuda was first surveyed and the island was divided into eight tribes or parishes, each named for an investor in the Bermuda Company, an offshoot of the Virginia Company, which controlled the island until 1684. The parishes are Sandys, Southampton, Warwick, Paget, Smith's, Hamilton, Pembroke, and Devonshire. St. George's, which was considered public land in the early days, is the ninth parish and includes the town of St. George's. Bermudians customarily identify sites on the island by the parish in which they are located: "It's in Pembroke," a resident will say, or "It's in Warwick." The main roads connecting the parishes are self-explanatory: North Shore Road, Middle Road, South Road, and Harbour Road. Almost all traffic traversing the island's 20-mile length uses these roads, although some 1,200 smaller roads crisscross the island. Visitors will see several "tribe roads" that date back to the initial survey of the island; many of these are now no more than country lanes, and some are dead ends. As you travel around the island you'll see small brown-and-white signs pointing to the Railway Trail. Built along the route of Bermuda's old railway line, the trail is now a peaceful route reserved for pedestrians and cyclists (*see* Off the Beaten Track, below).

## Tour 1: Hamilton

*Numbers in the margin correspond with points of interest on the Hamilton map.*

Historically, Bermudians were seafarers, and the government relied for revenues on the duties paid on ships' cargoes. Ships were required by law to anchor in the harbor at St. George's to declare their goods, but most captains preferred to anchor closer to their homes, and the law was largely ignored. To combat the loss of revenues, legislation was passed in 1790 to establish a second port and customs house at Crow Lane Harbour (now Hamilton Harbour). Largely because of Hamilton's excellent harbor and central location, the seat of government was moved from St. George's to Hamilton on January 1, 1815. Today, the capital is home to about a quarter of the island's 54,000 residents.

1 Your first stop should be the **Visitors Service Bureau** in the Ferry Terminal Building, where the friendly staff can provide you with maps and brochures. Step out of the bureau onto the capital's main avenue, **Front Street.** Running alongside the harbor, Front Street bustles with small cars, mopeds, bicycles, buses, pedestrians, and the occasional horse-drawn carriage. It's fun to imagine what the street must have looked like prior to the arrival of automobiles in 1946. From 1931 to 1946, railroad tracks ran along Front Street, carrying "Old Rattle and Shake," as the Bermuda Railway was called. Today, Front Street is lined with colorful little buildings, many with balconies and arcades that house shops and boutiques selling everything from imported woolens to perfumes and cosmetics. This is the main shopping area on the island, and shoppers will probably want to spend plenty of time—and money—here (*see* Chapter 4, Shopping).

The docks behind the Ferry Terminal are the departure points for ferries making the short trip to Paget and Warwick parishes, or the longer trip across the Great Sound to the West End. Next to the terminal are the slips for glass-bottom boats and other sightseeing vessels that take passengers on excursions to the Sea Gardens, St. George's, and Dockyard. Beyond these is **No. 1 Shed,** the pink passenger-ship terminal (two other terminals are situated farther east on Front Street). During high season, a cruise ship is usually moored in the harbor—all but the largest ships, such as the *QE2*, can sail right into Hamilton Harbour. During the low season (mid-November–March 31), No. 1 Shed is the site of regularly scheduled afternoon teas, fashion shows, and performances by the Gombey Dancers (*see* Chapter 9, The Arts and Nightlife).

The oddly shaped traffic box at Heyl's Corner, at the intersection of Front and Queen streets, is known as the **"Birdcage,"** from which the police (locally known as "bobbies" as in Great Britain) sometimes direct traffic. Named for its designer, Michael "Dickey" Bird, the traffic box has been a Hamilton landmark for more than 20 years. The corner itself is named for J. B. Heyl, a Southerner who came to Bermuda in the 19th century and opened an apothecary shop on Queen Street.

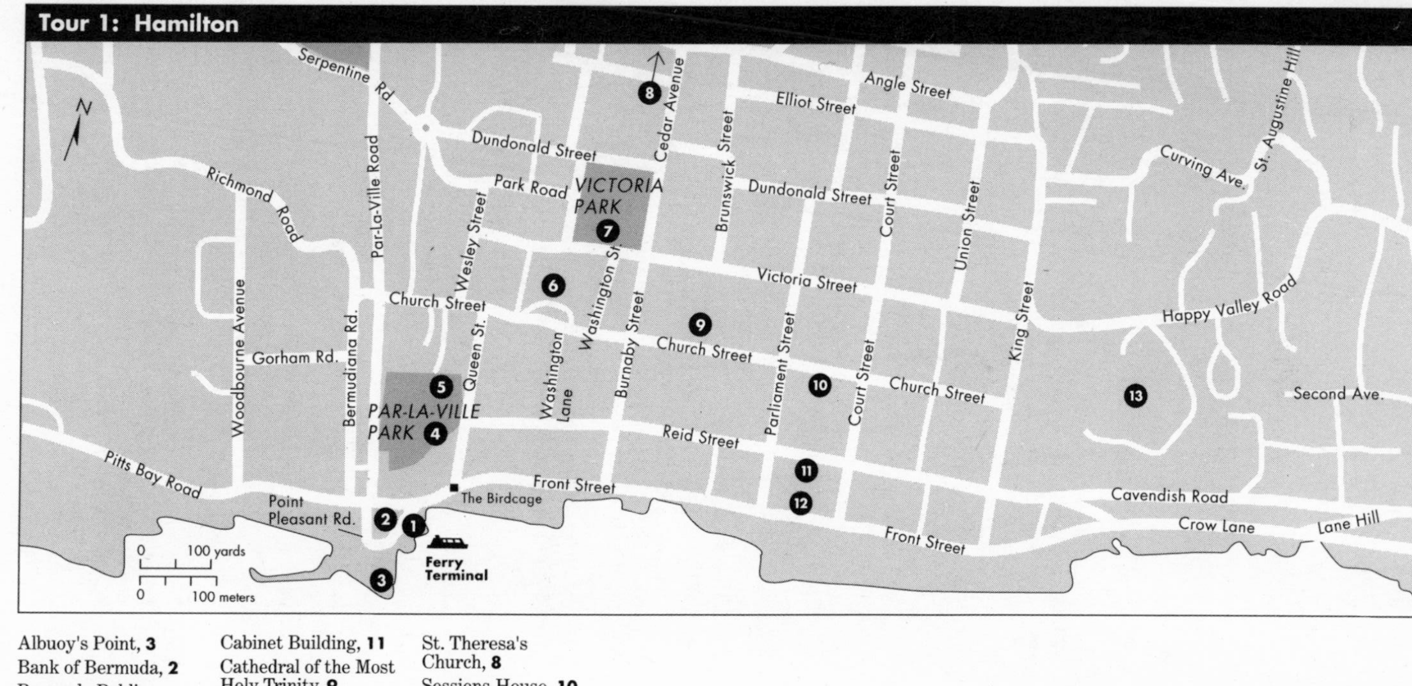


Albuoy's Point, **3**
Bank of Bermuda, **2**
Bermuda Public Library and Museum of the Bermuda Historical Society, **5**
Cabinet Building, **11**
Cathedral of the Most Holy Trinity, **9**
Cenotaph, **12**
City Hall, **6**
Fort Hamilton, **13**
Perot Post Office, **4**
St. Theresa's Church, **8**
Sessions House, **10**
Victoria Park, **7**
Visitors Service Bureau, **1**

Visitors interested in coins should cross Point Pleasant Road
2 and go up to the mezzanine of the **Bank of Bermuda**. British and Spanish coins, many of them ancient, are displayed in glass cases. The collection includes some pieces of "hog money," Bermuda's first currency, which was issued by the Bermuda Company in 1615. Hog money, the oldest of all British colonial coins, is stamped on one side with a replica of the *Sea Venture* and on the other with an unattractive wild hog ringed with the words "Somer Ilands." Pigs, which had survived a shipwreck or been released by Spanish sailors, were the only inhabitants encountered by Sir George Somers and his crew when they foundered on Bermuda's shores in 1609. *Admission free. Open weekdays. 9:30–3.*

Following Point Pleasant Road toward the water, you'll come to
3 **Albuoy's Point**, a pleasant waterfront park with benches, trees, and a splendid view of the activity in the harbor. Nearby is the **Royal Bermuda Yacht Club**, which was built in the 1930s. The idea for the yacht club was conceived in 1844 beneath the Calabash Tree at Walsingham (*see* Tour 4: The Parishes, below), and Prince Albert gave permission for the club to use the word "Royal" in 1845. Today, royalty, international yachting celebrities, and the local elite hobnob at the posh club, which sponsors the Newport–Bermuda Yacht Race.

If you plan to do a lot of exploring, visit the **Bermuda Book Store,** on Front and Queen streets, to buy a copy of the *Bermuda Islands Guide* ($4.95). The paperback atlas contains every lane, tribe road, alley, and landmark on the island. The bookstore, a marvelous Dickensian place with creaky wood floors, is filled with books about the island.

4 From the bookstore, continue along Queen Street to the **Perot Post Office,** a white two-story edifice that dates back to around 1842. Still a post office, this shuttered building is where Bermuda's first postage stamps originated. The island's first postmaster was William Bennet Perot. Appointed in 1821, Perot used to meet arriving steamers to collect the mail, stash it in his beaver hat, and then stroll around Hamilton to deliver it. Customers wishing to post a letter paid Perot, who hand-stamped each letter. Obviously, the postmaster had to be at his station to do this, which annoyed Perot, who preferred pottering around in the garden. Local historians credit Perot's friend, the pharmacist J. B. Heyl, for the idea for Bermuda's first book of stamps. Heyl suggested that Perot make a whole sheet of postmarks, write "Wm B. Perot" on each postmark, and sell the sheet for a shilling. People could then tear off a postmark, paste it on a letter, and post it—without having to extricate Mr. Perot from the garden shrubbery. The extremely rare Perot stamps, some of which are in the Queen's Royal Stamp Collection, are now coveted by collectors. In 1986, one of them sold at auction in Chicago for $135,000. *Queen St., tel. 809/295-5151. Admission free. Open weekdays 9–5.*

---

**Time Out** The garden where Perot liked to pass his time is now **Par-la-Ville Park**, a pleasant spot that occupies almost an entire block. The Queen Street entrance (there's another on Par-la-Ville Road) is next to the post office. Paths wind through the luxuriant gardens, and the park benches are ideal for picnicking or a short rest. At noon you may have trouble finding a place to sit, because this is a favorite lunch spot of Hamilton office workers.

One block along Queen Street is a Kentucky Fried Chicken franchise (open daily 11–10).

---

Next to the post office is a giant rubber tree from British Guiana (now Guyana) that was planted by Perot. On a visit to Bermuda, Mark Twain lamented that the rubber tree didn't bear fruit in the form of hot-water bottles and rubber overshoes. The tree is in the front yard of the Georgian house where Mr.
5 Perot and his family lived. Now the **Bermuda Public Library** and **Museum of the Bermuda Historical Society**, the house is a wonderful find for history buffs. The library, which was founded in 1839, moved to its present quarters in the 1940s. One early librarian was an eccentric gentleman with the Pickwickian name of Florentius Frith, who rode in from the country on horseback and struck terror into the heart of anyone who interrupted his chess games to check out a book. The reference section of the library has virtually every book ever written about Bermuda, as well as a collection on microfilm of Bermudian newspapers dating back to 1787. The collection of rare books contains a 1624 edition of John Smith's *Generall Histoire of Virginia, New England and the Somers Isles*. In the museum's entrance hall are portraits of Sir George Somers and his wife, painted about 1605; portraits of Postmaster Perot and his wife can be seen in the back room. Notice Admiral Sir George Somers's lodestone (circa 1600), used for magnetizing compass needles, and a Bermuda map from 1622 that shows the division of the island into 25-acre shares by the original Bermuda Company. The museum also contains an eclectic collection of old English coins and Confederate money; Bermuda silver; Oriental porcelains; portraits of the major investors in the Bermuda Company; and pictures of horse-and-buggy Bermuda juxtaposed with modern-day scenes. There are several cedar pieces, including two Queen Anne chairs from about 1740; a handsome grandfather clock; a Waterford chandelier; handmade palmetto hats; and a sedan chair from around 1770 that is beginning to show its age. Ask to see the letter from George Washington, written "to the inhabitants of Bermuda" in 1775, asking for gunpowder. *13 Queen St. Library: tel. 809/295–2905. Admission free. Open weekdays 9:30–6, Sat. 9:30–5. Museum: tel. 809/295–2487. Donation: $2. Open Mon., Tues., and Thurs.–Sat. 9:30–4:30; closed Wed.*

---

**Time Out** Decorated with lace curtains and white iron furniture, **Fourways Pastry Shop** (Reid St., at the entrance to Washington Mall) serves irresistible, diet-destroying pastries. The **Fourways Grill** (Windsor Pl., across Queen St. from the library) serves light lunches as well as desserts.

---

Continue up Queen Street, or cut through Washington Mall, to Church Street. Set back from the street behind a lawn, foun-
6 tains, and a lily pond is **City Hall**. Built in 1960, the large white structure is topped by a weather vane shaped like the *Sea Venture*. Massive cedar doors open into a large lobby that boasts huge chandeliers, high ceilings, and a portrait gallery. The regal portrait of Queen Elizabeth II was painted by Curtis Hooper and unveiled on April 29, 1987, by the Duke of Gloucester. Oil paintings of all Bermuda's mayors hang here as well. Behind tall cedar doors on the right is the Benbow Collection of

stamps. A handsome cedar staircase leads to an exhibition gallery where the Bermuda Society of Arts holds frequent shows. The City Hall Theatre is often the venue for musical, dance, and theatrical performances. At press time, plans had been announced for the establishment of a National Art Gallery to be housed in City Hall. *Church St., tel. 809/292–1234. Admission free. Open weekdays 9:30–5.*

7 Behind City Hall on Victoria Street, **Victoria Park** has a sunken garden, trees, and a Victorian bandstand, where concerts are sometimes held in the summer. The 4-acre park, built in 1887 in honor of Queen Victoria's Golden Jubilee, opened with great fanfare in 1890. The park is perfectly safe when filled with people, but it isn't a good place to wander alone—some fairly seedy-looking characters hang out here.

Cedar Avenue forms the eastern border of Victoria Park. Fol-
8 low it north for two blocks to **St. Theresa's Church**, a Roman Catholic church built in 1927 in Spanish Mission style. St. Theresa's serves as head of the island's six Roman Catholic churches. During a visit in 1968, Pope Paul VI presented Bermuda's Roman Catholic diocese with a gold and silver chalice that is housed in this church. *Cedar Ave. and Elliot St., tel. 809/292–0607. Open daily 8–7.*

Return to Victoria Street and walk down Washington Street, a one-block boulevard that is the site of the **Central Bus Terminal**. Pink-and-blue buses depart from here to all points on the island. Stop at the kiosk on the median to pick up bus and ferry schedules, and to buy discounted bus tokens for future use.

---

**Time Out** Executives, secretaries, shoppers, and store owners flock to **The Spot** for breakfast, plate lunches, burgers, sandwiches, and coffee. In business for more than 40 years, this simple little restaurant serves full meals for about $7 and sandwiches for about $3. *6 Burnaby St., tel. 809/292–6293. Open Mon.–Sat. 6:30–5.*

---

9 One of the island's most impressive structures is the **Cathedral of the Most Holy Trinity**, the seat of the Anglican Church of Bermuda. The cathedral is the second church to have been built on this site: Twelve years after its completion in 1872, Trinity Church was burned to the ground by an arsonist who torched several houses of worship on the island. Work began on the present church the following year, and it was consecrated in 1911. Designed in Early English style with Gothic flourishes, the church is constructed of Bermuda limestone and materials imported from Scotland, Nova Scotia, France, Ireland, and Indiana. The tower rises to a height of 143 feet, and the clerestory in the nave is supported by piers of polished Scottish granite. The four smaller columns in each aisle were added after a hurricane shook the cathedral—and its architect—during construction. The altar in the Lady Chapel is of Italian marble, and above it is a copy of Andrea del Sarto's *Madonna and Child*. In the south transept, the Warrior Chapel was dedicated in 1977 to honor those who serve in the armed forces of the Crown, and to commemorate those who died in service to their country. The Great Warrior Window is a memorial to 85 Bermudian men who died in World War I; the flags represent military units of Bermuda and England. The choir stalls and bishop's throne are of carved English oak, and the pulpit is a replica of the one in St.

Giles Cathedral, Edinburgh. On a wall near the lectern, the Canterbury Cross, set in stone taken from the walls of Canterbury Cathedral, is a copy of one made in Kent in the 8th century. The stained-glass windows are lovely; note especially the Angel Window on the east wall of the north transept, which was made by local artist Vivienne Gilmore Gardner. *Church St., tel. 809/292–4033. Open daily 8–7.*

10 The eye-catching Italianate edifice on the next block is **Sessions House**, home of the House of Assembly (the lower house of Parliament) and the Supreme Court. The original two-story structure was built in 1817; the Florentine towers and colonnade, decorated with red terra-cotta, were added in 1887 to commemorate Queen Victoria's Golden Jubilee. The Victoria Jubilee Clock Tower made its striking debut at midnight, December 31, 1893. Bermuda's Parliament, which is the world's third oldest after Iceland's and England's, met for the first time in 1620 in St. Peter's Church in St. George's. It later moved to the State House, where deliberations were held for almost 200 years until the capital was moved to Hamilton. In its present location, the House of Assembly meets on the second floor, where business is conducted in a style befitting such a venerable body. The Sergeant-at-Arms precedes the Speaker into the chamber, bearing a silver-gilt mace. Introduced in 1921, the mace is fashioned after a James I mace in the Tower of London. The Speaker, in wig and flowing black robe, solemnly calls the meeting to order with a cedar gavel made from an old belfry tree that has been growing in St. Peter's churchyard since 1620. The proceedings are no less ceremonious and colorful in the Supreme Court on the lower floor, where judges in red robes and full wigs hear the arguments of barristers in black robes and wigs. Visitors are welcome to watch the proceedings in the Assembly and the Supreme Court, but you must call to find out when sessions are scheduled. *Parliament St., between Reid and Church Sts., tel. 809/292–7408. Admission free. Open weekdays 9–5. Closed holidays.*

The next street over from Reid Street is Court Street. Although Court Street is safe during daylight hours, it is not advisable to wander around here at night. Bermuda doesn't have much of a drug problem, but what traffic there is centers on Court and Victoria streets after dark.

The Senate, which is the upper house of Parliament, sits in the
11 **Cabinet Building**, a dignified two-story structure surrounded by trees and gardens. Amid great ceremony, the official opening of Parliament takes place in the Senate Chamber in late October or early November. His Excellency the Governor, dressed in a plumed hat and full regalia, arrives on the grounds in a landau drawn by magnificent black horses and accompanied by a military escort. A senior police officer, carrying the Black Rod made by the Crown jewelers, summons the elected representatives to convene. The governor makes his Throne Speech from in front of a tiny cedar throne crudely carved with the words "Cap Josias Forstore Govornour of the Sumer Islands Anodo 1642" (Josias Foster was governor in 1642). The portraits above the dais are of King George III and Queen Charlotte. The chamber is open to visitors, but come on a Wednesday if you want to watch the Senate in action; call first to find out about scheduling. *Front St., tel. 809/292–5501. Admission free. Open weekdays 9–5. Closed holidays.*

12 In front of the Cabinet Building, the **Cenotaph** is a memorial to the war dead; on Remembrance Day (November 11), the governor and other dignitaries lay wreaths at the base of the monument. The Cenotaph is a smaller version of the famous one in Whitehall, London. The cornerstone was laid in 1920 by the Prince of Wales, who as King Edward VIII abdicated to wed Mrs. Simpson.

13 On the eastern outskirts of Hamilton is **Fort Hamilton,** an imposing old fortress, complete with a moat, 18-ton guns, and underground passageways that were cut through solid rock by Royal Engineers in the 1870s. If you've done enough walking, consider taking a taxi or moped there, because it's quite far. Head east on East Reid Street, turn left on King Street, and then right onto Happy Valley Road. The restored fort is one of several built by order of the Duke of Wellington. Outdated even before its completion, the fort never fired a shot in anger. Today, it affords splendid views of the capital and the harbor. Accompanied by drummers and dancers, the kilted Bermuda Isles Pipe Band performs a stirring skirling ceremony on the green every Monday at noon during the low season. Afterward the fort's "Tea Shoppe" is open for light refreshments. *Happy Valley Rd., Pembroke, no phone. Admission free. Open weekdays 9:30–5.*

## Tour 2: The Town of St. George's

*Numbers in the margin correspond with points of interest on the Town of St. George's map.*

The settlement of Bermuda began on the eastern end of the island in 1609, when the *Sea Venture* was wrecked off the coast. Despite its small size, St. George's encompasses much of historical interest, and visitors should plan to spend a full day poking around in the houses and museums. Much of the fun of St. George's is exploring the little alleys and walled lanes that wind through the town. The tour of the town is easily managed on foot.

14 **King's Square** is the hub of St. George's, although it is comparatively new. For 200 years after St. George's was settled, the square was a marshy part of the harbor—the area was filled in
15 only in the last century. Stop at the **Visitors Information Centre** for maps, brochures, and advice. A combination ticket for $4 buys admission to Tucker House and the Confederate Museum (and to Verdmont in Smith's Parish), which are all operated by the Bermuda National Trust.

Prominently displayed in King's Square is a cedar replica of the stocks and pillory originally used to punish criminals. Today, they serve as props for tourist photos and for the street theater staged here on Wednesdays during the low season. If you decide to take the walking tour (*see* Guided Tours in Chapter 1, Essential Information), you will be greeted in the square by the mayor of St. George's. The town crier, who has a voice to wake the dead (his voice is in the *Guinness Book of World Records),* is on hand in full colonial costume. After the official welcome, the crier bellows a few pronouncements and places any perceived malefactors in the stocks.

16 Stroll across the bridge to **Ordnance Island** and the splendid Desmond Fountain statue of Sir George Somers, titled *Land*

Bridge House, **19**
Carriage Museum, **29**
Confederate Museum, **27**
Featherbed Alley Printery, **24**
King's Square, **14**
Old Rectory, **25**
Old State House, **20**
Ordnance Island, **16**
St. George's Historical Society Museum, **23**
St. Peter's Church, **26**
Somers Garden, **21**
Town Hall, **18**
Tucker House, **28**
Unfinished Church, **22**
Visitors Information Centre, **15**
White Horse Tavern, **17**

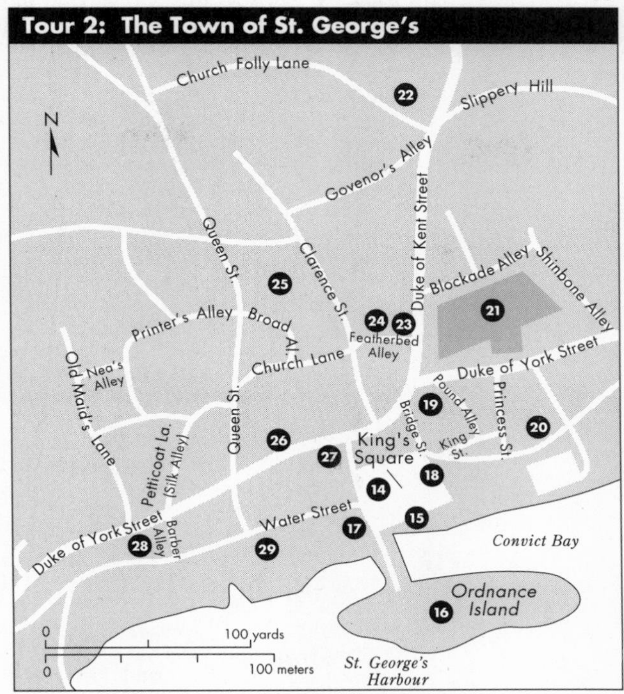


*Ho!* The **ducking stool** on the island is a replica of the one used to dunk gossips, nagging wives, and suspected witches in the water. Demonstrations are sometimes given, although volunteers say that getting dunked is no fun, even in fun.

Also on the island is the ***Deliverance II,*** a replica of the *Deliverance* built by the survivors of the wreck. After their shipwreck in 1609, Somers and his crew built two ships, the *Deliverance* and the *Patience*, to carry them to Jamestown, Virginia. Below deck, life-size mannequins in period costume are used to depict the realities of ocean travel in the 17th century—it's not the *QE2. Ordnance Island, no phone. Admission: $2 adults, 50¢ children under 12. Open daily 10–4. Closed Good Friday, Easter, and Christmas.*

17 The waterside **White Horse Tavern** is a popular restaurant today, but it was the Davenport home for much of the 19th century. After his arrival in St. George's in about 1815, John Davenport opened a small dry-goods store on the square. He was able to wangle a profitable contract to supply beef to the garrison, and gold and silver began to pour in. There were no banks on Bermuda, but Davenport wasn't the trusting sort anyway. He stashed the money in a keg that he kept beneath his bed. When the keg was full, he took it down to the cellar and put another one under his bed. By the time he was an old man, Davenport would spend hours each day gloating over the kegs that now filled his cellar. After his death, it was discovered that the old miser had amassed a fortune in gold and silver worth £75,000.

18 Across the square is **Town Hall**, a two-story building that houses administrative offices. Constructed in 1808 and subsequently restored, the hall is paneled and furnished with cedar, and there's a delightful collection of photographs of former mayors. Many years ago Town Hall was the scene of a memorable con. A gentleman calling himself Professor Trott appeared in town and announced a spectacular production of *Ali Baba and the Forty Thieves*. A great crowd collected at Town Hall for the play, and thievery was duly performed: Having lured the residents away from their homes, the wily "professor" made off with an iron safe. *The Bermuda Journey*, a worthwhile audiovisual presentation, is shown in the second-floor theater. *King's Sq. Admission to Town Hall free. Open Mon.–Sat. 9–4. Closed holidays.* Bermuda Journey, *tel. 809/297–0526. Admission: $3.50 adults, $2 senior citizens and children under 12. Open Mon.–Sat. 10:30–4:30, Sun. and public holidays noon–4:30 (shows every 45 min).*

---

**Time Out** **Pub on the Square** (King's Sq., tel. 809/297–1522) is exactly what its name implies. The balcony overlooking the square is a great place to knock back a beer, have a burger, and watch the action below.

---

19 On your left as you walk up King Street is **Bridge House,** so named for a bridge that once crossed a small creek here. Built around 1700, the house is a fine example of Bermudian architecture, has two verandas, and was the home of several governors. Now an art gallery and souvenir shop, the house is furnished with 18th- and 19th-century pieces. *King St., tel. 809/297–8211. Admission free. Open Mon., Thurs., Fri., Sat. 10–5, Tues.–Wed. 10–9, Sun. 11–3. Closed Christmas and Dec. 26. From mid-Jan. to mid-Feb. open Wed. and Sat. 10–5 only.*

20 At the top of King Street, the **Old State House** is the oldest stone house in Bermuda. Constructed in 1620 in what Governor Nathaniel Butler believed was the Italian style, the limestone building used a mixture of turtle oil and lime as mortar and set the style for future Bermudian buildings. Upon completion, it became home to the Parliament, which had been meeting in St. Peter's Church; dances and social gatherings were also held there. After the capital was moved to Hamilton, the old State House was rented to Lodge St. George's No. 200 of the Grand Lodge of Scotland. The annual rent charged by the city was one peppercorn, the payment of which is still made upon a velvet pillow amid much pomp and circumstance. The Peppercorn Ceremony takes place each April. *Princess St., no phone. Admission free. Open Wed. 10–4.*

Proceeding down Princess Street, you'll pass the place where a hotheaded tailor named Joseph Gwynn gunned down one Henry Folger in 1826. Enraged after his son had been sentenced to jail, Gwynn went out one night looking for the magistrate who had punished his son. Apparently blind with rage, he mistook Folger for the magistrate and shot him dead. A few months later, Gwynn was hanged near the very spot where the murder took place.

21 Nearby is **Somers Garden,** a pleasant tree-shrouded park where the heart of Sir George Somers is said to be buried. After sailing to Jamestown and back in 1610, Somers fell ill and

died. According to local lore, Somers told his nephew Matthew Somers that he wanted his heart buried in Bermuda, where it belonged. Matthew, who never seemed to pay much attention to his uncle's wishes, sailed for England soon afterward, sneaking Somers's body aboard in a cedar chest to avoid alarming the superstitious seamen. (Somers's body is buried near his birthplace in Dorset.) When the tomb where Somers's heart was supposedly interred was opened many years later, only a few bones, a pebble, and some bottle fragments were found—no one knows if Matthew Somers ever carried out his uncle's wishes. Nevertheless, ceremonies were held at the empty grave upon the 1920 visit of the Prince of Wales, during which the prince christened the park Somers Garden. *Bordered by Shinbone Alley, Blockade Alley, Duke of Kent and Duke of York Sts., no phone. Admission free. Open daily 7:30–4:30.*

---

**Time Out** Off the tourist beat, **Clyde's Cafe** (Duke of York St. at Somers Garden, tel. 809/297-0158) is popular with locals as a lunch spot. Nothing fancy is served here—just plate lunches, sandwiches, and burgers—but the prices aren't fancy, either.

---

Walk through Somers Garden and up the steps to Blockade Al-
22 ley. On the hill ahead is the **Unfinished Church**. Considering how much attention and affection are lavished on St. Peter's these days, it's hard to believe that residents in the 19th century wanted to replace the old church with a new one. Work began on this church in 1874, but construction was halted when a schism developed in the church. Money for construction was later diverted to rebuild Trinity Church in Hamilton when it burned down; work on the new church in St. George's was abandoned by the turn of the century.

At the corner of Featherbed Alley and Duke of Kent Street is
23 **St. George's Historical Society Museum.** A typical Bermudian structure from the early 1700s, the house is furnished much the same as when it was a private home. One of Bermuda's oldest pieces is a table believed to have been used as the High Court bench in the State House. The house is also filled with documents (including a doctor's bill from 1790), old letters, and displays of pewter, china, and rare books; there's even a whale-blubber cutter. A torpedo raft is one of the relics from the American Civil War. Constructed of heavy timber with projecting arms to hold torpedoes, the raft was part of a Union plan to blow up the submarine barricade in Charleston harbor. After breaking loose from its towing ship during a gale, the raft drifted for six years before washing ashore in Dolly's Bay on St. David's Island. When the captain of the towing ship later visited Bermuda, he recognized the raft and explained its purpose to the puzzled Bermudians. On the south wall of the house is an iron grate that is said to have come from the cell where Bermuda's first Methodist missionary, the Reverend John Stephenson, was confined for preaching to slaves. The persistent missionary continued to preach from his cell to a crowd that collected outside. Local artist Carole Holding has her studio and craft's shop in the former slave quarters of the house. *Featherbed Alley, tel. 809/297-0423. Admission: $1 adults, 50¢ children 6–16, children under 6 free. Open weekdays 10–4. Closed holidays.*

24 Around the corner, the **Featherbed Alley Printery** is as quaint as its name. Inside the cottage is a working printing press of the

kind invented by Johann Gutenberg in the 1450s. *Featherbed Alley, tel. 809/297-0009. Admission free. Open Mon.-Sat. 10-4. Closed holidays.*

Cross Clarence Street to Church Lane, and then turn right on
25 Broad Alley to reach the **Old Rectory,** now a private residence but owned by the Bermuda National Trust. Built around 1705 by a reformed pirate, it's a charming little house with Dutch doors, shutters, chimneys, and a welcoming-arms staircase. For many years it was the home of Alexander Richardson, the "Little Bishop," who was rector of St. Peter's from 1755 to 1805, except for a five-year stint on St. Eustatius. Richardson's diary is filled with anecdotes about 18th-century St. George's. *Broad Alley, tel. 809/297-0879. Admission free (donations appreciated). Open Wed. and Fri. 10-5. Closed holidays.*

Straight ahead (if "straight" is applicable among these twisted alleys) is **Printer's Alley**, where Bermuda's first newspaper was published. On January 17, 1784, less than a year after his arrival on the island, Joseph Stockdale printed the first copy of the *Bermuda Gazette*. The paper was published weekly for 20 years until Stockdale's death in 1805. The house where Stockdale worked is now a private home.

**Nea's Alley** is a short street connecting Printer's Alley with Old Maid's Lane. The 19th-century Irish poet Tom Moore lived on this street, then known as Cumberland Lane, during his four-month tenure as registrar of the admiralty court. Moore, who was endowed with considerable charm, had an impact on the island that endures to this day. He was invited to stay in the home of Admiral Mitchell, the neighbor of Mr. William Tucker and his wife, Hester—the "Nea" to whom Moore pours out his heart in several poems. Moore is thought to have first seen her in Cumberland Lane, which he describes in one of his odes as "the lime-covered alley that leads to thy home." However discreet Nea and Moore may have been about their affair, his odes to her were on the steamy side—much to the dismay of her husband. Although it was rather like locking the barn door after the horse has bolted, William Tucker refused to allow his former friend into his house again. Some Bermudians speculate that Nea was very much in love with Tom, but that he considered her merely a pleasant divertissement. He returned to Ireland after his assignment, and Nea died in 1817 at the age of 31. Bermudians are much enamored of the short-lived romance between Hester and Moore, and visitors are likely to hear a good deal about it.

26 Return to Church Lane and enter the churchyard of **St. Peter's Church.** The tombstones in Bermuda's oldest churchyard tell some interesting tales, indeed—this is the resting place of governors, doctors, simple folk, and pirates. East of the church is the grave of Hester, or "Nea," marked "Mr. William Tucker's Family Vault." One of the best-known monuments stands over the grave of Richard Sutherland Dale, who died in 1815 at age 20. An American navy midshipman, Dale was mortally wounded during a sea battle with the British in the War of 1812. The monument was erected by his parents as a tribute to the St. Georgians whose "tender sympathy prompted the kindest attentions to their son while living and honoured him when dead." In an enclosure to the west of the church is the slaves' graveyard. The ancient cedar tree, which dates back to 1620, is the old belfry tree. St. Peter's is the oldest Anglican church in

the Western Hemisphere, constructed in 1620. It was not the first church to stand on this site, however; it replaced a 1612 structure of posts and palmetto leaves that was destroyed in a storm. The present church was extended in 1713, and the galleries on either side were added in 1833. The oldest part of the church is the area around the 17th-century triple-tier pulpit. The dark-red cedar altar is the oldest piece of woodwork in the colony, carved under the supervision of Richard Moore, a shipwright and the first governor. The font, brought to the island by the early settlers, is about 500 years old, and the late-18th-century bishop's throne is believed to have been salvaged from a wreck. Among the treasures displayed in the vestry are a 1697 William of Orange communion set and a Charles I chalice, sent from England by the Bermuda Company in 1625. Commemorative plaques hang on the walls, and some of the names are wonderfully Pickwickian: One large memorial is to Governor Allured Popple. If you enter through the back door, be sure to look at the front of the church when you leave. *Duke of York St., tel. 809/297–8359. Donations appreciated. Open daily.*

27 Across the street, the **Confederate Museum** has a colorful history. Built in 1700 by Governor Samuel Day, the building served for 150 years as the Globe Hotel. During the American Civil War, the house was occupied by Major Norman Walker, who came to Bermuda as a Confederate agent. St. George's—which had suffered a depression after the capital moved to Hamilton in 1815—sided with the South for economic reasons, and the town became a hotbed of blockade-running activity. The first woman to run the blockade was Major Walker's pregnant wife, who risked capture by the North to join him in Bermuda. She was determined to have their baby born on Confederate soil, however, beneath the Stars and Bars. In the room where she gave birth, therefore, the four-poster bed was draped with the Confederate flag, and it's said that Confederate soil was spread beneath the bed. A wall map, designed by Desmond Fountain, shows the blockade-running routes from Bermuda to Southern ports. Also on display are a model of a blockade-runner, a replica of the Great Seal of the Confederacy, and an antique Victorian Seal Press, which makes reproductions of the Great Seal as souvenirs for visitors. *Duke of York St., tel. 809/297–1423. Donation: $2. Open Mon.–Sat. 10–5. Closed holidays.*

Continuing down Duke of York Street, you come to **Barber Alley**, named for Joseph Hayne Rainey, a former slave from South Carolina. Rainey's father had bought him his freedom, so when the Civil War broke out, Rainey and his French wife fled to Bermuda. Living in the kitchen of the Tucker House, Rainey became a barber and his wife made fashionable clothes. After the Civil War, they returned to South Carolina, where he went into politics. Elected to the House of Representatives in 1870, Rainey was the first black to serve in Congress.

**Petticoat Lane,** which is also called Silk Alley, received its name in 1834 after the emancipation of Bermudian slaves. Legend has it that two freed slaves, who had always wanted petticoats like those worn by their mistresses, strolled down the lane on Emancipation Sunday amid much rustling of petticoat skirts.

28 Antiques aficionados will find much of interest in the **Tucker House,** one of the showplaces of the Bermuda National Trust. Built of native limestone in 1711, the house sat above green hills that sloped down to the waterside (the area is now all built up).

Henry Tucker, president of the Governor's Council, lived in the house with his family from 1775 to 1800. His grandson donated most of the furnishings, which date from the mid-18th and early 19th centuries. Much of it is cedar, but there are some handsome mahogany pieces as well: The mahogany dining table was crafted from a tree grown in Cuba, and an English mahogany breakfront holds a collection of Tucker-family silver engraved with their coat of arms. Notice the tiny wig rooms off the dining room, where ladies and gentlemen went to fix their wigs after dinner. A short flight of stairs leads down to the kitchen, where Joseph Rainey lived and ran his barber shop. There is a small bookstore in the cellar. The Tucker name has been important in Bermuda since the island's beginnings (Henry Tucker's son St. George built the Tucker House in Williamsburg, Virginia), and a number of interesting family portraits hang in the house. Henry Tucker's father and brother were both involved in the famed "Gunpowder Plot" of 1775. The Continental Congress had imposed a ban on exports to all British colonies not taking part in the revolt against England. Bermuda depended upon the American colonies for grain, so a delegation of Bermudians traveled to Philadelphia offering salt in exchange for the resumption of grain shipments. Congress rejected the salt but agreed to lift the ban if Bermuda sent gunpowder instead. A group of Bermudians, including the two Tuckers, then sneaked into the island's arsenal, stole the gunpowder, and shipped it to Boston. The ban was soon lifted. *Water St., tel. 809/297–0545. Donation: $2. Open Mon.–Sat. 10–5. Closed holidays.*

With the arrival of cars on Bermuda in 1946, horse-drawn carriages were put out to pasture, so to speak. Across the street
29 from the Tucker House, the **Carriage Museum** offers a fascinating look at some of the island's old carriages. Yes, there's a surrey with a fringe on top as well as isinglass curtains that roll down. Among the other displays are a dignified Brougham; a six-passenger enclosed Opera Bus; and a small two-wheeler for children, called the Little Red Dog Cart. The carriages are labeled, but it's fun to hear the curator, Mr. Frith, describe them. *Water St., tel. 809/297–1367. Admission free (donations appreciated). Open Mon.–Sat. 10–4. Closed holidays.*

**Somers Wharf**, where the Carriage Museum is located, is part of a multimillion-dollar waterfront restoration that includes several shops and the pleasant Carriage House Restaurant. At press time, Penno's Wharf was being renovated as a major passenger-ship terminal.

## Tour 3: The West End

*Numbers in the margin correspond with points of interest on the West End map.*

In contrast to Hamilton and St. George's, the West End is a rather bucolic part of Bermuda. With the notable exception of Dockyard, many of the attractions here are natural rather than manmade: nature reserves, wooded areas, and beautiful harbors and bays. In the waters off Daniel's Head, the Sea Gardens are regularly visited by glass-bottom boats from Hamilton: With its bow jutting out of the water, the coral-wrapped wreck of HMS *Vixen* is a major attraction. The ship was deliberately sunk by the British to block the channel and protect Dockyard from attack. The West End is part of Sandys

Parish, named after Sir Edwin Sandys, an investor in the Bermuda Company. Local lore contends that Sir George Somers took a keen interest in this region, and in the early days it was known as "Somers's seate"—hence the name of Somerset Village. Today, Somerset is a sleepy little hamlet with a few shops and not much else. The West End's big attraction is Dockyard, a bastion of the British Royal Navy for 150 years. You should plan to spend at least a day exploring this area.

If you take the ferry to Somerset, look closely at the ferry schedule: The trip can take anywhere from a half hour to more than an hour, depending on which ferry you take. However, there are worse ways to while away an hour than churning across Bermuda's Great Sound. Take your bicycle or moped aboard the ferry, too, because you will need wheels in the West End. Bus service is available for those without their own transport.

The Somerset ferry stops at Somerset Bridge, Cavello Bay,
30 Watford Bridge, and Dockyard. This tour begins at **Dockyard** on Ireland Island, a sprawling complex housing several notable attractions. After the American Revolution, Britain found itself with neither an anchorage nor a major ship-repair yard in the western Atlantic. When Napoleon started to make threatening noises in Europe and British ships became increasingly vulnerable to pirate attack, Britain began construction of a major stronghold in Bermuda in 1809. The work was done by slaves and English convicts toiling under appalling conditions—thousands of workers died before the project was completed. The Royal Navy maintained a presence here for nearly 150 years, finally leaving in 1951. With the opening of the Maritime Museum (*see* below) in 1975, the decision was made to transform the entire naval port into a tourist attraction. Current plans call for the development of a minivillage at Dockyard. Bermudians are enormously proud of the Dockyard project, but the area lacks the warmth and charm of, for example, Nelson's Dockyard in Antigua; instead it has the barren feel of a shopping mall. Dockyard is still being developed, however, and it may blossom over time. New additions include a shopping arcade and visitor center in the century-old Clock Tower (which *is* a handsome edifice); a cruise-ship terminal; a marina and deep-water berth. Also planned are trips aboard scuba-diving facilities and a snorkel park; horse-drawn carriage tours; and the tourist submarine *Enterprise*. A new half-hour express bus service leaves Hamilton for Dockyard every 15 minutes. Hold on to your hair when you're strolling around Dockyard—it's very windy, particularly along the water.

Opened by Queen Elizabeth II in 1975, the sprawling 6-acre
31 **Maritime Museum** is housed in the huge fortress built to defend Dockyard. Entry to the museum is over a moat. The exhibition rooms are in old magazines and munitions warehouses arranged around the parade grounds. Several exhibits pertain to the *Sea Venture* and the early history of the island. Treasures and relics from some of the approximately 300 ships wrecked on the island's reefs are exhibited, as are maps, diving gear, ship models, uniforms, and costumes. Sailors will particularly enjoy the Bermuda dinghies (14-foot sailboats which can carry as much as 1,000 feet of canvas) on display in the Boat Loft. Visitors can also explore the ramparts, although this walk is only for dedicated (and hardy) fortress buffs. Currently undergoing

Bermuda Arts Centre, **33**
Dockyard, **30**
Ely's Harbour, **42**
Heydon Trust property, **40**
Lagoon Park, **34**
Long Bay Park and Nature Reserve, **36**
Maritime Museum, **31**
Neptune Cinema and Craft Market, **32**
St. James Church, **39**
Scaur Hill Fort, **41**
Somerset Bridge, **43**
Somerset Village, **35**
Somerset Visitors Information Centre, **38**
Springfield Library and Gilbert Nature Reserve, **37**

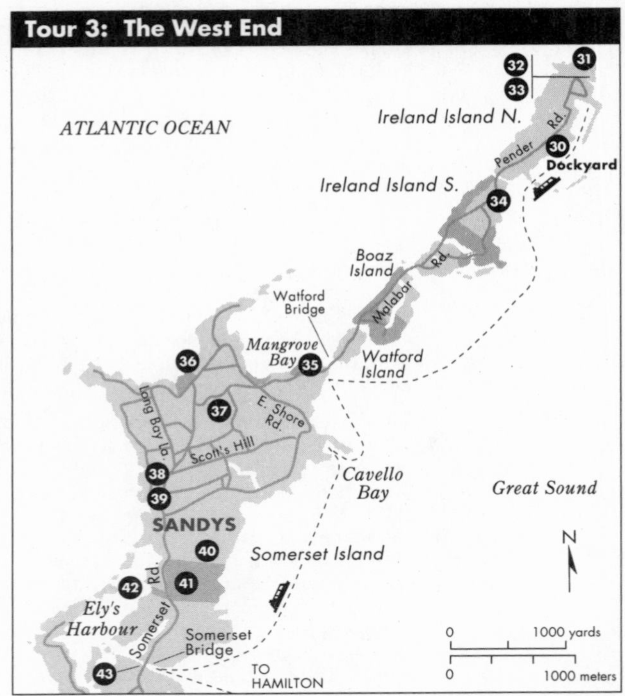


renovation, the 19th-century Commissioner's House is an elaborate cast-iron affair set high on a bluff. The house is slated for completion by 1992, in time for the 500th anniversary of Christopher Columbus's voyage to the New World. *Dockyard, tel. 809/234–1418. Admission: $5 adults, $2 senior citizens and children under 12. Open daily 10–5. Closed Christmas.*

Across the street from the Maritime Museum is the Old Cooperage, or barrel-maker's shop. Dating back to 1831, the recon-
32 structed building houses the **Neptune Cinema** and **Craft Market**.

The Neptune Cinema features *The Attack on Washington*, a spirited multimedia show detailing the role Bermuda and Dockyard played in the War of 1812. Angered by American raids on York (now Toronto), the British laid plans to retaliate. Bermuda was the departure point for a mighty fleet and some 35,000 troops that sailed over to sack and burn the U.S. capital in 1814. Shows are run continuously every half hour. *Neptune Cinema, the Cooperage, tel. 809/238–9432. Admission: $2.50 adults, $1.50 senior citizens and children under 12. Shows daily 10–4. Closed Easter and Christmas Day.*

Adjacent to the theater, the Craft Market displays the works of local artists. Jaded tourists, for whom "craft" usually means tacky souvenirs, are in for a pleasant surprise. Despite a poor presentation and layout, some delightful items are on sale here, including stained glass and miniature cedar furniture (*see* Chapter 4, Shopping). *Dockyard, tel. 809/234–3208. Admis-*

*sion free. Open daily 11–4. Closed Christmas, Boxing Day, New Year's Day, Good Friday.*

33 Since its opening by Princess Margaret in 1984, the **Bermuda Arts Centre** has been a showcase for local artists and artisans, and an excellent place to see Bermudian work (*see* Chapter 4, Shopping). Exhibits, which cover such subjects as underwater photography, change monthly. *Dockyard, tel. 809/234–2809. Admission: $1 adults, 50¢ senior citizens, students, and children under 12. Open Tues.–Fri. 10–4:30; weekends 10–5. Closed Christmas, Boxing Day, New Year's Day, and Good Friday.*

Take the main road out of Dockyard along Ireland Island
34 South. Turn left on Craddock Road and cycle down to **Lagoon Park.** Hidden in the mangroves are a lovely lagoon, footpaths, wild birds, and places to picnic. Next to the park, **The Crawl** is a picturesque inlet with fishing boats bobbing in the water and lobster pots on the dock. The park is always open, and there's no admission charge.

Cross over Boaz and Watford islands to Somerset Island. The largest of all these islets, Somerset Island is fringed on both sides with beautiful secluded coves, inlets, and bays. Beside
35 pretty Mangrove Bay, **Somerset Village** is a quiet retreat, quite different from St. George's, Hamilton, and Dockyard. Only one road runs through the village, and the few shops are mostly branches of Hamilton stores. During the low season walks, tour guides concentrate on the area's natural beauty and the unusual and medicinal plants on the island. Somerset Island itself is heavily populated, laced with roads and pathways through quiet residential areas.

---

**Time Out** Overlooking Mangrove Bay, the **Somerset Country Squire Restaurant** (Mangrove Bay Rd., tel. 809/234–0105) is an English-style pub with a great atmosphere. Diners can rely on good sandwiches and burgers, as well as such traditional British dishes as steak and kidney pie and bangers (sausages) and mash. Desserts are sensational.

---

**Cambridge Beaches**, Bermuda's original cottage colony, sits on its own 25-acre peninsula northwest of Somerset Village. Nestled among the trees near the entrance is a branch of the **Irish Linen Shop** (Cambridge Rd., tel. 809/234–0127). The little cottage was one of the original units of Cambridge Beaches.

36 A short distance farther along Cambridge Road is **Long Bay Park and Nature Reserve,** which has a great beach, shallow water, and picnic areas. The Bermuda Audubon Society owns the adjacent nature reserve and its pond, which attracts migrating birds in the spring and fall. Peaceful as this area is now, it was the scene of one of Bermuda's most sensational murders. Skeeters' Corner, at the end of Daniel's Head Road, was the site of a cottage once owned by a couple of the same name. One night in 1878, Edward Skeeters strangled his wife and dumped her in the water. His long, rambling confession revealed that he was irked because she talked too much!

Continue along Cambridge Road (which becomes Somerset
37 Road), until you see the arched gateway leading to the **Springfield Library and Gilbert Nature Reserve.** Set in 5 heavily wooded acres, Springfield is an old plantation home that dates back to around 1700. The restored house and outbuildings—

the kitchen, slave quarters, and buttery—are built around an open courtyard. The most interesting rooms are in the main house, which also contains the Somerset branch of the public library. Named after the family that owned the property from 1700 to 1973, the nature reserve was acquired by the Bermuda National Trust in conjunction with the Bermuda Audubon Society. *Main Rd., Somerset, tel. 809/234–1980. Admission free. Nature reserve always open. Library open Mon., Wed., and Sat. 10–4. Closed 1–2 PM, and holidays.*

38 Somerset Road winds around to the **Somerset Visitors Information Centre** (Somerset Rd., tel. 809/234–1388), where you can get information about this area from May through November.

39 High atop a promontory against a backdrop of the sea, **St. James Church** is one of the loveliest churches on the island. The entrance on the main road is marked by handsome iron gates that were forged by a Royal Engineer in 1872; the long driveway curls past glistening white tombs in the churchyard. The first church on this site was a wood structure destroyed by a hurricane in 1780. The present church was consecrated in 1789, and its tall, slender spire was added in 1880. *Main Rd., Somerset, no phone. Open dawn–dusk.*

40 Shortly after the church, you'll see the entrance to the **Heydon Trust property,** opposite Willowbank guest house. Among its 43 acres are citrus orchards, banana groves, flower and vegetable gardens, and bird sanctuaries. The quiet, peaceful property has been maintained as undeveloped "open space"—a reminder of what the island was like in its early days. Pathways dotted with park benches wend through the preserve, affording some wonderful views of the Great Sound. If you persevere along the main path, you'll reach the tiny, rustic **Heydon Chapel,** which dates from before 1620. An old rugged cross is planted in the hillside, and a welcome mat lies at the door. Inside are a few wooden pews, cedar beams, and an ancient oven and hearth in a small room behind the altar. Services are still held in the chapel. *Somerset Rd., tel. 809/234–1831. Admission free. Open during daylight hours.*

41 Just around the bend on your left is **Scaur Hill Fort.** Perched on the highest hill in Somerset, the fort was built in the 1870s to protect the Royal Naval Dockyard. Little remains to be seen here, although the 22 acres of gardens are quite pretty, and the view of the Great Sound is fantastic. Almost worth the long climb is the Early Bermuda Weather Stone, the "perfect weather indicator." The plaque reads: "A wet stone means . . . it is raining; a shadow under the stone . . . means the sun is shining; if the stone is swinging, it means there is a strong wind blowing; if the stone jumps up and down it means there is an earthquake; if ever it is white on top . . . believe it or not . . . it is snowing." *Somerset Rd., Ely's Harbour, tel. 809/234–0908. Admission free. Open daily 10–4:30. Closed Christmas and Boxing Day.*

42 At the bottom of the hilly, twisting road lies spectacular **Ely's Harbour,** with pleasure boats dotting its brilliant turquoise waters. Pronounced "Ee-lees," the small sheltered harbor was once a hangout for smugglers. From the main road you can take a right turn on rugged Scaur Hill Drive to visit the aptly named **Cathedral Rocks**, which overlook the harbor. This is one of the prettiest scenes in Bermuda.

43 Linking Somerset Island with the rest of Bermuda is **Somerset Bridge,** reputed to have the smallest draw in the world. It opens a mere 18 inches, just wide enough to accommodate a sailboat mast. Near the bridge is the Somerset ferry landing, where you can catch a ferry back to Hamilton. Across the bridge, Somerset Road becomes Middle Road, which leads into Southampton Parish (*see* Tour 4: The Parishes, below).

**Time Out** At the Somerset Bridge Hotel, the **Blue Foam** (162 Somerset Rd, tel. 809/234–2892) is a pleasant lunch spot in a greenhouse setting. In high season, an expensive alternative is the sumptuous lunch at the **Lantana Colony Club** (Somerset Rd., tel. 809/234–0141). Reservations are necessary at Lantana.

## Tour 4: The Parishes

*Numbers in the margin correspond with points of interest on The Parishes map.*

Bermuda's other points of interest—and there are many—are scattered across the island's parishes. This final tour takes you across the length and breadth of the colony, commenting only on the major sights. Half the fun of exploring Bermuda, though, is wandering down forgotten lanes or discovering some little-known beach or cove. A moped or bicycle is ideal for this kind of travel, although most of the island is covered by bus and ferry service. It would be foolish to try to see all the sights here in just one day. The tour, which leaves from Hamilton, can easily be broken into two halves: The first half explores those parishes in the eastern part of the island; the second travels through the western parishes. Even so, vacationers may find it more rewarding to do the tour piecemeal—a couple of sites here, a church there, and a day at the beach in between.

44 Follow Cedar Avenue north out of Hamilton to **St. John's Church,** consecrated in 1826 as the parish church of Pembroke. Another church, which dated to 1625, stood on this site before. During a funeral in 1875, the churchyard was the scene of a verbal duel between the Anglican rector and a Wesleyan minister. The Anglican church insisted that all burial services in parish churchyards be conducted by the rector, but the Wesleyans challenged the church in the case of a deceased woman named Esther Levy. Claiming he'd been asked by her friends to perform the funeral service, a Wesleyan minister appeared in the churchyard despite the efforts of the Anglican rector to stop him. Simultaneous services were held over poor Mrs. Levy's body, with the minister and the adamant Anglican trying to out-shout each other. The rector subsequently filed charges of trespassing against the Wesleyan, and the celebrated case went before the Supreme Court. The jury found for the rector, and fined the minister one shilling. *St. John's Rd., Pembroke. Open daily 8–7.*

By following Marsh Folly Road, which runs between the church
45 and Bernard Park, you'll come to **Black Watch Pass.** The Public Works Department excavated about 2.5 million cubic feet of solid limestone during construction of the pass. The tunnel re-
46 ceived its name from **Black Watch Well,** at the intersection of Black Watch Pass and North Shore Road. During a severe

## Tour 4: The Parishes

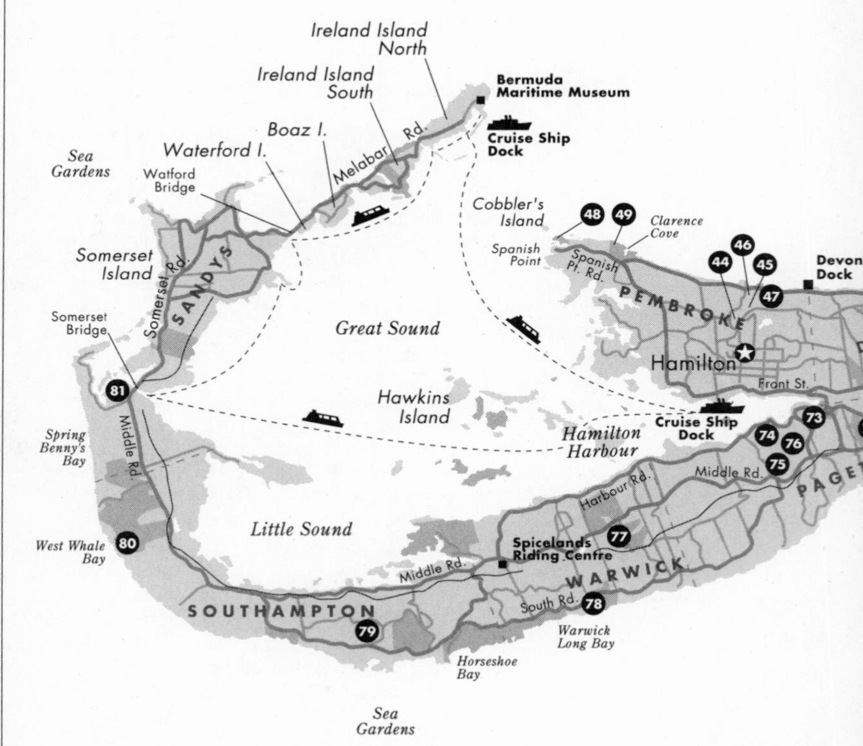


Admiralty House Park, **49**
Amber Caves of Leamington, **63**
Aquarium, Museum and Zoo, **52**
Astwood Park, **78**
Bermuda Biological Station for Research, **55**
Bermuda National Trust, **73**
Bermuda Perfumery and Gardens, **54**
Black Watch Pass, **45**
Black Watch Well, **46**
Botanical Gardens, **72**
Carter House, **59**
Castle Island, **66**
Christ Church, **77**
Clermont, **74**
Crystal Caves, **61**
Devil's Hole Aquarium, **67**
Flatts Village, **51**
Fort St. Catherine, **57**
Gates Fort, **56**
Gibb's Hill Lighthouse, **79**
Government House, **47**
Holy Trinity Church, **53**
Natural Arches, **65**
Old Devonshire Church, **71**
Overplus Street, **81**

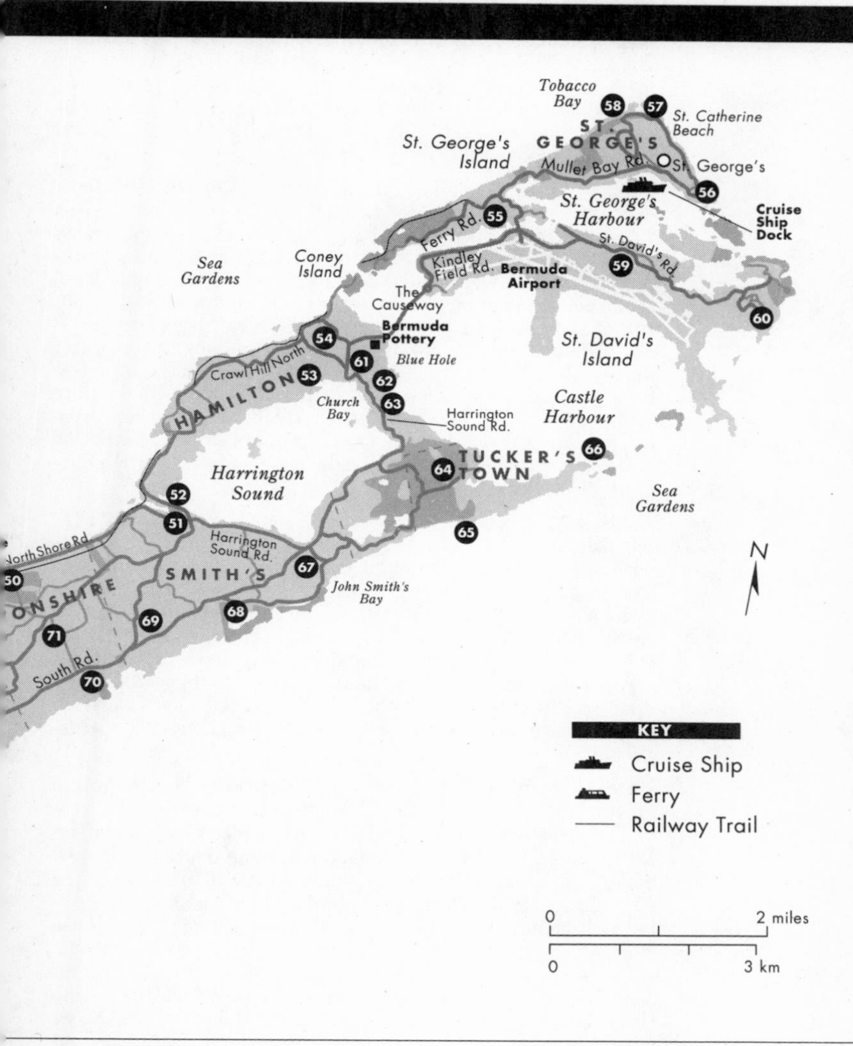
Tobacco Bay
58
57
St. Catherine Beach
ST. GEORGE'S
St. George's Island
Mullet Bay Rd.
St. George's
56
Cruise Ship Dock
St. George's Harbour
Ferry Rd.
55
St. David's Rd.
Sea Gardens
Coney Island
Kindley Field Rd.
Bermuda Airport
59
The Causeway
60
Bermuda Pottery
54
St. David's Island
61
Blue Hole
Crawl Hill North
53
62
HAMILTON
Church Bay
63
Harrington Sound Rd.
Castle Harbour
66
TUCKER'S TOWN
64
Harrington Sound
Sea Gardens
52
51
65
North Shore Rd.
Harrington Sound Rd.
50
SMITH'S
67
ONSHIRE
John Smith's Bay
68
69
71
South Rd.
70
N
KEY
Cruise Ship
Ferry
Railway Trail
0
2 miles
0
3 km

drought in 1849, the governor ordered a well dug on government ground to alleviate the suffering of the poor in the area. Excavated by a detachment of the famed Black Watch regiment, the well is marked by a commemorative plaque and shaded by a tiered concrete slab. The site is not particularly inspiring, however, and only the most dedicated well-wishers will want to make the pilgrimage to see it.

47 From its position on Langton Hill, imposing **Government House** overlooks North Shore Road, Black Watch Well, and the sea. The house is the residence of the governor and is not open to the public. The land was purchased when the capital was transferred from St. George's to Hamilton in 1815. A simple, two-story house served as the governor's home until the present, rather austere mansion was built. Various royals and other distinguished visitors planted the trees and shrubs on the pretty landscaped lawns. Among the guests who have been entertained in Government House are Queen Elizabeth II and Prince Philip, Prince Charles, Winston Churchill, and President Kennedy. The mansion was also the scene of the 1973 assassination of Governor Richard Sharples and his aide, Captain Hugh Sayers.

North Shore Road merges with Spanish Point Road near
48 **Spanish Point,** at the tip of the peninsula. The survivors of the wrecked *Sea Venture* thought they found evidence here of an earlier visit by the Spanish. Apparently they were right: Historians now believe that Captain Diego Ramirez landed here in 1503. There is a small park for picnicking, a sheltered bay for swimming, public facilities, and a lovely view of Somerset across the sound. Cobbler's Island, across Cobbler's Cut from Spanish Point, has a grisly history—executed slaves were exhibited there as a warning to others of the consequences of disobedience.

49 En route to Spanish Point you pass **Admiralty House Park,** a pretty spot with several caves and sheltered coves. Little remains of the house, originally the 19th-century estate of John Dunscombe. Dunscombe, who later became lieutenant governor of Newfoundland, sold the property in 1816 to the Bermuda government, which decided to build a house for the commanding British admiral of the naval base at Dockyard. The house was reconstructed several times over the years, notably in the 1850s by an eccentric admiral with a weakness for subterranean tunnels—he had several caves and galleries cut into the cliffs above the sea. The house was closed when the Royal Navy withdrew in 1951. Within the park, Clarence Cove offers a sheltered beach and pleasant swimming.

Head back along North Shore Road to Devonshire Parish. Ideal for cycling and quiet picnics, Devonshire is a serene part of the island, with much to offer in the way of natural beauty. Locals come to **Devonshire Dock** to buy fresh fish (something to bear in mind if you're staying in a housekeeping apartment).

50 A short distance farther along North Shore Road is **Palmetto House,** an 18th-century cruciform house. It was believed that a house built in the shape of a cross warded off evil spirits. Three rooms, furnished with fine pieces of Bermudian furniture, are on view. *North Shore Rd., tel. 809/295–9941. Admission free. Open Thurs. 10–5.*

51 If you continue along North Shore Road, you will reach **Flatts Village,** one of the earliest settlements on the island. The House of Assembly sometimes met in Flatts, although much of the village's activities involved flaunting the law rather than making it. Hoping to avoid customs officers, Bermudians returning from the West Indies would sometimes sail into the village in the dead of night to unload their cargoes.

52 The **Aquarium, Museum and Zoo** at Flatts Village is one of the island's most popular attractions. Pick up an audio "wand" at the aquarium entrance for a self-guided tour of the tanks and exhibits. Sea creatures native to Bermudian waters are on display, including sharks, barracuda, and grumpy-looking giant grouper. Just outside the aquarium, you'll see three harbor seals (Charlotte, Archie, and their pup) splashing in a small pond. The natural-history museum features a geology display that explains Bermuda's volcanic origins, and a deep-sea exhibit that documents the half-mile dive of marine biologist Dr. William Beebe in the early 1930s. The odd-looking contraption outside the museum is the bathysphere in which Dr. Beebe made his dive. In the zoo, a reptile walkway gives visitors a close look at alligators, Galapagos tortoises, and lizards. Other attractions include an aviary, a monkey house, and a number of Caribbean flamingos and strutting peacocks. A petting zoo is open only in the summer. *Flatts, tel. 809/293–2727. Admission: $4 adults, $1 senior citizens and children 5–12. Open daily 9–5 (last admission at 4:30). Closed Christmas.*

Continuing east, North Shore Road climbs **Crawl Hill**, a high point offering spectacular views over the island and sea. "Crawl" derives from the Afrikaans word "kraal," meaning animal enclosure; on Bermuda, the word was applied to several ponds containing turtles and fish. This part of Hamilton Parish was also a site for shipbuilding during the early days of the colony.

53 Turn right on Trinity Church Road to see **Holy Trinity Church.** Built in 1623 as one long room with a thatched roof, it is said to be the oldest Anglican church on Bermuda. The church has been much embellished over the past 368 years, but the original building remains at its core. The small graveyard is encircled by palms, royal poinciana, and cherry trees. *Church Bay, Harrington Sound, no phone. Not open to the public.*

Just off Trinity Church Road is **Mount Wyndham**, the peak from which Admiral Sir Alexander Cochrane surveyed the British fleet prior to its attack on Washington, DC, in 1814.

54 Follow North Shore Road as it dips south to the **Bermuda Perfumery and Gardens.** On a guided tour, visitors learn how the Lili Perfume Factory, which began extracting natural fragrances from the island's flowers in 1929, blossomed into the present perfumery/tourist attraction. The factory is in a 200-year-old cottage with cedar beams, but the biggest draw is the aromatic nature trail that you can walk on your own. A complimentary map helps you sniff your way around the oleanders, frangipani, jasmine, orchids, and passionflower that are the raw material for the factory. *212 North Shore Rd., tel. 809/293–0627. Admission free. Open Apr.–Oct., Mon.–Sat. 9–5, Sun. 10–4; Nov.–Mar., Mon.–Sat. 9–4:30, closed Sun. and holidays.*

**Time Out** Just up the road, **Bailey's Ice Cream Parlour & Food D'Lites** (Blue Hole Hill, tel. 809/293–9333) offers 40 varieties of freshly made natural ice cream, as well as shakes, sodas, yogurts, and sorbets. For something a bit stronger, cross the road for a rum swizzle and a "swizzleburger" at the **Swizzle Inn** (Blue Hole Hill, tel. 809/293–9300).

---

Blue Hole Hill leads to the causeway over Castle Harbour. Once on the other side you are in St. George's Parish. Take Kindley Field Road around the airport, turn left onto Mullet Bay Road, and cross Swing Bridge over Ferry Reach. The
55 **Bermuda Biological Station for Research** will be of interest to anyone who cares about the environment. Scientists here have conducted research on marine life since 1932, and the center has been given a five-year, $2 million grant from the U.S. National Science Foundation to study the greenhouse effect. Extensive research has been conducted here on acid rain. Guided tours of the grounds and laboratory are conducted every Wednesday at 10 AM, beginning in the main building. Coffee and snacks are served. *17 Biological La., Ferry Reach, St. George's, tel. 809/297–1880.*

The scenery is magnificent along the stretch of road that runs between Mullet Bay and the sea. A little farther east, Mullet Bay Road becomes Wellington Road, and finally Duke of York Street when you reach St. George's (*see* Tour 2: The Town of St. George's, above). East of town, Duke of York Street becomes Barrack Hill Road. From the road, the views of the town, St. David's Island, and Castle Harbour are splendid. Barrack Hill
56 Road turns into Cut Road, which leads all the way to **Gates Fort.** St. George's has always had the greatest concentration of fortifications on the island. Gates Fort is a reconstruction of a small militia fort dating from the 1620s. Don't expect turrets, towers, and tunnels, however; there is little to see here apart from the sea. The fort and Gates Bay, which it overlooks, were named for Sir Thomas Gates, the first of the survivors of the *Sea Venture* to reach dry land. Upon doing so, he is reputed to have shouted, "This is Gates, his bay!" Public speaking was obviously not his forte, although Gates was by profession a politician—he later became governor of Virginia. *Cut Rd., no phone. Admission free. Open daily 10–4.*

The main camp of the *Sea Venture* survivors is believed to have been in this general area. Leaving Gates Fort via Barry Road, you'll pass **Buildings Bay**. One of the two ships that carried Sir George Somers and his crew to Virginia was built here in 1610, hence the bay's name.

57 Continue up Barry Road to **Fort St. Catherine.** Apart from Dockyard, this restored fortress is the most impressive on the island: It has enough cannons, tunnels, and ramparts to satisfy the most avid military historian. One of a host of fortifications constructed in St. George's, the fort was begun around 1614 and work continued on it throughout the 19th century. As you travel through the tunnels, you'll come across some startlingly lifelike figures tucked into niches. Several dioramas depict the island's development, and an audiovisual presentation describes the building and significance of the fort. There is also a small but elaborate display of replicas of the crown jewels of England. *Barry Rd., tel. 809/297–1920. Admission: $2.50*

*adults, children under 12 free, but must be accompanied by an adult. Open daily 10–4:30. Closed Christmas.*

**St. Catherine's Beach**, where the survivors from the *Sea Venture* scrambled ashore, is a pleasant place for a swim and quiet contemplation of the events of July 28, 1609. Another fine beach, with changing facilities and a refreshment stand, is at
58 nearby **Tobacco Bay**, where the Tuckers secretly loaded the gunpowder bound for Boston in 1775 (*see* Tour 2: The Town of St. George's, above). Retrace your route through St. George's to Swing Bridge that connects St. George's with St. David's Island. In addition to Bermuda's airport, about 2 square miles of St. David's is occupied by a U.S. Naval Air Station. In 1940, during World War II, Churchill agreed to give the United States a 99-year lease to operate a base on Bermuda in exchange for destroyers. The entire area taken up by the air station is now called St. David's, but construction of the base actually required linking three separate islands—St. David's, Longbird, and Cooper's—with landfills.

Christopher Carter, one of three men left behind when the *Deliverance* and the *Patience* sailed for Jamestown in 1610, was offered St. David's Island in 1612 as a reward for revealing the "Ambergris Plot." Before the ships returned to Bermuda, it seems, one of the three men, Edward Chard, found 80 pounds of ambergris (a precious sperm-whale product used for perfumes) washed up on the beach. In collusion with Carter and the third man, Chard planned to smuggle the ambergris off the island (when a ship arrived) and sell it in London at enormous profit. At the last minute, however, Carter squealed on his co-conspirators to Governor Moore, who had arrived in 1612 with new settlers. Instead of St. David's Island, Carter opted for Cooper's Island, which is also now part of the naval base. Built
59 by Carter's descendants in 1640, **Carter House** is one of the oldest houses in Bermuda and should not be missed. The stone-and-cedar house has been refurbished with new floors and period furnishings, including a 17th-century bedding chest, a mortar and pestle, and an 18th-century tavern table, and is maintained by the naval base as a museum. You can reach Carter House through the main gate of the air station; you'll need a photo identification and proof of vehicle insurance to get in. *Kindley Field Rd., tel. 809/297–1150 (ask for Ms. Lyndell O'Dey). Admission free. Open Wed. 11–4.*

Apart from the naval base, St. David's is a rustic spot where the inhabitants have always led an isolated life—some are said to have never visited St. George's, let alone the other end of the island. A number of residents had to be relocated when the base was built, but they refused to leave St. David's. Therefore, a section of St. David's called "Texas" was purchased by the government, which built cottages there for the displaced islanders. The area is just off the naval base; you can see Texas Road at the tip of the island near the lighthouse.

60 **St. David's Lighthouse** occupies the highest point on the island's eastern end. Built in 1879 of Bermuda stone, the lighthouse rises 280 feet above the sea. Although only about half the height of Gibb's Hill Lighthouse in Southampton Parish, it nevertheless affords spectacular views: From the balcony you can see St. David's and St. George's, Castle Harbour, and the reef-fringed south shore. The lighthouse is not always open;

check with the Visitors Service Bureau in the Visitors Information Centre in Hamilton or St. George's.

**Time Out** Right on the water near the lighthouse, the **Black Horse Tavern** (Clarkes Hill, tel. 809/293–9742) is a spot that's popular with the locals. Seafood is the specialty, and shark hash and curried conch stew are featured items. The fish sandwiches are delicious. There are outdoor picnic tables as well as indoor dining.

Head back across the causeway and turn left on Wilkinson Avenue. A network of caves, caverns, and subterranean lakes runs beneath the hills in this part of the island. Two of them are on the property of the nearby Grotto Bay Beach Hotel (*see* Chap-
61 ter 8, Lodging). Just south of the hotel are the **Crystal Caves,** discovered in 1907 by two boys playing ball. When the ball disappeared down a hole, the boys burrowed after it and found themselves in a vast cavern 120 feet underground, surrounded by fantastic stalagmite and stalactite formations. Today, the approach is along a wet, sloping walkway and a wood pontoon bridge across the underground lake. After explaining the formation of stalactites and stalagmites, a tour guide uses a lighting system to make silhouettes. People who suffer from claustrophobia will probably want to give the caves a miss, because space can be quite tight. *8 Crystal Caves Rd., off Wilkinson Ave., tel. 809/293–0640. Admission: $3 adults, $1.50 senior citizens and children 5–11. Open daily 9:30–4:30. Closed Christmas and New Year's Day. From mid-Nov. to mid-March, hours may vary.*

Harrington Sound Road runs along the strip of land between the Sound and Castle Harbour. At Walsingham Lane, you'll see
62 a white sign for **Tom Moore's Tavern,** a popular restaurant. The restaurant was originally the home of Samuel Trott, who constructed it in the 17th century and named it Walsingham. (The harbor nearby was named for Robert Walsingham, a sailor on the *Sea Venture* who apparently became enamored of the bay.) The house is surrounded by woods that are much the same as they were three centuries ago. When Tom Moore, the Irish poet, arrived in Bermuda in 1804, the house was occupied by a descendant of the original owner (also named Samuel Trott) and his family. The Trotts befriended the poet, who became a frequent visitor to the house. In Epistle V, Moore immortalized the Calabash Tree on the Trott estate under which he liked to write his verses. In 1844, the idea for the Royal Bermuda Yacht Club was conceived under the very same tree.

63 Harrington Sound Road leads southward to the **Amber Caves of Leamington,** smaller and less impressive than Crystal Caves. However, they do have their share of stalagmites and stalactites in fanciful formations, one of them an amber-tinted Statue of Liberty. Above ground, the Plantation Restaurant serves some of the island's best food—worth a trip whether you visit the caves or not. *Harrington Sound Rd., tel. 809/293–1188. Admission: $3 adults, $1.50 senior citizens and children 4–12. Open Mon.–Sat. 9:30–4:30, Sun. noon–3. Closed late Nov.–late Feb., holidays.*

64 Farther south on Harrington Sound Road is **Tucker's Town,** named for Governor Daniel Tucker, who wanted to abandon St. George's in 1616 in favor of a new settlement on the shores of Castle Harbour. A few streets were laid out and some cottages

were built, but the plan was eventually shelved. For 300 years Tucker's Town remained a small fishing and farming community: Cotton was grown for a while, and a few whaling boats operated from here. Dramatic change overtook the community soon after World War I, however. Seeking to raise the island's appeal in order to attract passengers on its luxury liners to Bermuda, a steamship company called Furness, Withy & Co. purchased a large area of Tucker's Town for a new country club. The result was the exclusive Mid Ocean Club, with its fine golf course. Members of the club started building residences nearby, and the Tucker's Town boom began. Today, only members of the club can buy a house in the area, and private residences have been known to sell for more than $2 million.

65 Below the clubhouse on the south shore are the **Natural Arches,** one of the island's oldest and most photographed attractions. Carved over the centuries by the wind and ocean, the two limestone arches rise 35 feet above the beach. Look for the signs near the end of South Shore Road pointing to Castle Harbour Beach and the Natural Arches.

A chain of islands dots the entrance channel to the harbor between St. David's and Tucker's Town Bay. In the colony's early days, these islands were fortified to protect Castle Harbour
from possible enemy attack. Soon after his arrival in 1612, Gov-
66 ernor Moore built his first and best fort on **Castle Island.** Ac-
cording to an oft-told tale, two Spanish ships appeared outside the channel in 1614 and attempted to attack the colony. Two shots were fired from the fort: One fell into the water, and the other hit one of the ship's hulls. The Spaniards fled, unaware that the fortress had expended two-thirds of its stock of ammunition—the colonists had one cannonball left.

67 Touted as Bermuda's first tourist attraction, **Devil's Hole Aquarium** was started by a Mr. Trott in 1830. After building a wall around his fish pond—manifestly to prevent people from fishing in it—Mr. Trott was besieged with questions about what he was hiding. In 1843, yielding to the curiosity of the Bermudians, Mr. Trott permitted people to view his fish pond—at a fee. These days, the deep pool contains about 400 sea creatures, including giant grouper, sharks, and huge turtles. Visitors can play at fishing, using baited—but hookless—lines. *Harrington Sound Rd., tel. 809/293–2072. Admission: $5 adults, $3 children 6–12. Open daily 9–5. Closed Good Friday and Christmas Day.*

Take Ashwood Drive to South Shore Road, and turn right to
68 reach **Spittal Pond.** A showcase of the Bermuda National Trust,
this nature park has 60 acres in which visitors can roam, although visitors are requested to keep to the walkways. More than 25 species of waterfowl winter here between November and May. On a high bluff, overlooking the ocean, is an oddity known as Spanish Marks. Early settlers found a rock crudely carved with the date 1543 and other markings that were unclear. It is now believed that a Portuguese ship was wrecked on the island in 1543, and that her sailors built a new ship on which they departed. The carvings are thought to be the initials *RP* (for Rex Portugaline), and the cross to be a badge of the Portuguese Order of Christ. The rock was removed to prevent further damage by erosion, and a plaque now marks the spot. A plaster-of-paris cast of the Spanish Marks is on display at the Museum of Bermuda Historical Society in Hamilton (*see* Tour 1:

Hamilton, above). *South Shore Rd., no phone. Admission free. Open daily sunrise–sunset.*

West of Spittal Pond on South Shore Road is the turnoff to **Collector's Hill**, which is a very steep climb indeed. The hill is named for Gilbert Salton, a 19th-century customs collector who lived in a house near the top; the house has long since disappeared.

69 At the very top of Collector's Hill is **Verdmont,** Bermuda's finest house museum. It was built around 1710, possibly by a prominent shipowner named John Dickinson. At the end of the War of Independence, Verdmont was the home of John Green, an American Loyalist who fled to Bermuda from Philadelphia. Green married one of Dickinson's granddaughters and was appointed judge of the Court of Vice Admiralty. Green was also a portrait painter, and the only furnishings in the house from the 18th century are family portraits by him. The house, which resembles a small English manor house, has an unusual double roof and four large chimneys—all eight rooms have their own fireplace. Elegant cornice moldings and paneled shutters grace the two large reception rooms downstairs, originally the drawing room and formal dining room. The sash windows reflect a style that was fashionable in English manor houses. Although it contains none of the original furnishings, Verdmont is a treasure house of Bermudiana. Some of the furniture is mahogany imported from England—there are two exquisite early 19th-century pianos—but most of it is fine 18th-century cedar, crafted by Bermuda cabinetmakers. In particular, notice the desk in the drawing room, the lid and sides of which are made of single planks. Also displayed in the house is a china coffee service, said to have been a gift from Napoleon to President Madison. The president never received it: The ship bearing it across the Atlantic was seized by a Bermudian privateer and brought to Bermuda. Look carefully, too, at the handmade cedar staircase, with its handsomely turned newels and posts. The newel posts on each landing have removable caps to accommodate candles in the evening. Upstairs is a nursery: It's easy to imagine a child at play with the antique toys, riding the hand-propelled tricycle (circa 1840), or napping in the cedar cradle. The last occupant of Verdmont was an eccentric old woman, who lived here for 75 years without electricity or any other modern trappings. After her death, her family sold the house to the Bermuda Historic Monuments Trust—the forerunner of the Bermuda National Trust—which opened it as a museum in 1956. *Collector's Hill, tel. 809/236–7369. Admission: $2. Open Mon.–Sat. 9–5. Closed holidays.*

**Time Out** Popular with the locals, **Specialty Inn** (South Shore Rd., foot of Collector's Hill, tel. 809/236–3133) is a simple spot that serves pasta, pizza, sandwiches, soups, shakes, and ice cream.

A singular delight of Devonshire Parish are the gardens at
70 **Palm Grove,** a private estate. There is a splendid pond, within which is a relief map of the island—each parish is divided by carefully manicured grass sections. Desmond Fountain statues stand around the edge, peering into the pond's depths. *South Shore Rd., across from Brighton Hill, no phone. Admission free. Open weekdays 9–5.*

Brighton Hill Road, just west of Palm Grove, runs north to
71 Middle Road and the **Old Devonshire Church,** the parish's biggest attraction. A church has stood on this site since 1612, although the original was replaced in 1716. That replacement church was almost completely destroyed in an explosion on Easter Sunday in 1970, and the present church is a faithful reconstruction. A small, simple building of limestone and cedar, it looks much like an early Bermuda cottage. The three-tier pulpit, the pews, and the communion table are believed to be from the original church. Some pieces of church silver date back to 1590 and are said to be the oldest on the island. A cedar chest, believed to have once held the church records, dates from the early 17th century. Other pieces that have survived include an old cedar armchair, a candelabra, a cross, and a cedar screen. *Middle Rd., Devonshire, tel. 809/236–0537. Admission free. Open daily, 9–5:30.*

Turn left off Middle Road onto Tee Street, and then right onto Berry Hill Road. One mile farther on the left is the turnoff to
72 Point Finger Road and the **Botanical Gardens,** a landscaped park laced with roads and paths. The gardens are a fragrant showcase for the island's exotic subtropical plants, flowers, and trees. Within the 36 acres are a miniature forest, an aviary, a hibiscus garden (with more than 150 species of the flower), and a special Garden for the Blind, which is filled with the scent of lemon, lavender, and spices. Ninety-minute walking tours of the gardens leave the Tavern on the Green parking lot at 10:30 AM on Tuesday, Wednesday, and Friday (Tuesday and Friday only from November 15 to March). *Point Finger Rd., tel. 809/236–4201. Admission free. Open daily sunrise–sunset.*

The pretty white home on the grounds of the Botanical Gardens is **Camden**, the official residence of Bermuda's premier. A large two-story house, Camden is more typical of West Indian estate architecture than traditional Bermudian building. The house is open for tours, except when official functions are scheduled. *Botanical Gardens, tel. 809/236–5732. Admission free. Open Apr.–Nov. 14, Tues. and Wed. noon–2 PM; Nov. 15–Mar. 31, Tues. and Fri. noon–2 PM.*

73 A few minutes away by moped are the offices of the **Bermuda National Trust,** a nonprofit organization that oversees the restoration and preservation of many of the island's gardens and historic homes. The trust is also a wonderful source of information about the island. The offices are in the rear of a rambling 18th-century house built by the Trimingham family. *"Waterville," 5 The Lane, Paget, tel. 809/236–6483. Open weekdays 9–4:30.*

The first half of the tour ends here: Hamilton is just a few hundred yards up the road. The second part of the tour heads west through the parishes of Paget, Warwick, and Southampton.

74 On Harbour Road near the Lower Ferry Landing, **Clermont** is an imposing house noted for its fine woodwork. Once the residence of Sir Brownlow Gray, Chief Justice of Bermuda, the house is also famous for having Bermuda's first tennis courts. During a visit from New York in 1874, Miss Mary Outerbridge learned to play here. Upon her return to the United States, she asked the Staten Island Cricket Club to build a court; armed with her racquet and a book of rules, she introduced tennis to America. This house is not open to the public, although it is

sometimes included in the spring House and Gardens Tour (*see* Guided Tours in Chapter 1, Essential Information).

75 Turn left on Valley Road to reach **St. Paul's,** built in 1796 to replace an earlier church on the site. Around the turn of the century, the "Paget Ghost" began to be heard in and around St. Paul's. Nothing could be seen, but the mysterious sound of tinkling bells was plainly audible, coming from several directions. The ghost became quite famous, and a veritable posse—armed with firearms and clubs— gathered to find it; vendors even set up refreshment stands. Finally, a visiting American scientist proclaimed that the tinkling sound came from a rare bird, the fililo. According to the scientist, the fililo was a natural ventriloquist, which explained why the sound jumped around. No one ever saw the fililo, however, and no one saw the ghost either—it disappeared as mysteriously as it had appeared.

76 St. Paul's sits on the edge of **Paget Marsh,** 18 acres of unspoiled woodland that look much as they did when the first settlers arrived. Protected by the Bermuda National Trust, the marsh contains cedars and palmettos, endangered plants, and a mangrove swamp. *Middle Rd., tel. 809/236–6483. Admission by arrangement with the Bermuda National Trust.*

From St. Paul's, head west into Warwick Parish along Middle Road. Just after the intersection with Ord Road (opposite the Belmont Hotel, Golf & Country Club), look to your left to see
77 **Christ Church.** Built in 1719, it is reputedly the oldest Presbyterian church in any British colony or dominion.

Turn left off Middle Road onto Camp Hill Road, which winds down to the south shore beaches. Along the way is **Warwick Camp,** built in the 1870s to guard against any enemy landing on the beaches. The camp was used as a training ground and rifle range during World War I. In 1920, Pearl White of *The Perils of Pauline* fame came to Bermuda to shoot a movie, bringing along an entourage that included lions, monkeys, and a host of other exotic fauna. Scenes for the film were shot on Warwick Bay, below the rifle range. Most Bermudians had never seen either a lion or a movie star, and huge crowds collected to watch the filming.

---

**Time Out** An inexpensive roadside restaurant, **Tio Pepe's** (South Shore Rd., near the entrance to Horseshoe Bay, tel. 809/238–1897) serves Spanish and Italian foods and pizza to go. It's closed on Tuesday.

---

Bermuda's beaches tend to elicit the most effusive travel-writing clichés—simply because they are so good. A 3-mile chain of sandy beaches, coves, and inlets begins at Warwick Long Bay and extends to Horseshoe Bay in the east (*see* Chapter 5,
78 Beaches and Water Sports). Just east of Warwick Bay, **Astwood Park** is a lovely public park with picnic tables and two beaches, one of them ideal for snorkeling.

Two miles west along South Shore Road is the turnoff for Light-
79 house Road. High atop Gibb's Hill, **Gibb's Hill Lighthouse** is the second cast-iron lighthouse ever built. Designed in London and opened in 1846, the tower stands 133 feet high and 360 feet above the sea. The original light mechanism had to be wound every three hours, a process that took three minutes. Today, the beam from the 1,500-watt bulb can be seen by ships 40 miles

out to sea, and by planes 120 miles away at 10,000 feet. You can climb to the top of the lighthouse, although this is not a trip for anyone who suffers from vertigo. It's a long haul up the 185 spiral stairs—you have to climb another 30 steps just to reach the entrance—but you can stop to catch your breath at platforms along the way, where photographs and drawings of the lighthouse are displayed. At the top you can stroll on the balcony for a spectacular view of Bermuda. The wind may snatch you baldheaded—the tower is known to sway in high winds—and you may find it hard to concentrate on the view knowing that a tiny guard rail is the only thing between you and a swan dive. (An alternative is to inch around with your back pressed against the tower, clinging to it for dear life). *Lighthouse Rd., Southampton, tel. 809/238–0524. Admission: $1.50 adults, 75¢ children under 8. Open daily 9–4:30. Closed Christmas.*

If you're still feeling adventurous, turn left off Middle Road onto Whale Bay Road (just before the Port Royal Golf & Coun-
80 try Club), and go down the hill to **Whale Bay Fort.** Overgrown with grass, flowers, and subtropical plants, this small 19th-century battery offers little in the way of a history lesson, but it does overlook a secluded pink-sand beach, gin-clear water, and craggy cliffs. The beach is accessible only on foot, but it's a splendid place for a swim. Bear in mind that you have to climb back up the hill to your moped or bike.

Just before Somerset Bridge is a little street with the odd name
81 of **Overplus,** which harks back to the 17th century. When Richard Norwood surveyed the island in 1616, he divided the island into shares and tribes. He allotted 25 acres to each share, and 50 shares to each tribe. When the survey was completed, 200 acres (too small to form a tribe) remained unalloted and were listed as "overplus." Governor Tucker apparently directed the surveyor to keep an eye peeled for an attractive chunk of territory that could be designated as the surplus land. Norwood recommended a piece of real estate in the western part of the island, whereupon the governor claimed it and built a fine house on it. Upon hearing of the governor's action, the Bermuda Company lodged a complaint, forcing Tucker to return to London to sort everything out. The surplus land was eventually divided into seven parts, with Tucker retaining the section on which his house sat; the remainder was given to the church.

Across Somerset Bridge is the West End (*see* Tour 3: The West End, above). If you are traveling by bike or by moped, you can catch a ferry from Somerset Bridge back to Hamilton. Otherwise, take your choice of Middle, Harbour, or South Shore roads, to find your way back to the capital.

## Bermuda for Free

Bermuda is an expensive vacation destination. The cost of lodging and food aside, however, many of the island attractions are free. Certainly, Bermuda's greatest attractions—the sea and its beaches—don't cost a penny, but there is also a host of historical sites and museums that don't charge admission fees. Large portions of the exploring tours in this guide can be enjoyed for a few dollars at most. During the low and shoulder seasons (October–April), the government and the Department of Tourism sponsor a whole range of free or inexpensive activities, from walking tours and house tours to fashion shows.

Listed below are attractions described in the exploring tours and elsewhere that can be enjoyed for free.

**Astwood Park** (*see* Tour 4: The Parishes)
**Beaches** (*see* Chapter 5, Beaches and Water Sports)
**Bermuda Public Library** (*see* Tour 1: Hamilton)
**Black Watch Well** (*see* Tour 4: The Parishes)
**Botanical Gardens** (*see* Tour 4: The Parishes)
**Cabinet Building and Sessions House** (*see* Tour 1: Hamilton)
**Camden** (*see* Tour 4: The Parishes)
**Carter House** (*see* Tour 4: The Parishes)
**City Hall** (*see* Tour 1: Hamilton)
**Featherbed Alley Printery** (*see* Tour 2: The Town of St. George's)
**Fort Hamilton** (*see* Tour 1: Hamilton)
**Gates Fort** (*see* Tour 4: The Parishes)
**Heydon Chapel** (*see* Tour 3: The West End)
**Old Rectory** (*see* Tour 2: The Town of St. George's)
**Par-la-Ville Park** (*see* Tour 1: Hamilton)
**St. Peter's Church** (*see* Tour 2: The Town of St. George's)
**Scaur Hill Fort** (*see* Tour 3: The West End)

## What to See and Do with Children

Bermuda is not an ideal vacation spot for children. Aside from the obvious attractions of surf and sand, Bermuda does not offer much in the way of fairs, amusement parks, or other diversions. Two books are available, however, that can make exploring the island with children much easier. The first, *The Bermuda Coloring Book*, by Diana Watlington Ruetenik, is an educational book with historical sites for small children to color. The second, *A Child's History of Bermuda*, by E. M. Rice, puts the island's history into words that are easy to understand. Both books are available at A. S. Cooper & Son (59 Front St., Hamilton, 809/295–3961). Listed below are some of the attractions in the exploring tours and elsewhere that will appeal to children.

**Aquarium, Museum and Zoo** (*see* Tour 4: The Parishes)
**Beaches** (*see* Chapter 5, Beaches and Water Sports)
**Botanical Gardens** (*see* Tour 4: The Parishes)
**Ferries** (*see* Getting Around Bermuda in Chapter 1, Essential Information)
**Glass-bottom boat ride** (*see* Guided Tours in Chapter 1, Essential Information)

## Off the Beaten Track

The **Railway Trail** is a secluded 18-mile track that runs the length of the island along the route of the old Bermuda Railway. Restricted to pedestrians, horseback riders, and cyclists, the trail is a delightful way to see the island, away from the traffic and noise of the main roads. The Bermuda Department of Tourism has published *The Bermuda Railway Trail Guide*, which is available at all Visitors Service Bureaus and Information Centres. The pamphlet includes seven separate walking tours, ranging from about two to four hours, and an outline of what you can expect to see along the way. (For more information about sights along the way, refer to the appropriate section of the exploring tours, above. See also "Following in the Tracks of the Bermuda Railway," in Chapter 2, Portraits of

Bermuda.) It should be noted that many of the trails are quite isolated, and none is heavily trafficked. Although Bermuda has no major crime problem, unpleasant incidents do sometimes occur; women travelers especially should avoid striking out on remote trails alone. Apart from reasons of safety, the Railway Trail is much more enjoyable shared with a companion.

The history of the railway that ran along this trail is fascinating. Aside from horse-drawn carriages, boats, and bikes, the Bermuda Railway—"Old Rattle and Shake" as it was called—was the primary means of transportation on the island from 1931 to 1948. As early as 1899, however, the Bermuda Public Works Department bandied about proposals for a railroad. In 1922, over the objections of livery stable owners, the Bermuda Parliament finally granted permission for a narrow-gauge railroad to run from Somerset to St. George's.

The laying of the tracks was a formidable undertaking, requiring the construction of long tunnels and swing bridges. By the time it was finished in 1931, the railway had cost the investors $1 million. Mile for mile it was the most expensive railroad ever built, and the construction, which proceeded at a somnolent 2½ miles per year, was the slowest ever recorded. Nevertheless, on October 31, 1931, the little train got off to a roaring start with festive opening ceremonies at Somerset Bridge.

Passengers in the first-class carriages sat in wicker chairs, and the second-class cars were outfitted with benches. An American visitor reported in glowing terms of her first train ride in Bermuda, waxing lyrical about rolling cedar-covered hills, green velvet lawns, and banks of pink oleanders. Certainly, it was a vast improvement over the 19th-century horse buses that lumbered from Somerset to St. George's, carrying freight as well as passengers. Not everyone was happy, however. One writer groused that the train was "an iron serpent in the Garden of Eden." "Old Rattle and Shake" began going downhill during World War II. While the train was put to hard use by all the military personnel on the island, it proved impossible to obtain the necessary maintenance equipment. At the end of the war, the government acquired the distressed railway for £115,000. After the arrival of the automobile on Bermuda in 1946, the government sold the railway in its entirety to British Guiana (now Guyana).

# Sightseeing Checklists

## Historical Buildings and Sights

**"Birdcage"** (*see* Tour 1: Hamilton)
**Black Watch Well** (*see* Tour 4: The Parishes)
**Bridge House** (*see* Tour 2: The Town of St. George's)
**Cabinet Building** (*see* Tour 1: Hamilton)
**Camden** (*see* Tour 4: The Parishes)
**Cenotaph** (*see* Tour 1: Hamilton)
**City Hall** (*see* Tour 1: Hamilton)
**Clermont** (*see* Tour 4: The Parishes)
***Deliverance II*** (*see* Tour 2: The Town of St. George's)
**Featherbed Alley Printery** (*see* Tour 2: The Town of St. George's)
**Gibb's Hill Lighthouse** (*see* Tour 4: The Parishes)

**Government House** (*see* Tour 4: The Parishes)
**Old Rectory** (*see* Tour 2: The Town of St. George's)
**Old State House** (*see* Tour 2: The Town of St. George's)
**Palmetto House** (*see* Tour 4: The Parishes)
**Perot Post Office** (*see* Tour 1: Hamilton)
**Printer's Alley** (*see* Tour 2: The Town of St. George's)
**Royal Bermuda Yacht Club** (*see* Tour 1: Hamilton)
**Sessions House** (*see* Tour 1: Hamilton)
**St. David's Lighthouse** (*see* Tour 4: The Parishes)
**Tom Moore's Tavern** (*see* Tour 4: The Parishes)
**Town Hall** (*see* Tour 2: The Town of St. George's)
**White Horse Tavern** (*see* Tour 2: The Town of St. George's)

## Churches

**Cathedral of the Most Holy Trinity** (*see* Tour 1: Hamilton)
**Christ Church** (*see* Tour 4: The Parishes)
**Heydon Chapel** on the grounds of the Heydon Trust property (*see* Tour 3: The West End)
**Holy Trinity Church** (*see* Tour 4: The Parishes)
**Old Devonshire Church** (*see* Tour 4: The Parishes)
**St. James Church** (*see* Tour 3: The West End)
**St. John's Church** (*see* Tour 4: The Parishes)
**St. Paul's** (*see* Tour 4: The Parishes)
**St. Peter's Church** (*see* Tour 2: The Town of St. George's)
**St. Theresa's Church** (*see* Tour 1: Hamilton)
**Unfinished Church** (*see* Tour 2: The Town of St. George's)

## Forts

**Castle Island** (*see* Tour 4: The Parishes)
**Fort Hamilton** (*see* Tour 1: Hamilton)
**Fort St. Catherine** (*see* Tour 4: The Parishes)
**Gates Fort** (*see* Tour 4: The Parishes)
**Maritime Museum** (*see* Tour 3: The West End)
**Scaur Hill Fort** (*see* Tour 3: The West End)
**Warwick Camp** (*see* Tour 4: The Parishes)
**Whale Bay Fort** (*see* Tour 4: The Parishes)

## Museums and Galleries

**Aquarium, Museum and Zoo** (*see* Tour 4: The Parishes)
**Bank of Bermuda** (*see* Tour 1: Hamilton)
**Bermuda Public Library** and **Museum of the Bermuda Historical Society** (*see* Tour 1: Hamilton)
**Carriage Museum** (*see* Tour 2: The Town of St. George's)
**Carter House** (*see* Tour 4: The Parishes)
**Confederate Museum** (*see* Tour 2: The Town of St. George's)
**Maritime Museum** (*see* Tour 3: The West End)
**St. George's Historical Society Museum** (*see* Tour 2: The Town of St. George's)
**Tucker House** (*see* Tour 2: The Town of St. George's)
**Verdmont** (*see* Tour 4: The Parishes)

## Parks and Gardens

**Admiralty House Park** (*see* Tour 4: The Parishes)
**Astwood Park** (*see* Tour 4: The Parishes)
**Botanical Gardens** (*see* Tour 4: The Parishes)
**Gilbert Nature Reserve** (*see* Tour 3: The West End)

**Heydon Trust property** (*see* Tour 3: The West End)
**Lagoon Park** (*see* Tour 3: The West End)
**Long Bay Park and Nature Reserve** (*see* Tour 3: The West End)
**Paget Marsh** (*see* Tour 4: The Parishes)
**Palm Grove** (*see* Tour 4: The Parishes)
**Par-la-Ville Park** (*see* Tour 1: Hamilton)
**Somers Garden** (*see* Tour 2: The Town of St. George's)
**Spittal Pond** (*see* Tour 4: The Parishes)
**Victoria Park** (*see* Tour 1: Hamilton)

# 4 Shopping

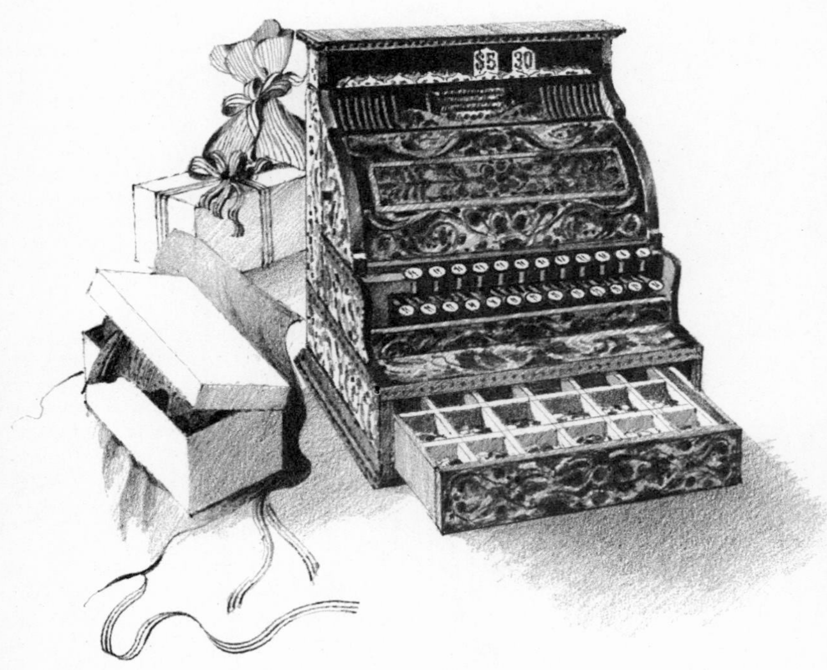

*by Honey Naylor*

If you're looking for colorful street markets where you can haggle over the price of low-cost goods and souvenirs, find another island. Shopping in Bermuda is characterized by sophisticated department stores and boutiques that stock top-quality—and expensive—merchandise. Cheap bargains are a rarity, and only products actually made in Bermuda (and antiques more than 100 years old) can be sold duty-free. If you're accustomed to shopping in Saks Fifth Avenue, Neiman-Marcus, and Bergdorf-Goodman, the prices in Bermuda's elegant shops won't come as a surprise. Actually, the prices on many items in Bermuda's stores are discounted, but a $600 dress discounted by 20% is still $480. But if you are looking for high-end merchandise, Bermuda does offer substantial savings on many items, particularly British-made clothing. Woolens and cashmere are good buys, especially in February when there is a host of sales during which many stores offer two-for-one sweater deals. Bermuda shorts are hot items, obviously, as are kilts.

European-made crystal and china—Wedgwood, Royal Crown Derby, Villeroy & Boch, Waterford, and Orrefors, to name a few—are available at prices at least 25% lower than those in the United States. Figurines from Lladro, Royal Doulton, and Hummel are also sold at significantly discounted prices. European fragrances and cosmetics are priced about 20%–25% less than in the United States, as are Rolex, Tissot, Patek Philippe, and other watches.

Bermuda has a thriving population of artists and artisans, whose work ranges from sculpture and paintings to miniature furniture, hand-blown glass, and dolls (*see* Arts and Crafts, below). Bermuda also has a number of noteworthy products to offer. Outerbridge's Sherry Peppers condiments add zip to soups, stews, drinks, and chowders. The original line has been expanded to include Bloody Mary mix, pepper jellies, and barbecue sauce; gift packs are available all over the island.

Bermuda rum is another popular item, and a variety of rum-based liqueurs is available, including Bermuda Banana, Banana Coconut Rum, and Bermuda Gold. Gosling's Black Seal Rum is excellent mixed with ginger beer to make a Dark 'n' Stormy, a famous Bermuda drink that should be treated with respect and caution. Rum is also found in quantity in Horton's Rum Cakes, which are made from a secret recipe and sold island-wide. U.S. citizens aged 21 or older, who have been out of the country for 48 hours, are allowed to bring home one liter of duty-free liquor each (*see* Customs and Duties in Chapter 1, Essential Information). In a bizarre catch-22, however, Bermuda requires a minimum purchase of two liters. Some liquor stores tell tourists that they must buy a minimum of four or five bottles to qualify for in-bond (duty-free) prices, but it isn't true. Although liquor prices are identical island-wide, some stores allow customers to create their own mixed packs of various liquors at in-bond prices, while others offer a selection of prepackaged sets (the five-pack is most common). Duty-free liquor must be purchased at least 24 hours before your departure, and it can be picked up only in the airport departure lounge or on board your cruise ship. The airport has no duty-free shop of its own. Below are some sample prices at press time for one liter of liquor: Tia Maria, $13.55; Grand Marnier, $20.40; Chivas Regal, $20.85; J&B Rare, $14.25; Johnnie Walker Black, $21.20;

Stolichnaya vodka, $8.80; Beefeater gin, $12.15; and Bermuda rum, $7.

Comparison shopping is probably a waste of time in Bermuda because the merchants' association keeps prices almost identical island-wide. However, it's worth checking the price of items at home—especially crystal and china—before you embark on a shopping spree in Bermuda. Ask your local department store if any sales are scheduled and check the prices of designer and name-brand products at local factory outlets. Remember that Bermuda, unlike most U.S. states, has no sales tax, which means that the price on the tag is the price you pay.

Buildings and houses in Bermuda are numbered rather whimsically. If you check the phone directory for a store address, you may find a listing on Front Street or Water Street, for example, but no street number. To complicate matters further, some Front Street buildings have two numbers, one of them an old historic address that has nothing to do with the building's present location. Fortunately, almost all Bermudians can give you precise directions.

In general, shops are open Monday–Saturday 9–5 or 9–5:30. Some of the Front Street shops in Hamilton stay open until about 10:30 PM, and open on Sunday when cruise ships call.

In most cases in this chapter, if a store has several branches or outlets, only the main branch phone number has been listed. Unless otherwise noted the shops listed below accept American Express, MasterCard, and Visa.

## Shopping Districts

Hamilton boasts the greatest concentration of shops in Bermuda, and **Front Street** is its pièce de résistance. Lined with small, pastel-colored buildings, this most fashionable of Bermuda's streets houses sedate department stores and snazzy boutiques, with several small arcades and shopping alleys leading off it. **The Emporium** on Front Street, a renovated old building arranged around an open atrium, is home to an eclectic collection of dress and jewelry shops. The statue on top of the atrium fountain is of Bermudian Gina Swaison, who ruled as Miss World in 1979–80. **Windsor Place** is a new mall on Queen Street where customers can shop while taped classical music plays in the background.

In St. George's, **Water Street and Somers Wharf** are the site of numerous renovated buildings that now house boutiques and branches of Front Street stores. **King's Square** is also dotted with shops selling everything from dresses to sweaters and ties. In the West End, **Somerset Village** has a few shops, but they hardly merit a special shopping trip. Restoration continues on the 19th-century **Dockyard** area, however, and recent additions include a large luxury mall. Dockyard is also home to the Craft Market, the Bermuda Arts Centre, and Island Pottery, where local artisans display their wares and visitors can sometimes watch them at work. Several other small plazas are sprinkled over the island, featuring a few shops, and often a grocery store and post office.

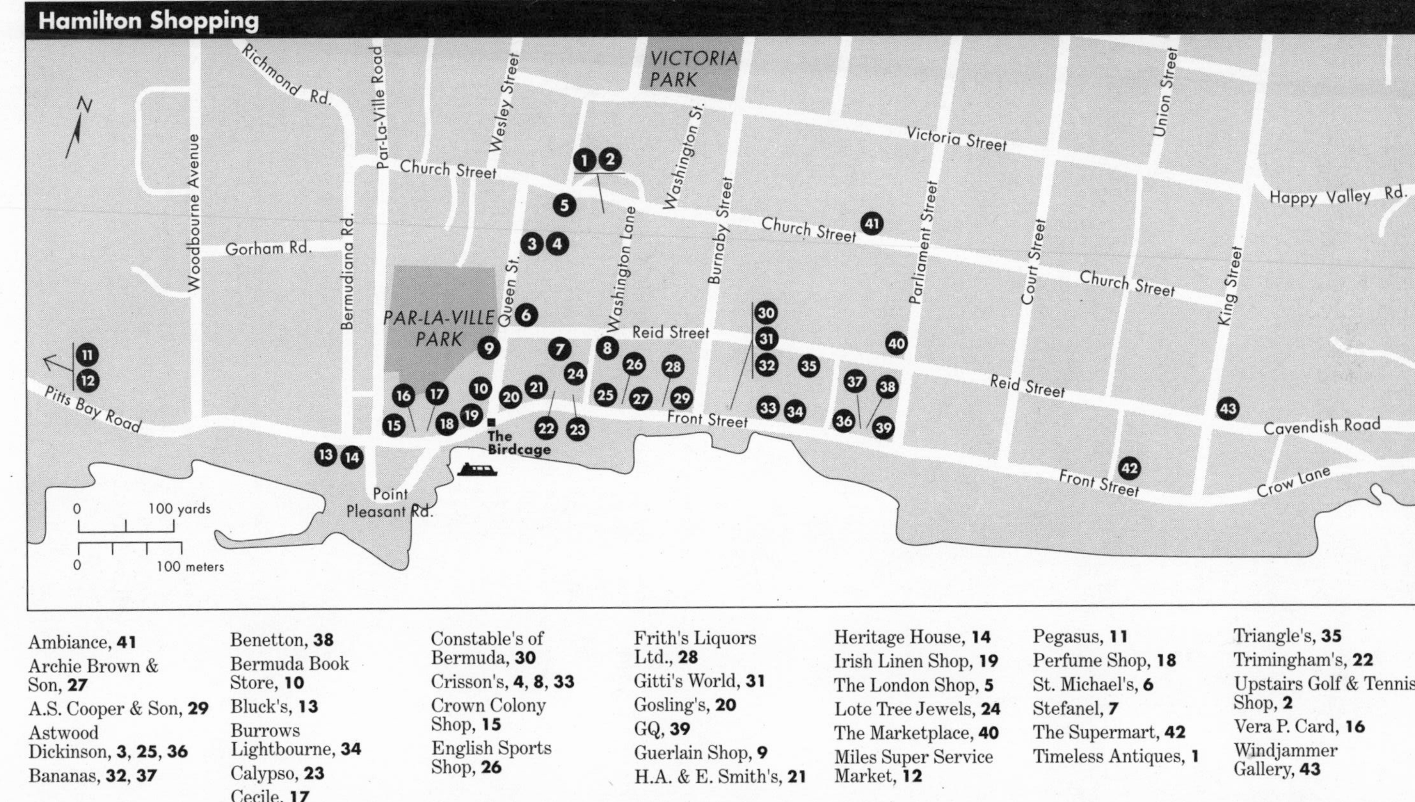


Ambiance, **41**
Archie Brown & Son, **27**
A.S. Cooper & Son, **29**
Astwood Dickinson, **3**, **25**, **36**
Bananas, **32**, **37**
Benetton, **38**
Bermuda Book Store, **10**
Bluck's, **13**
Burrows Lightbourne, **34**
Calypso, **23**
Cecile, **17**
Constable's of Bermuda, **30**
Crisson's, **4**, **8**, **33**
Crown Colony Shop, **15**
English Sports Shop, **26**
Frith's Liquors Ltd., **28**
Gitti's World, **31**
Gosling's, **20**
GQ, **39**
Guerlain Shop, **9**
H.A. & E. Smith's, **21**
Heritage House, **14**
Irish Linen Shop, **19**
The London Shop, **5**
Lote Tree Jewels, **24**
The Marketplace, **40**
Miles Super Service Market, **12**
Pegasus, **11**
Perfume Shop, **18**
St. Michael's, **6**
Stefanel, **7**
The Supermart, **42**
Timeless Antiques, **1**
Triangle's, **35**
Trimingham's, **22**
Upstairs Golf & Tennis Shop, **2**
Vera P. Card, **16**
Windjammer Gallery, **43**

Bananas, **9**
Bluck's, **2**
Bridge House Gallery, **11**
Cow Polly, **6**
Crisson's, **7, 10**
Frangipani, **5**
Gosling's, **1**
Irish Linen Shop, **3**
Perfume Shop, **8**
Trimingham's, **4**

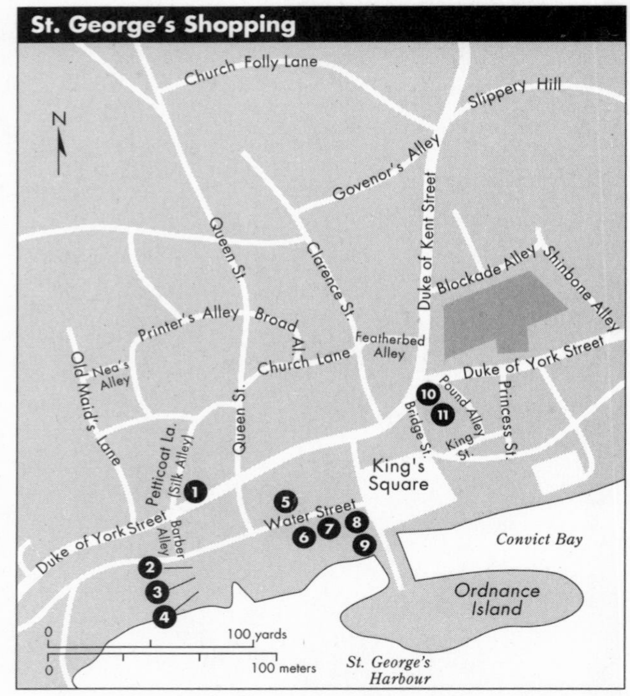


## Department Stores

Bermuda's three leading department stores are A. S. Cooper & Son, Trimingham's, and H. A. & E. Smith's, the main branches of which are on Front Street in Hamilton. These elegant, venerable institutions are operated by the third or fourth generation of the families that founded them, and customers stand a good chance of being waited on by a Cooper, a Trimingham, or a Smith. In addition, many of the salespeople have worked at the stores for two or three decades; they tend to be unobtrusive, but polite and helpful when you need them.

**A. S. Cooper & Son** (59 Front St., Hamilton, tel. 809/295–3961) is best known for Wedgwood bone china, which is sold exclusively on the island by this store. A five-piece place setting of the Wedgwood strawberry-and-vine pattern costs $51.20, or $64 (including duty, freight, and insurance) if you want it shipped to the United States. Prices on other well-known brands of china, as well as crystal, are similarly attractive. The store's own private-label collection of clothing can be found in the well-stocked men's and women's departments. Hungry shoppers can head for The Balcony, a tiny pink-and-white restaurant just off the second floor that has a magnificent view of the harbor. Open Monday–Friday from noon to 2, The Balcony serves quiches, salads, and sandwiches. Other branches of the department store can be found in all major hotels and in St. George's at 22 Water Street.

Bermuda Arts Centre, **8**
Craft Market, **7**
Frith's, **4**
Gosling's, **1**
Irish Linen Shop, **2**
Island Pottery, **6**
Trimingham's, **3**, **5**

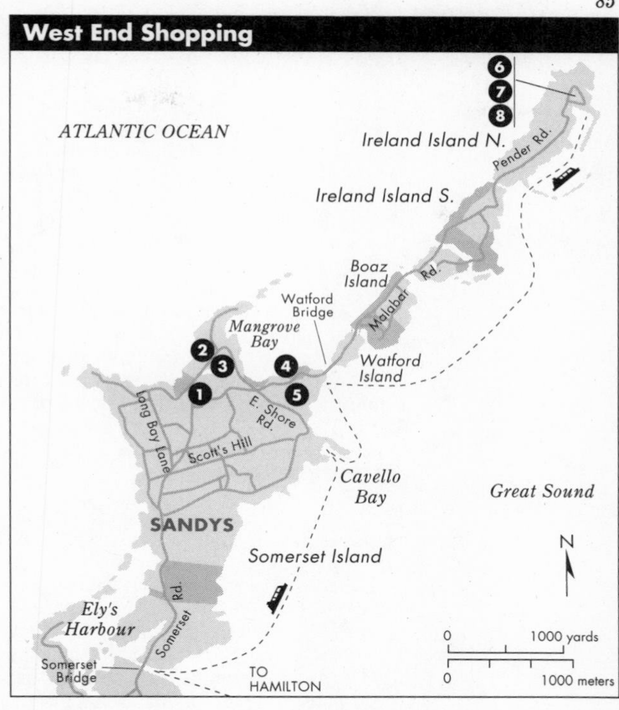


**H. A. & E. Smith's** (35 Front St., Hamilton, tel. 809/295–2288), founded in 1889 by Henry Archibald and Edith Smith, is arguably the best men's store in Bermuda—and exclusive agents for Burberry and Alan Paine. Burberry raincoats are priced from $295 to $495, and Alan Paine cable-knit sweaters sell for about $375; a Chester Barrie cashmere jacket costs around $650. You can buy Harris Tweed jackets for $175 and Italian silk ties for $12. There is a large selection of Shetland sweaters, which go for about $30 each. Smith's is also a good place to buy kilts. Ladies can find Christian Dior handbags for about $300, but the store also stocks Bermuda bags—the kinds with the detachable cedar handle and interchangeable cloth satchel—for about $30. Ladies' cashmere-lined leather gloves cost $65 (unlined $45). Unfortunately, the store's confusing layout makes it easy to get lost. The staff here is especially genteel, however, and they will help orient you. Branches can be found in the Belmont and Southampton Princess hotels and at 18 York Street in St. George's.

**St. Michael's** (7 Reid St., Hamilton, tel. 809/295–0031), an offshoot of Britain's Marks & Spencer, is called Marks and Sparks by everyone in Bermuda. This large store is usually filled with thrift-minded Britons attracted by its moderate prices for men's, women's, and children's clothing. Summer wear, including swimsuits, cotton jerseys, and polo shirts, is a good buy. High-quality men's and women's cashmere and woolen sweaters are also sold at substantial discounts.

**Trimingham's** (37 Front St., Hamilton, tel. 809/295–1183) has been a Hamilton fixture since 1842. The first store in the world to tailor madras for Western clothing, this is the place to look for men's colorful madras blazers and trousers. The store also has its own line of sportswear, and Bermuda shorts are good buys. In womenswear, savings can be found on Shetland and lamb's wool sweaters, but prices for Dean's of Scotland woolens are about the same, or even a bit less, in the United States. Liberty of London and Hermès scarves are definitely worth a look. The store has an impressive display of perfumes and cosmetics, and it is the exclusive Bermuda distributor for Tiffany and Boucheron fragrances. La Prairie, the beauty treatment from Montreux, is discounted by about 20%. Head for the excellent gift boutique to buy Outerbridge's Sherry Pepper Sauce or a box of Trimingham's hand-baked assorted cookies. Trimingham branches have sprouted up all over the island, including at Somers Wharf in St. George's and in Somerset Village.

## Grocery Stores

Most of the accommodation on Bermuda, from cottage colonies to guest houses and housekeeping apartments, offers guests the opportunity to do their own cooking. Self-catering vacations are cheaper than those where you pay full board or dine out at every meal; considering how expensive Bermuda is, this option has widespread appeal for both families and budget travelers. Don't expect the same prices as at home, however—foodstuffs in Bermuda are also quite expensive. For example, a dozen large eggs costs $2.30, a six-pack of Coke is $4.10, a pound of Maxwell House coffee $4.50, and a quart of Tropicana orange juice $3.10 (a local brand is slightly cheaper). Listed below are some of the major supermarkets in Bermuda.

**A-1 Fine Food Market** (South Shore Rd., Paget, tel. 809/236–0351) features a take-out counter that serves inexpensive ($6–$9) chicken dinners, French fries, burgers, hot dogs, and sandwiches. The store is near Barnsdale Guest Apartments and the Sky Top Cottages, but you will need a vehicle to carry heavy groceries up the hill.

**The Friendly Store** (Middle Rd., Warwick, tel. 809/236–1344) is a medium-size convenience store within walking distance of the Pretty Penny guest house.

**Harrington Hundreds Grocery & Liquor Store** (South Rd., Smith's, tel. 809/293–1635) is near Spittal Pond, not far from Angel's Grotto apartments; it may be too far to walk, however.

**The Marketplace** (Reid St., near Parliament St., Hamilton, tel. 809/292–3163) is part of a moderately priced chain with stores around the island. Customers can get hot soups to go.

**Miles Super Service Market** (Pitts Bay Rd., near The Princess, Hamilton, tel. 809/295–1234) has expensive steaks and Häagen-Dazs ice cream. The market makes deliveries anywhere on the island.

**The Supermart** (Front St., near King St., Hamilton, tel. 809/292–2064) has a well-stocked salad bar, prepackaged sandwiches, and hot coffee. This store and the two immediately below are a five-minute ferry ride across the harbor from the Greenbank Cottages and Salt Kettle House.

## Specialty Stores

**Antiques**

**Heritage House** (2 W. Front St., Hamilton, tel. 809/295–2615). Browsers will find it difficult to tear themselves away from this small shop, which features an array of both antique and modern pieces. Among the antiques recently featured were a 17th-century chest for $9,000, an 18th-century harp for $2,250, a 19th-century sewing machine for $277, and a six-piece Royal Worcester demitasse set priced at $575. Staffordshire silver is usually available, too; a Spode plate goes for about $75. The shop is also home to the Litchfield Collection, a fascinating array of tall ships in glass bottles, including a beautiful model of HMS *Victory* (Admiral Nelson's ship) for $325. The original works of several local artists are also on display. Shoppers who don't want to make a major purchase can search through bins of prints. The shop has its own framing department.

**Pegasus** (63 Pitts Bay Rd., Hamilton, tel. 809/295–2900). A Dickensian place with creaky wood floors, this store has racks and racks of antique prints and maps. In particular, look for the "Spy" *Vanity Fair* caricatures from the late 19th and early 20th centuries ($10–$100) and the Dickens characters by 19th-century artist Frederick Barnard ($50–$100). Among the antique maps are some 18th-century representations of the United States priced at $300, and others showing the castles of Ireland, Scotland, and England. There are several racks of children's books (about $4) by British authors, as well as a good selection of postcards. Shoppers can browse here to their hearts' content. Diners Club cards are accepted here in addition to those credit cards mentioned above.

**Timeless Antiques** (26 Church St., Hamilton, tel. 809/295–5008). Across the street and down the steps from City Hall, you'll find this small, Old World shop, where the walls are lined with 200- to 300-year-old grandfather (or long-case) clocks. Among the store's collection of antiques are carved Early English oak tables, chests, chairs, candelabra, and exquisite reproductions of medieval tapestries. Time is of the essence here, however, and clock aficionados will want to spend hours talking with proprietor Peter Durhager. If $8,000 for a long-case clock is a little too rich for your blood, take a look at the collection of antique pocket watches.

**Arts and Crafts**

*Artists*

Buying artwork by someone you know is always more satisfying than buying it blind, and some of Bermuda's resident artists encourage visits to their studios. Call ahead first, however, to find out if it's convenient to stop by, and be sure to check which credit cards each artist accepts. Remember that there are no duties levied on Bermudian arts and crafts.

**Celia and Jack Arnell** (tel. 809/236–4646). The miniature cedar furniture crafted by this husband-and-wife team is displayed in a dollhouse at the Craft Market (*see* below). The fine details on the breakfronts and chests of drawers include tiny metal drawer knobs, and the wonderful four-poster bed comes complete with a canopy. A breakfront sells for $140; the four-poster bed for $100; and chairs for $27.

**Kathleen Kemsley Bell** (tel. 809/236–3366). A director of the Bermuda Arts Centre, Ms. Bell creates exquisite dolls of a particular person or period in Bermuda's history. Each doll is researched for historical accuracy and is unique. The bodies are sculpted of papier-mâché and hand-painted. The faces of the dolls are marvelously expressive, and the costumes are all hand-stitched. The base of each doll is signed and carries a description of the historical period on which the doll's fashions are based. Ms. Bell works on commission and will visit your hotel with samples of her work. Prices start at $185.

**Alfred Birdsey Studio** ("Stowe Hill," Paget, tel. 809/236–6658). An island institution, Mr. Birdsey is a recipient of the Queen's Certificate of Honour and Medal in recognition of "valuable services given to Her Majesty for more than 40 years as an artist of Bermuda." His watercolors of Bermuda hang in the Bank of Bermuda and Cambridge Beaches cottage colony, as well as in the building at 2 Wall Street in New York. His studio is open weekdays 9–5.

**Liz Campbell** (tel. 809/236–8539). Lovely stained-glass butterflies, mirrors, panels, and boxes created by Ms. Campbell are displayed at the Dockyard Craft Market (*see* below). Prices range from $30 to about $200 for larger, more elaborate pieces.

**Ronnie Chameau** (tel. 809/292–1387). Ms. Chameau creates Christmas angels and dolls from dried palm, banana, and grapefruit leaves gathered from her yard. The 9-inch dolls ($35), with palmetto leaf baskets and hats, Spanish moss hair, and pecan heads with painted faces, are intended as table ornaments, while the dainty little 4-inch angels ($5–$20) are designed to hang on the Christmas tree. The angels and dolls are available year-round at Trimingham's (*see* above) and at Carole Holding's studio in St. George's (*see* below).

**Gayle Sherwood Cooke** (Tee Street Studio, 1 Tee St., Devonshire, tel. 809/236–4321). Ms. Cooke crafts glass plates, bowls, cups, perfume bottles, and Christmas ornaments in vibrant, swirling colors. The perfume bottles, with individually made stoppers for an airtight seal, cost between $15 and $125; bowls are $20–$200; and plates $60–$200. Her work can also be seen at Flameworks (3 Chancery La., Hamilton, tel. 809/295–9679).

**Joan Forbes** (Art House, South Shore Rd., Paget, tel. 809/236–6746). Watercolors and lithographs are the specialty of Ms. Forbes, whose work focuses on Bermudian architecture, horticulture, and seascapes. Her lithographs sell for $10–$45. She also produces cards, notepaper, and envelopes.

**Desmond Fountain** (tel. 809/292–3955). This award-winning sculptor's works are on display all over the island, whether it's a life-size bronze statue perched beside a lagoon or a lolling figure seated in a garden chair. Fountain created the *Land Ho!* statue of Sir George Somers on Ordnance Island in St. George's, and other of his works can be seen in the Sculpture Gallery on the mezzanine of the Southampton Princess. Prices start at about $5,000 for a small bronze and soar to dizzying heights.

**Carole Holding Studio** (3 Featherbed Alley, St. George's, tel. 809/297–1833, after hours 809/236–6002). Ms. Holding uses pastel watercolors to paint the flowers and homes of Bermuda. In addition to her own watercolors, signed prints, and limited editions, her studio displays works, including cedar crafts, by local artists. Housed in the slave quarters of an 18th-century home that now serves as the St. George's Historical Society, Holding's studio is open to the public Monday–Saturday 10–4.

**Graeme Outerbridge** (tel. 809/238–2411). A photographer who contributed to the acclaimed *Day in the Life* book series, Mr. Outerbridge captures Bermuda in original photographic prints, silk screens, and posters.

**Mary Zuill** (10 Southlyn La., Paget, tel. 809/236–2439). In a tiny studio attached to her house, Ms. Zuill paints delightful watercolors of Bermuda's flowers, alleyways, and cottages. She accepts commissions and will either design a painting or work from a photograph you've taken in Bermuda. Original watercolors cost from $60 to $600. She welcomes visitors Tuesday–Friday from April to November only.

*Galleries and Crafts Shops*

**Bermuda Arts Centre** (Dockyard, Ireland Island, tel. 809/234–3208). Sleek and modern, with well-designed displays of local art, this gallery is housed in one of the stone buildings of the former naval yard. The walls are adorned with pictures and photographs, and glass display cases contain costume dolls, jewelry, and other crafts. Visitors are provided with a printed list with descriptions and prices of the various works. Changing exhibits are frequently held.

**Bridge House Gallery** (1 Bridge St., St. George's, tel. 809/297–8211). Housed in a Bermuda mansion that dates to 1700, this gallery is of historical and architectural interest in its own right. In the 18th century, the two-story white building was the home of Bermuda's governors; today it is maintained by the Bermuda National Trust. Displayed amid 18th- and 19th-century furnishings are works of Bermudian artists: original paintings, hand-blown glass, Bermuda costume dolls, antique bottles and maps, jewelry, and books.

**Craft Market** (Dockyard, Ireland Island, tel. 809/234–3208). Occupying part of what was once the cooperage, this large stone building dates to 1831. Although some lovely work is to be found here—miniature cedar furniture, stained glass, and costume dolls, in particular—the displays are poorly arranged on simple wooden tables and in drab booths. As a result, even high-quality work seems unimpressive.

**Island Pottery** (Dockyard, Ireland Island, tel. 809/234–3208). This workshop establishment takes up a single room in a large stone building. A counter separates the workshop from the gift shop in the front of the room, where crude tables and shelves are piled with ashtrays, bowls, and vases. Behind the counter, artisans in aprons and work clothes toil over potter's wheels.

**Windjammer Gallery** (King and Reid Sts., Hamilton, tel. 809/292–7861). A cluttered, three-room shop on the ground floor of a small cottage, this is the place to go to find out about upcoming art shows. The staff can help you choose from the huge range of prints, lithographs, oils, watercolors, and photographs that fill the walls and bins. Jewelry and sculpture—most notably by Desmond Fountain—are also on display.

**Bookstores**

**Bermuda Book Store** (Queen and Front Sts., Hamilton, tel. 809/295–3698). Book lovers, beware! Once you set foot inside this musty old place, you'll have a hard time tearing yourself away. Stacked on a long table are a host of books about Bermuda. Proprietor Jim Zuill, whose father wrote the acclaimed *Bermuda Journey*, can probably answer any questions you have about the island.

**Boutiques**

**Ambiance** (Armoury Bldg., Reid St., Hamilton, tel. 809/292-4132). Ladies who like hats should head for this tiny shop. Prices average around $75.

**Archie Brown & Son** (49 Front St., Hamilton, tel. 809/295-2928). Top-quality woolens, Pringle of Scotland cashmeres, Shetland and lamb's wool sweaters, and 100% wool tartan kilts are among the specialties at this store.

**Bananas** (93 W. Front St., 7 E. Front St., Hamilton, and 3 King's Sq., St. George's, tel. 809/295-1106 or 809/292-7268). Sportswear and T-shirts make this place a teenager's dream. Brightly colored Bermuda umbrellas cost about $25.

**Benetton** (95 Front St., Hamilton, tel. 809/292-5878). In this link in the ever-lengthening Italian chain are colorful Benetton fashions at prices considerably lower than in the United States.

**Calypso** (45 Front St., Hamilton, tel. 809/295-2112). Available only in Bermuda, owner Polly Hornburg's ladies' fashions are created from splashy fabrics imported from Europe, India, and Africa. Her casually elegant dresses sell for $145 and more. The store has an exclusive arrangement to sell Louis Vuitton merchandise in Bermuda. Expect to shell out $180 for a small wallet; $1,145 for an attaché case.

**Cecile** (15 Front St., Hamilton, tel. 809/295-1311). Specializing in upscale off-the-rack ladies' fashions, this shop carries designer labels such as Ciao and Ciaosports, Nina Ricci, Geiger of Austria, and Louis Feraud of Paris. There's a good selection of swimwear, too, including swimsuits by Gottex.

**Constable's of Bermuda** (Emporium, Front St., Hamilton, tel. 809/295-8060). Icelandic woolen clothing is the specialty of this store, and prices are generally 30%-50% lower than those in the United States. This is *the* place to come for heavy woolen coats, ski sweaters, ponchos, jackets, and skirts in smoky colors. Travel blankets are also a hot item.

**Cow Polly** (Somers Wharf, St. George's, tel. 809/297-1514). Phoebe and Sam Wharton's store is an upscale novelty shop that carries only imported items. You won't find their unusual pottery, jewelry, or men's ties sold anywhere else on the island.

**English Sports Shop** (95 Front St., Hamilton, tel. 809/295-2672). Bermuda has several branches of this store, which specializes in British woolens: Harris Tweed jackets for men cost $175, while Shetland woolen sweaters are priced at $45; more expensive cashmere sweaters go for $99. The Crown Colony Shop (1 Front St., Hamilton, tel. 809/295-3935), a branch of the store that focuses on women's clothing, sells Lady Clansmen Scottish Shetland sweaters for $45 and silk dresses made in Hong Kong for about $300.

**Frangipani** (Water St., St. George's, tel. 809/297-1357). Exotic men's and women's clothing from Greece and Indonesia give this little shop a distinctly non-Bermudian feel. Colorful cotton sweaters from Greece come in more than 100 designs. The shop also has a collection of unusual jewelry.

**Gitti's World** (Emporium, Front St., Hamilton, tel. 809/295-8056). This tiny, rather inconspicuous boutique is a real find. It's overflowing with modestly priced hand-embroidered blouses, beaded sweaters, sequined evening bags, and tie-dyed dresses. Casual cottons cost $30; cocktail dresses are about

$60. The shop also has a collection of chunky costume jewelry and children's dresses and sleepwear for about $15.

**GQ** (99 Front St., Hamilton, tel. 809/292–6655). Rap and rock music attract a trendy young crowd to this small boutique, which stocks the latest fashions from Smak and Williwear, Italian shoes, knit suits, high-quality leather jackets (around $275), and jazzy cocktail dresses.

**The London Shop** (22 Church St., Hamilton, tel. 809/295–1279). This small, cluttered shop has shelves piled high with Pierre Cardin dress shirts for about $35 and sweaters for $45. Countess Mara short-sleeve sport shirts are priced at $19, and herringbone caps cost $35.

**Stefanel** (12 Reid St., Hamilton, tel. 809/295–5698). This very smart, very expensive boutique stocks the snazzy cotton knits of Italian trendsetter Carlo Stefanel. Imported from Italy, the clothing includes men's cotton and linen suits and cotton dress shirts; women's patterned wool skirts with handknit, contrasting jackets; and children's sweaters and sweats.

**Triangle's** (48 Reid St., Hamilton, tel. 809/292–1990). The star attractions of this boutique are Diane Freis's original, colorful, and crushable mosaic dresses, priced between $220 and $260—almost half what they cost in the United States.

**Upstairs Golf & Tennis Shop** (26 Church St., Hamilton, tel. 809/295–5161). As befits Bermuda's role as a golfing paradise, this store stocks clubs and accessories from some of the best brands available including Hogan, Ping, MacGregor, and Spalding. Tennis players can choose a racquet by Head, Wilson, Square Two, or Nike. Men's and women's sportswear is also available.

### Crystal, China, and Porcelain

**Bluck's** (4 W. Front St., Hamilton, tel. 809/295–5367). A dignified establishment that has been in business for more than 140 years, this is the only store on the island devoted exclusively to the sale of crystal and china. Royal Doulton, Royal Copenhagen, Villeroy & Boch, Herend, Lalique, Minton, Waterford, Baccarat, and others are displayed on two floors. The courteous staff will provide you with price lists upon request. As an example, a five-piece place setting of Limoges Roulette costs $119.75, while eight place settings of Hermès Peonies are priced at $1,587.

**Vera P. Card** (11 Front St., Hamilton, and 9 Water St., St. George's, tel. 809/295–1729). Lladro and Royal Doulton's "Reflections" figurines are widely available all over the island at almost identical prices, but this store has the most extensive selection. The shop's collection of Hummel figurines is, without a doubt, the best on the island.

### Jewelry

**Astwood Dickinson** (83–85 Front St., Windsor Pl. on Queen St., and Walker Arcade, Hamilton, tel. 809/292–5805). In addition to 18-karat gold Omega watches that sell for $7,125, this store carries less expensive items such as Le Clip Swiss quartz watches ($35) and alarm Le Clips ($60). Most interesting of all, however, is the store's Bermuda Collection of 18-karat gold mementos that sell for $50–$600. The collection includes the Bermuda dinghy pendant for $300 (earrings are $230); a tall ship pin or pendant for $600; a Bermuda Island pendant for $50; and a Gibb's Hill Lighthouse tie-pin for $150.

**Crisson's** (71 Front St., 20 Reid St., Hamilton, and five other locations, tel. 809/295–2351). The exclusive Bermuda agent for Rolex, Cartier, and Raymond Weil, this upscale establishment offers discounts of 20%–25% on expensive merchandise, but don't expect to find cheap Timex or Swatch watches. The gift department carries English flatware, Saint Louis crystal, and imported baubles, bangles, and beads.

**Lote Tree Jewels** (Walker Arcade, Hamilton, tel. 809/292–8525). Opened by owner Mary Walker in 1980 to showcase her own Marybeads—14-karat gold beads intertwined with semi-precious gems or freshwater pearls—the shop now emphasizes ethnic jewelry from around the world: African trade beads combined with tooled silver beads from Afghanistan, Bali, and India; and handmade, hand-painted Peruvian clay beads strung with hand-carved stone beads from Ecuador. There are baskets of bangles from Burkina Faso, Mali, and Kenya; a "jungle collection" that includes tortoise twin combs and hair bows; and tribal jewelry from Afghanistan that features lapis lazuli and silver chokers, earrings, rings, and brooches. Marybeads are still available—a 14-karat necklace sells for $495.

**Linens**

**Irish Linen Shop** (31 Front St., Hamilton, and Cambridge Rd., Somerset, tel. 809/295–4089). In a cottage that looks as though it belongs in Dublin, the Hamilton branch is *the* place for Irish linen double damask tablecloths. Prices range from $38 to $410 (not including napkins), although antique tablecloths can cost as much as $1,600. From Madeira come exquisite hand-embroidered handkerchiefs ($17); cotton and organdy pillowcases; and a cotton organdy christening robe with slip and bonnet, hand embroidered with garlands and tiers of Valenciennes lace ($210). Pure linen hand-rolled handkerchiefs from Belgium with Belgian lace are priced under $20, while Le Jacquard Français cotton kitchen towels cost less than $10. The shop's Bermuda Cottage Collection includes quilted place mats, tea cozies, and pot holders—most for less than $12. The store has an exclusive arrangement with Souleiado, maker of the vivid prints from Provence that are available in skirts, dresses, place mats, bags, as well as by the yard.

**Liquors and Liqueurs**

The following liquor stores sell at identical prices, and each will allow you to put together your own package of Bermuda liquors at in-bond (duty-free) prices: **Burrows Lightbourne** (Front St., Hamilton, tel. 809/295–0176), **Frith's Liquors Ltd.** (57 Front St., Hamilton, tel. 809/295–3544), **Gosling's** (33 Front St., Hamilton, tel. 809/295–1123).

**Perfumes**

**Bermuda Perfumery** (North Shore Rd., Bailey's Bay, tel. 809/293–0627 or 800/527–8213). This highly promoted perfumery is on all the taxi-tour itineraries. Guided tours of the facilities are given continuously, during which you can see how the fragrances of flowers are distilled into perfume and take a walk through the ornamental gardens. At the Cobweb gift shop you can purchase the factory's Lili line of fragrances.

The **Perfume Shop** (23 W. Front St., Hamilton, tel. 809/295–0570) and the **Guerlain Shop** (19 Queen St., Hamilton, tel. 809/295–5535 and 6 Water St., St. George's, tel. 809/297–1525), which is the exclusive agent for Guerlain products, stock more than 127 lines of French and Italian fragrances, as well as soaps, bath salts, and bubble bath.

# 5 Beaches and Water Sports

## Introduction

*by Peter Oliver*

*Peter Oliver is a New York–based freelance writer, specializing in sports and the outdoors. His articles have appeared in* Backpacker, The New York Times, Skiing, *and* Travel-Holiday.

Bermuda boasts that it has "water scientifically proven to be the clearest in the western Atlantic." Whether this is true or not, the water is certainly clear enough to make Bermuda one of the world's great centers for snorkeling and scuba diving. Clear water also gives fishermen a distinct advantage—a fish has almost nowhere to hide in the island's shallow, translucent water. For whatever reasons, however, the water around Bermuda was apparently *not* clear enough to allow many ship captains to see the barrier reefs encircling the island. Consequently, the reefs today are a veritable smorgasbord of marine wreckage, guaranteed to whet the appetite of any diving enthusiast. Some wrecks are in less than 30 feet of water and are accessible even to snorkelers. The reefs also help keep the water close to shore relatively calm, acting as a fortress wall against the pounding swells of the Atlantic and reducing beach erosion. And Bermuda's beaches are definitely worth saving—fine-grain sand tinted pink with crushed coral. But Bermuda's reefs remain as dangerous as ever. Boat rentals are available at several island locations, but only the most experienced yachtsmen should venture beyond the safe waters of Great Sound, Harrington Sound, and Castle Harbour. To go anywhere else without a full knowledge of Bermuda's considerable offshore hazards is pure folly.

Thanks to Bermuda's position close to the Gulf Stream, the water stays warm year-round, although Bermudians consider anything under 75°F frigid. In summer, the ocean is usually above 80°F, and even warmer in the shallows between the reefs and shore. In winter, the water temperature only occasionally drops below 70°F, but it seems cooler because the air temperature is usually in the mid-60s—a wet suit is recommended for anyone who plans to spend an extended period of time in the water. Lack of business, more than a drop in water temperature, is responsible for the comparative dearth of water-sports activity during the winter months. The winter does tend to be windier, however, which means water conditions can be less than ideal. Rough water creates problems anchoring or stabilizing fishing and diving boats, and visibility underwater is often clouded by sand and debris. High season runs from April through October, during which time fishing, diving, and yacht charters fill up quickly. Most boats carry fewer than 20 passengers, so it's advisable to sign up early. March–April and October–November are shoulder seasons, and December–February is the off-season, when many operators close to make repairs and perform routine maintenance. During these months, a few operators stay open on a limited basis, scheduling charters only when there are enough people to fill a boat; if too few people sign up, the charter is canceled. For this reason, water-sports enthusiasts have to be flexible during the winter months.

Take advantage of the activities director at your hotel or your ship's cruise director—he or she can make arrangements for you long before you arrive. The **"Sportsman's Guide,"** a 24-page booklet available free from the Bermuda Department of Tourism (*see* Chapter 1, Essential Information), has extensive listings and information on all water sports in Bermuda; it's worth obtaining a copy before you make any plans.

# Water Sports

## Boating and Sailing

Visitors to Bermuda can either rent their own boat or charter a boat with a skipper. Rental boats, which are 17 feet at most, range from sailboats (typically tiny Sunfish) to motorboats (typically 13-foot Boston Whalers), glass-bottom boats, kayaks, and pedal boats. Such vessels are ideal for exploring the coves and harbors of the sounds or, in the case of motorboats, waterskiing. In **Great Sound,** several small islands, such as Hawkins Island and Long Island, have tiny secluded beaches that are usually empty during the week. If the wind is fresh, the islands are about a half hour's sail from **Hamilton Harbour** or **Salt Kettle.** These beaches are wonderful places to have a picnic, although many are privately owned and visitors are not always welcome. Check with the boat-rental operator before planning an island outing.

The trade winds pass well to the south of Bermuda, so the island does not have predictable air currents. Channeled by islands and headlands, the winds around Hamilton Harbour and the Great Sound can be particularly unpredictable; **Mangrove Bay** has far more reliable breezes. The variability of the winds has no doubt aided the education of Bermuda's racing skippers, who are traditionally among the world's best. To the casual sailor, however, wind changes can be troublesome, although you can be fairly confident you won't be becalmed: The average summer breeze is 10–15 knots, usually out of the south or southwest. Encircled by land, **Harrington Sound** has the calmest water, ideal for novice sailors, pedal boaters, and waterskiers. Anyone wanting a small taste of open water should head for **Pompano Marina** (Pompano Beach Club, Southampton, tel. 809/234–0222) on the western ocean shore.

**Boat Rentals** Rates for small powerboats range between $20 and $25 an hour, or about $100 for a full day; sailboat rentals cost $12–$20 an hour, or $50–$80 for a full day. A refundable deposit of about $50 is usually required. Several of the larger hotels, such as **Marriott's Castle Harbour Resort** (Paynters Rd., Hamilton Parish, tel. 809/293–2040), the **Sonesta Beach Hotel & Spa** (Sinky Bay Rd., Southampton, tel. 809/238–8122), and the **Southampton Princess** (off South Rd., Southampton, tel. 809/238–8000) have their own fleets of rental boats. Otherwise, the best places for renting sailboats or powerboats are **Grotto Bay Water Sports** (Grotto Bay Hotel, 11 Blue Hole Hill, Hamilton Parish, tel. 809/293–8333, ext. 37), **Mangrove Marina** (Cambridge Rd., Sandys, tel. 809/234–0914), **Robinson's Marina** (Somerset Bridge, Sandys, tel. 809/234–0709), and **Salt Kettle Boat Rentals** (off Harbour Rd., Salt Kettle Rd., Paget, tel. 809/236–4863).

**Charter Boats** More than 20 large power cruisers and sailing vessels, piloted by local skippers, are available for charter. Typically between 35 and 50 feet long, charter sailboats can carry up to 18 passengers, with overnight accommodations available in some cases. Meals and drinks can be included on request, and a few skippers offer dinner cruises for the romantically inclined. Rates generally range between $200 and $250 for a half-day cruise, or $350–$475 for a full-day cruise, with additional per-person

## Beaches and Water Sports

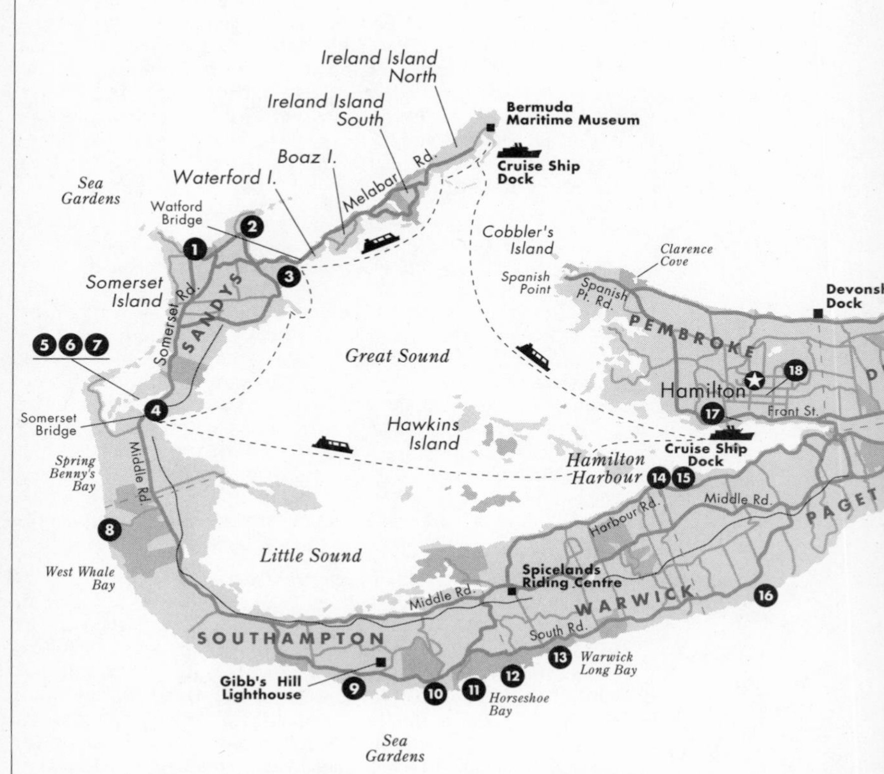


**Beaches**
Chaplin Bay, **12**
Elbow Beach Hotel, **16**
Horseshoe Bay Beach, **11**
John Smith's Bay, **21**
St. Catherine Beach, **27**
Shelley Bay Beach, **19**
Somerset Long Bay, **1**
Tobacco Bay Beach, **26**
Warwick Long Bay, **13**

**Water Sports**
A & J Watersports, **20**
Bermuda Waterski Centre, **5**
Bermuda Water Skiing, **22**
Bermuda Water Tours Ltd., **17**
Blue Water Divers Ltd., **7**
Fly Bridge Tackle, **18**
Greg Hartley's Under Sea Adventure, **3**
Mangrove Marina, **2**
Grotto Bay Diving, **23**
Grotto Bay Water Sports, **24**
Nautilus Diving Ltd., **10**
Pitman's Snorkelling, **4**
Pompano Marina, **8**
Robinson's Marina, **6**
Salt Kettle Boat Rentals, **15**
South Side Scuba, **9**
Tobacco Bay Beach House, **25**
Watlington's Windsurfing Bermuda, **14**

Tobacco Bay
Fort St. Catherine
25
26
27
St. Catherine Beach
ST. GEORGE'S
St. George's Island
Mullet Bay Rd.
St. George's
St. George's Harbour
Cruise Ship Dock
Ferry Rd.
St. David's Rd.
Kindley Field Rd.
Bermuda Airport
Coney Island
Sea Gardens
22
23
24
The Causeway
Bermuda Perfumery
Bermuda Pottery
Blue Hole
St. David's Island
St. David's Lighthouse
Crawl Hill North
Crystal Caves
Leamington Caves
HAMILTON
Church Bay
Harrington Sound Rd.
Castle Harbour
19
TUCKER'S TOWN
Aquarium, Museum, and Zoo
Harrington Sound
20
Sea Gardens
North Shore Rd.
Harrington Sound Rd.
SMITH'S
21
John Smith's Bay
N
VONSHIRE
South Rd.
KEY
Cruise Ship
Ferry
Railway Trail
0
2 miles
0
3 km

charges for large groups. Where you go and what you do—exploring, swimming, snorkeling, cruising—is up to you and your skipper. In most cases, cruises travel to and around the islands of Great Sound. Several charter skippers advertise year-round operations, but the off-season (December–February) schedule can be haphazard. Skippers devote periods of the off-season to maintenance and repairs or close altogether if bookings lag. Be sure to book well in advance. A full listing of charter-boat operators is included in the "Sportsman's Guide," available from the Bermuda Department of Tourism (*see* Chapter 1, Essential Information).

## Diving

Bermuda has all the ingredients necessary for classic scuba diving—reefs, wreckage, underwater caves, a variety of coral and marine life, and clear, warm water. Although diving is possible year-round, the best months are May–October, when the water is calmest and warmest. No prior certification is necessary; novices can learn the basics and be diving in water up to 25 feet deep on the same day. The easiest day trips, offered by **South Side Scuba** (Sonesta Beach Hotel, Sinky Bay Rd., Southampton, tel. 809/238–1833) and **Nautilus Diving Ltd.** (Southampton Princess Hotel, off South Rd., Southampton, tel. 809/238–2332), involve exploring the south-shore reefs that lie close inshore. These reefs may be the most dramatic in Bermuda: In places, the oceanside drop-off exceeds 60 feet, and the coral is so honeycombed with caves, ledges, and holes that exploratory possibilities are infinite. Also infinite are the chances of becoming lost in this coral labyrinth, so it is important to stick with your guide. Despite concerns in recent years about dying coral and fish depletion, most of Bermuda's reefs are still in good health—anyone eager to swim with multicolored schools of fish or the occasional barracuda will not be disappointed. In the interest of preservation, however, the removal of coral or coral objects is illegal.

Prominently displayed in any dive shop in Bermuda is a map of nautical carnage, showing the outlying reef system and wreck sites. The map shows 38 wrecks spanning three centuries, but these are only the larger wrecks that are still in good condition. There are reportedly more than 300 wreck sites in all, many of them well preserved. As a general rule, the more recent the wreck or the more deeply submerged it is, the better its condition. Most of the well-preserved wrecks are to the north and east, and dive depths range between 25 and 80 feet. Several wrecks off the western end of the island are in relatively shallow water—30 feet or less—making them accessible to novice divers and even snorkelers. The major dive operator for wrecks on the western side of the island is **Blue Water Divers Ltd.** (Robinson's Marina, Somerset Bridge, Sandys, tel. 809/234–1034); for wrecks off the east coast, contact **Grotto Bay Diving** (Grotto Bay Beach Hotel, 11 Blue Hole Hill, Hamilton Parish, tel. 809/293–2915). Costs range from $35 for a one-tank dive to $65 for introductory dives for novices or two-tank dives for experienced divers. With two tanks, divers can explore two or more wrecks during the same four-hour outing. Rates usually include all equipment—mask, fins, snorkel, scuba apparatus, and wet suit (if necessary). Some operators also offer night dives.

**Helmet Diving** A different, less technical type of diving that is popular in Bermuda is "helmet diving." Underwater explorers, wearing helmets that are fed air through hoses leading to the surface, walk along the sandy bottom in 15 feet of water or less. Although cruises last three hours or more, actual underwater time is about a half hour. A morning or afternoon tour costs $32. Contact **Greg Hartley's Under Sea Adventure** (Village Inn dock, Bridgeview La., Sandys, tel. 809/234–2861).

## Fishing

Fishing in Bermuda falls into three basic categories: shore or shallow-water fishing, reef fishing, and deep-sea fishing. No license is required, although some restrictions apply, particularly regarding the use of spear guns and the fish you can keep (for instance, only commercial fishers are permitted to take lobsters). In recent years, some concern has been expressed about the decline in the number of reef and shore fish in Bermudian waters. New government measures to restore fish populations have adversely impacted some commercial fishers, but sportfishing has been largely unaffected. Indeed, the deep-sea fishing for which Bermuda is famed remains as good as ever.

**Shore Fishing** The principal catches for shore fishers are pompano, bonefish, and snapper. Excellent sport for saltwater fly-fishing is the wily and strong bonefish, which is found in coves, harbors, and bays—almost anywhere it can find food and shelter from turbulent water. Among the more popular spots for bonefish are **West Whale Bay** and **Spring Benny's Bay,** which feature large expanses of clear, shallow water, protected by reefs close inshore. Good fishing holes are numerous along the south shore, too, although fishing is not permitted on major south-shore swimming beaches. Fishing in the calm waters of the **Great Sound** and **St. George's Harbour** can be rewarding, but enclosed **Harrington Sound** is less promising. Ask at local tackle shops about the latest hot spots and the best baits to use. Rod and reel rentals for shore fishing are available for about $10 a day from **Fly Bridge Tackle** (Church St., Hamilton, tel. 809/ 295–1845) and **Salt Kettle Boat Rentals** (off Harbour Rd., Salt Kettle Rd., Paget, tel. 809/236–4863). Rental arrangements can also be made through hotel activities directors.

**Reef Fishing** Three major reef bands lie at various distances from the island: The first is anywhere from a half mile to 5 miles offshore; the second, the Challenger Bank, is about 15 miles offshore; the third, the Argus Bank, is located about 30 miles offshore. As a rule, the farther out you go, the larger the fish—and the more expensive the charter. Most charter fishers work the reefs and deep water to the north and northwest of the island, because most of Bermuda's harbors face in those directions. Catches over the reefs include snapper, amberjack, grouper, and barracuda. Of the most sought-after deep-water fish—marlin, tuna, wahoo, and dolphin—wahoos are the most common and blue marlin the least. Trolling is the usual method of deep-water fishing, and charter-boat operators offer various tackle setups, with test-line weights ranging from 20 to 130 pounds. The boats, which range between 35 and 55 feet long, are fitted with a wide array of gear and electronics to track fish, including depth sounders, lorans, video fish finders, radar, and computer scanners. Half-day or full-day charters are offered by most operators, but full-day trips offer the best chance for a big catch, because the boat can reach waters that are less frequently fished. Rates vary widely, as do policies about keeping the catch. The Bermuda Game Fishing Association runs a year-long **Game Fishing Tournament,** open free to all fishers. Catches of any of 26 game varieties can be registered with the Bermuda Department of Tourism, and prizes are awarded at the end of the year. Charter bookings can be arranged through three organizations: the **Bermuda Charter Fishing Boat Association** (Box SB 145, Sandys SB BX, tel. 809/292–6246); the **Bermuda Sport Fishing Association** ("Creek View House," 8 Tulo La., Pembroke HM 02, tel. 809/295–2370); and the **St. George's Game Fishing & Cruising Association** (Box GE 107, St. George's GE BX, tel. 809/297–1622). In addition, several independent charter boats operate out of Hamilton Harbour and harbors in Sandys at the western end of the island. For more information about chartering a fishing boat in Bermuda, obtain a copy of the "Sportsman's Guide" from the Bermuda Department of Tourism (*see* Chapter 1, Essential Information).

## Snorkeling

The clarity of the water, the stunning array of coral reefs, and the shallow resting places of several wrecks make snorkeling in the waters around Bermuda—both close inshore and offshore—particularly rewarding. Snorkeling is possible year-round, although a wet suit is advisable for anyone planning to spend a long time in the water in winter, when the water temperature can dip into the 60s. During the winter, too, the water tends to be rougher, often restricting snorkeling to the protected areas of Harrington Sound and Castle Harbour. Underwater caves, grottoes, coral formations, and schools of small fish are the highlights of these areas. When Bermudians are asked to name a favorite snorkeling spot, however, **Church Bay** is invariably ranked at or near the top of the list. A small cove cut out of the coral cliffs, this protected bay is full of nooks and crannies in the coral, and the reefs are relatively close to shore. Snorkelers should exercise caution here, as they should everywhere along the south shore, because the water can be rough. Other popular snorkeling areas close inshore are the beaches of **John Smith's Bay** at the eastern end of the south shore, and **Tobacco Bay** at the eastern end of the north shore. Despite its small size, **West Whale Bay** is also worth a visit.

Having a boat at your disposal can improve your snorkeling experience immeasurably. Otherwise, long swims are necessary to reach some of the best snorkeling sites from shore, while other sites are inaccessible from anything but a boat. Small boats, some with glass bottoms, can be rented by the hour, half day, or day (*see* Boat Rentals, above). As the number of wrecks attests, navigating around Bermuda's reef-strewn waters is no simple task, especially for inexperienced boaters. If you rent a boat yourself, stick to the protected waters of the sounds, harbors, and bays. For trips to the reefs, let someone else do the navigating—a charter-boat skipper (*see* Charter Boats, above) or one of the snorkeling-cruise operators (*see* Snorkeling Cruises, below). Some of the best reefs for snorkeling, complete with shallow-water wrecks, are to the west. Where the tour guide or skipper goes, however, often depends on the tide, weather, and water conditions. For snorkelers who demand freedom of movement and privacy, a boat charter (complete with captain) is the only answer, but the cost is considerable—$400 a day or more. Divided among eight or more passengers, however, the expense may be worthwhile. By comparison, half-day snorkeling cruises (*see* Snorkeling Cruises, below) generally cost $35 or less, including equipment and instruction.

Snorkeling equipment is available for rental at most major hotels; the **Grotto Bay Hotel, Palmetto Hotel, Sonesta Beach Hotel,** and **Southampton Princess** have dive operators on site. Rates for mask, flippers, and snorkel are usually $6 per hour, or $18 per day from the dive operators; however, snorkels and masks can be rented for $2 an hour at the concession stand at **Horseshoe Bay Beach**. Equipment, including small boats and underwater cameras, can also be rented at several dive shops or marinas. The two best places for equipment rentals on the western end of the island are **Blue Water Divers Ltd.** (Robinson's Marina, Somerset Bridge, Sandys, tel. 809/234–1034) and **Mangrove Marina** (Cambridge Rd., Sandys, tel. 809/234–0914), both of which also rent small boats. In the central part of the island, boats and gear can be rented at **Salt Kettle Boat Rentals** (off Harbour Rd., Salt Kettle Rd., Paget, tel. 809/236–4863). At the eastern end of the island, contact **Tobacco Bay Beach House** (Tobacco Bay, Naval Tanks Hill, St. George's, tel. 809/293–9711).

**Snorkeling Cruises**

Snorkeling cruises, which are offered from May to November, may be too touristy for many visitors. Some boats carry 20 passengers or more, and feature music and bars (complimentary beverages are usually served on the return trip from the reefs). Smaller boats limit capacity to 10 passengers, but they offer few amenities and their travel range is shorter. To make sure you choose a boat that's right for you, ask for all the details before booking. Half-day snorkeling tours cost approximately $35. **Bermuda Water Tours Ltd.** (Albuoy's Point, Hamilton, tel. 809/295–3727) operates two boats out of Hamilton, and **Pitman's Snorkelling** (Somerset Bridge Hotel, Main Rd., Sandys, tel. 809/234–0700) offers half-day and shorter evening cruises, departing from the Somerset Bridge Hotel dock next to Robinson's Marina. Half-day cruises are also available from **Salt Kettle Boat Rentals Ltd.** (off Harbour Rd., Salt Kettle Rd., Paget, tel. 809/236–4863).

## Waterskiing

Winds on the island vary considerably, making it difficult to predict when the water will be calmest, although evening breezes are usually the lightest. Head for the **Great Sound** when the winds are coming from the south or southwest, the prevailing winds on Bermuda. In the event of northerly winds, however, **Castle Harbour** and **Harrington Sound** are protected bodies of water. If possible, make friends with a Bermudian with a boat—many visitors are invited boating by Bermudians they have only recently met. Otherwise, contact **Bermuda Water Skiing** (Grotto Bay Hotel, 11 Blue Hole Hill, Hamilton Parish, tel. 809/293–8333, ext. 37) or **Bermuda Waterski Centre** (Robinson's Marina, Somerset Bridge, Sandys, tel. 809/234–3354). Rates fluctuate with fuel costs, but average $70–$75 an hour, with lessons extra.

### Windsurfing

**Great Sound, Somerset Long Bay, Mangrove Bay,** and **Harrington Sound** are the favorite haunts of board sailors in Bermuda. For novices, the calm, enclosed waters of Harrington Sound are probably the best choice. The Great Sound, with its many islands, coves, and harbors, is good for board sailors of all abilities, although the quirky winds that sometimes bedevil yachts in the sound obviously affect sailboards as well. When the northerly storm winds blow, the open bays on the north shore are popular among wave-riding enthusiasts. Only experts should consider windsurfing on the south shore. Wind, waves, and reefs make the south shore so dangerous that rental companies are prohibited from renting boards there. Experienced board sailors might want to try their luck in the open races at **Salt Kettle** from April through mid-October every Thursday at 6 PM.

Even the most avid board sailors should rent sailboards rather than attempt to bring their own. Transporting a board around the island is a logistical nightmare: There are no rental cars on Bermuda, and few taxi drivers are willing to see their car roofs scoured with scratches in the interest of sport. Rental rates range between $15 and $17.50 an hour, or about $50 a day. Contact **Grotto Bay Water Sports** (Grotto Bay Hotel, 11 Blue Hole Hill, Hamilton Parish, tel. 809/293–8333), **Mangrove Marina** (Cambridge Rd., Sandys, tel. 809/234–0914), **Pompano Marina** (Pompano Beach Club, Southampton, tel. 809/234–0222), or **A & J Watersports** (Palmetto Hotel & Cottages, Flatts Village, Smith's, tel. 809/293–2323). **Watlington's Windsurfing Bermuda** (Glencoe Harbour Club, Salt Kettle La., Paget, tel. 809/236–5274 or 809/295–0808) rents high-performance boards at a premium. A & J Watersports and Watlington's also offer instruction: A two- or three-lesson program costs about $105, including on-land simulation and instruction on water.

## Beaches

The beaches of Bermuda fall into two categories: those on the south shore and those on the north shore. The water on the south-shore beaches tends to be a little rougher, because the prevailing winds come from the south and southwest. However, most people would agree that the typical south-shore beach is also more scenic—fine pinkish sand, coral bluffs topped with summer flowers, and gentle, pale-blue surf. Most Bermudian beaches are relatively small compared with ocean beaches in the United States. Although sizes vary considerably, an average Bermudian beach might be 300 yards long and 30 yards wide. In winter, when the weather is more severe, beaches may erode—even disappear—only to be replenished as the climate eases into spring.

Bermudian beaches offer little shade, either in the way of palm trees or thatched shelters, so bring hats, umbrellas, and plenty of sunscreen. Unfortunately, tar is a regular nuisance on many beaches. South-shore beaches seem more prone to the sticky black globs, although the amount of tar varies widely from beach to beach, depending on the tide, the season, and the level of marine traffic. Some hotels include a tar-removal solvent among the usual complimentary toiletries, but it's a good idea to bring along a bottle of rubbing alcohol. Below are reviews of the major beaches on the island that are open to the public. (For information about the many private beaches owned by hotels on the south shore, *see* Chapter 8, Lodging.)

## South-Shore Beaches

**Chaplin Bay.** In a secluded bay east of Horseshoe Bay (*see* below), this tiny beach disappears almost entirely at high tide or after a storm. Its most distinguishing feature is a high coral wall that reaches across the beach to the water, perforated by a 10-foot high, arrowhead-shaped hole. Like Horseshoe Bay, the beach fronts South Shore Park. *Off South Rd., Southampton. Bus no. 2 or 7 from Hamilton.*

**Elbow Beach Hotel.** The $3 fee for nonguests ensures that this beach remains relatively quiet, even on weekends. Shielded from big ocean swells by reefs, the beach has almost no surf, except in heavy winds. The Elbow Beach Surf Club sells refreshments, and has umbrellas and beach chairs to rent; toilet facilities are available. A free public beach lies adjacent. *Off South Rd., Paget. Bus no. 2 or 7 from Hamilton.*

**Horseshoe Bay Beach.** Horseshoe Bay has everything you would expect of a Bermudian beach: A ¼-mile crescent of pink sand, clear water, a vibrant social scene, and an uncluttered backdrop provided by South Shore Park. This is the most popular beach with visitors and locals alike, a place where adults arrive with coolers and teenagers come to check out the action. The presence of lifeguards—the only other beach with lifeguards is John Smith's Bay (*see* below)—and toilet facilities adds to the beach's appeal; in fact, it can become uncomfortably crowded here on summer weekends. Parents should keep a close eye on their children in the water: The undertow can be strong, especially when the wind is blowing. *Off South Rd., Southampton. Bus no. 2 or 7 from Hamilton.*

**John Smith's Bay.** Backed by houses and South Road, this beach consists of a pretty strand of long, flat, open sand. The presence of a lifeguard in summer makes this an ideal place to bring children. As the only public beach in Smith's Parish, John Smith's Bay is also popular among locals. *South Rd., Smith's. Bus no. 1 from Hamilton.*

**Warwick Long Bay.** Very different from covelike Chaplin and Horseshoe bays, this beach features the longest stretch of sand—about ½ mile—of any beach on the island. And instead of a steep backdrop, low grass- and brush-covered hills slope away from the beach, exposing the beach to the wind. Despite the wind, the waves are rarely big here because the inner reef is close inshore. An interesting feature of the bay is a 20-foot coral outcrop, less than 200 feet offshore, that looks like a sculpted boulder balancing on the surface of the water. The emptiness of South Shore Park, which surrounds the bay, heightens the beach's sense of isolation and serenity. *Off South Rd., Southampton. Bus no. 2 or 7 from Hamilton.*

## North-Shore Beaches

**St. Catherine Beach.** Nestled beneath Fort St. Catherine and St. George's Golf Club, this is the prettiest beach near St. George's. Unfortunately, this eastern-facing beach is considered the property of a nearby hotel, most recently managed by Club Med. At press time, however, the hotel was not in operation and swimmers could use the beach at their discretion. Whether the beach will be open to the public in future years remains unclear. *Off Barry Rd., St. George's. Bus no. 10 or 11 from Hamilton.*

**Shelley Bay Beach.** As at Somerset Long Bay (*see* below), the water at this beach near Flatts is well protected from prevailing southerly winds. In addition, a sandy bottom and shallow water make this a good place to take small children. Shelley Bay also boasts shade trees—something of a rarity at Bermudian beaches. A beach house has rest rooms, showers, and changing areas. One drawback is the traffic noise from busy North Shore Road, which runs nearby. *North Shore Rd., Hamilton Parish. Bus no. 10 or 11 from Hamilton.*

**Somerset Long Bay.** Popular with Somerset locals, this beach sits on the quiet northwestern end of the island—far from the airport, the bustle of Hamilton, and major tourism hubs. In keeping with the area's rural atmosphere, the beach is low-key and unprepossessing. Undeveloped parkland shields the beach from light traffic on Cambridge Road. The main beach is crescent-shaped and long by Bermudian standards—nearly ¼ mile from end to end. Instead of the great coral outcroppings common on the south shore, grass and brush make up the main backdrop here. Although exposed to northerly storm winds, the bay water is normally calm and shallow—ideal for children. However, the bottom is not sandy everywhere nor is it even. *Cambridge Rd., Sandys. Bus no. 7 or 8 from Hamilton.*

**Tobacco Bay Beach.** The most popular beach near St. George's's, this small north-shore beach is huddled in a coral cove similar to those found along the south shore. Like Shelley Bay (*see* above), Tobacco Bay has a beach house with toilets, showers, and changing rooms. *Naval Tanks Hill, St. George's. Bus no. 10 or 11 from Hamilton.*

# 6 Sports and Fitness

*by Peter Oliver*

When high jumper Nicky Barnes won a gold medal in the 1990 Commonwealth Games, Bermuda welcomed him home with a degree of adoration normally reserved for martyrs and deities. Bermudians champion their sports heroes, but—more significantly—they champion sports, both as participants and spectators. Every taxi driver seems to be a single-handicap golfer; tennis courts outnumber banks by more than three to one; and runners, cyclists, and horseback riders fill the roads and countryside in the mornings, especially on weekends. Bermuda might not have the world's fittest population but, at sunrise on Saturday, it certainly seems that way.

Washed by the Atlantic, Bermuda is probably best known as a beach destination, offering a host of water sports and activities (*see* Chapter 5, Beaches and Water Sports). However, the island is also a golfing center—eight courses are jammed onto this tiny island—and the popularity of tennis, squash, and riding are a further testament to Bermudians' love affair with land-based sports. As a Crown Colony, Bermuda tends to favor pursuits with a British flavor. In addition to several golf tournaments, cricket, soccer, rugby, field hockey, equestrian events, and even badminton, are popular spectator sports in season. Visitors can enter some of these events, primarily races and golf and tennis tournaments, although it is usually necessary to qualify.

Perhaps more than any other single factor, climate is what makes Bermuda such a sporting hive. In winter (December–February), temperatures hover between 50°F and 70°F, often climbing higher. While this might prove too chilly for many water sports, the cool air is ideal for activities on land. And although it is not immune to the occasional hurricane or storm, Bermuda does not have an extended storm season. Island residents like to boast, with some justification, that if you enjoy sport, you can enjoy it here 365 days of the year.

Most visitors can arrange sporting activities (tee times, for example) through their hotel's or ship's activities director, although arrangements can be made independently as well. For this purpose, the Bermuda Department of Tourism issues two excellent publications, the *Sportsman's Guide* and *Golfer's Guide*. Available through the Department of Tourism (*see* Government Tourist Offices in Chapter 1, Essential Information), the guides offer descriptions of sports facilities and golf courses on the island, addresses, phone numbers, and prices.

# Participant Sports

## Bicycling

In Bermuda, bicycles are called pedal or push bikes, to distinguish them from the more common motorized two-wheelers. Many of the cycle liveries around the island (*see* Chapter 1, Essential Information) also rent three-speed and 10-speed pedal bikes, but they can be difficult to find—it makes sense to reserve a bike a few days in advance. Rental rates start at $10 for the first day, and $5 per day thereafter.

Bermuda is not the easiest place in the world to bicycle. Riders should be prepared for some tough climbs—the roads running north–south across the island are particularly steep and winding—and the wind can sap even the strongest rider's strength, especially along South Road in Warwick and Southampton parishes. Bermudian roads are narrow, with heavy traffic (especially near Hamilton during rush hours) and no shoulder. Most motorists are courteous to cyclists—arbitrary horn-honking is against the law—and stay within 10 mph of the 20-mph speed limit. Despite the traffic, bicycle racing is a popular sport in Bermuda, and club groups can regularly be seen whirring around the island on evening and weekend training rides. Bermudian roads are no place for novice riders, however, and parents should think twice before allowing preteen children to hop on a bike.

Bermuda's premier cycling route, the Railway Trail (*see* Chapter 3, Exploring Bermuda), requires almost no road riding. Restricted to pedestrian and bicycle traffic, the paved trail runs intermittently for almost the length of the island along the route of the old Bermuda Railway. The Bermuda Department of Tourism publishes *The Bermuda Railway Trail Guide*, a free pamphlet that features a series of short exploring tours along the trail. The pamphlet is available at all Visitors Service Bureaus and Information Centres.

Tribe roads—small side roads that are often unpaved—are also good for exploring, although don't be surprised if many of these roads, which date back to the earliest settlement of Bermuda, are dead ends. Well-paved South Road has relatively few climbs and some excellent ocean views, although it is one of Bermuda's most heavily traveled thoroughfares. The "Bermuda Handy Reference Map," also available at Visitors Service Bureaus and Information Centres, is as essential to cyclists as two inflated tires and an oiled chain.

## Golf

Bermuda is justifiably renowned for its golf courses. The scenery is spectacular, and the courses are challenging. However, visitors should not expect the manicured, soft fairways and greens typical of U.S. courses. Just as courses in Scotland have their own identity, the same is true of courses on this Atlantic isle. Bermudian golf courses are distinguished by plenty of sand, firm fairways and greens, relatively short par fours, and wind—*especially* wind. Elsewhere, golf courses are usually designed with the wind in mind—long downwind holes and short upwind holes. Not so on Bermuda's eight courses, where the wind is anything but consistent or predictable. Quirky air currents make a Bermudian course play differently every day. On some days, a 350-yard par four may be driveable; on other days, a solidly hit drive may fall short on a 160-yard par three. Regardless, the wind puts a premium on being able to hit the ball straight; any slice or hook becomes disastrously exaggerated in the wind.

The island's water supply is limited, so irrigation is done sparingly and the ground around the green tends to be quite hard. For success in the short game, therefore, players need to run the ball to the hole, rather than relying on high, arcing chips, which require plenty of club face under the ball. Typically, Bermudian greens are elevated and protected by sand traps rather than thick grass. Most traps are filled with the pulverized coral that has made the island's beaches so famous. Such fine sand

## Sports and Fitness

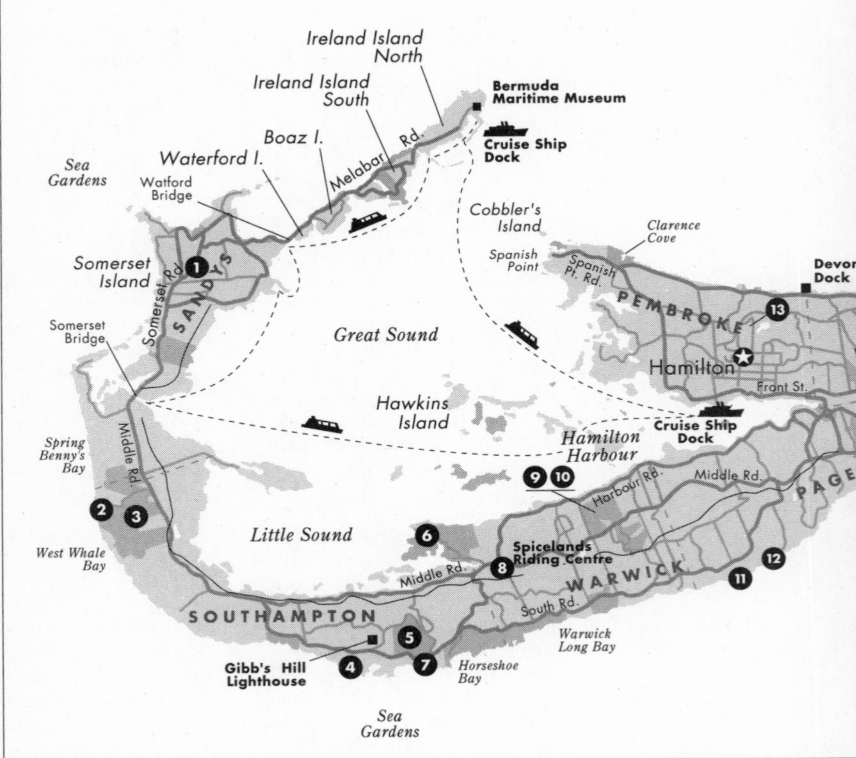


**Golf Courses**
Belmont Golf & Country Club, **9**
Castle Harbour Golf Club, **18**
Mid Ocean Club, **19**
Ocean View Golf & Country Club, **14**
Port Royal Golf & Country Club, **3**
Princess Golf Club, **5**
Riddell's Bay Golf & Country Club, **6**
St. George's Golf Club, **21**

**Tennis and Squash Courts**
Belmont Hotel, Golf & Country Club, **10**
Bermuda Squash Club, **16**
Coral Beach & Tennis Club, **11**
Elbow Beach Hotel, **12**
Government Tennis Stadium, **13**
Marriott's Castle Harbour Resort, **17**
Pompano Tennis Club, **2**
Sonesta Beach Hotel & Spa, **4**
Southampton Princess Hotel, **7**

**Horseback Riding**
Spicelands Riding Centre, **8**

**Spectator Sports**
National Sports Club, **15**
St. George's Cricket Club, **20**
Somerset Cricket Club, **1**

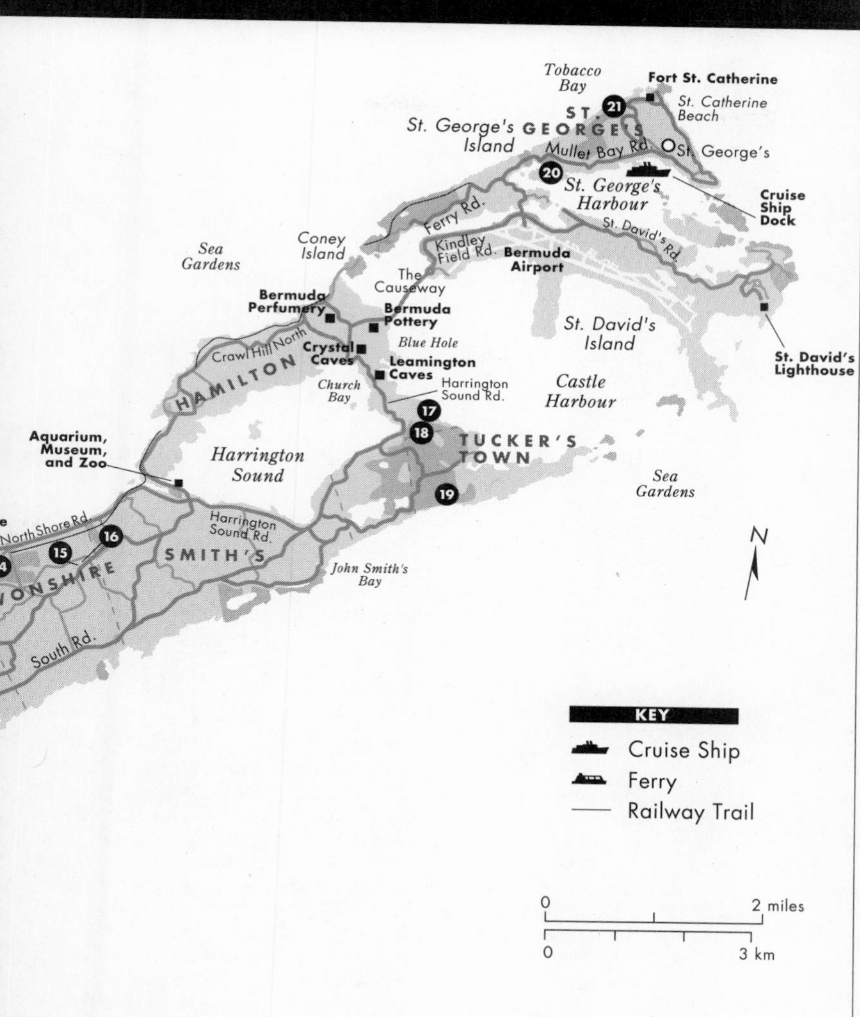

Tobacco Bay
Fort St. Catherine
St. Catherine Beach
ST. GEORGE'S
St. George's Island
Mullet Bay Rd.
St. George's
St. George's Harbour
Cruise Ship Dock
Ferry Rd.
St. David's Rd.
Coney Island
Sea Gardens
Kindley Field Rd.
Bermuda Airport
The Causeway
Bermuda Perfumery
Bermuda Pottery
Blue Hole
St. David's Island
St. David's Lighthouse
Crawl Hill North
Crystal Caves
Leamington Caves
HAMILTON
Church Bay
Harrington Sound Rd.
Castle Harbour
TUCKER'S TOWN
Aquarium, Museum, and Zoo
Harrington Sound
Sea Gardens
North Shore Rd.
Harrington Sound Rd.
SMITH'S
John Smith's Bay
VONSHIRE
South Rd.
N
KEY
Cruise Ship
Ferry
Railway Trail
0
2 miles
0
3 km

may be unfamiliar to visiting golfers, but it tends to be consistent from trap to trap and from course to course.

Greens are usually seeded with Bermuda grass and then overseeded with rye. Golfers putt on Bermuda grass during the warmer months (March–November) and on rye when the weather cools and the Bermuda grass dies out. For a couple of weeks between October and January, depending on the weather, temporary greens or limited putting areas may be used during reseeding. Greens in Bermuda tend to be much slower than the bent-grass greens prevalent in the United States, and putts tend to break less.

Another characteristic of Bermudian courses is the preponderance of rolling, hummocky fairways, making a flat lie the exception rather than the rule. Little effort has been made to flatten the fairways, because much of the ground beneath the island's surface is honeycombed with caves; bulldozer and backhoe operators are understandably uneasy about doing extensive landscaping.

How should golfers prepare for a Bermuda trip? In anticipation of the wind, practice hitting lower shots—punching the ball or playing it farther back in the stance may be helpful. Working on chip-and-run shots (a seven iron is ideal for this), especially from close-cropped lies, should also help. You can save yourself some strokes, too, by practicing iron shots from awkward, hillside lies. On the greens, a long, firm putting stroke may save you from the bugaboo that haunts many first-time visitors: gently stroked putts dying short of the hole or drifting off-line with the grain of the Bermuda grass. As Allan Wilkinson, the professional at the Princess Golf Club, says: "In Bermuda, ya gotta slam 'em into the back of the cup."

Tournaments for pros, seniors, juniors, women, and mixed groups fill Bermuda's golfing schedule from February through December. Some competitions, such as the Bermuda Open in early October, are high-level competitions with prize money for professional participants. Handicap limits are usually imposed for the more serious tournaments, and entry fees range between $90 and $120 (not all events are open to non-Bermudian players). A schedule, with entry forms, is available from the **Bermuda Golf Association** (Box HM 433, Hamilton HM BX, tel. 809/238–1367). A low-key event for golfers of all abilities is the **Bermuda Golf Festival**, a two-week affair in late February that gives players a chance to compete on several of the island's courses. Greens fees are reduced for festival participants, and several hotels offer reduced package rates. For more information, contact the Bermuda Golf Festival (GD/T Sports Marketing, 5520 Park Ave., Trumbull, CT 06611, tel. 800/282–7656). Another easygoing tournament in mid-February is the **Valentine's Mixed Foursomes**, for which tournament/hotel packages are also available. For information or entry forms, contact the tournament chairman, Kim Swan (St. George's Golf Club, 1 Park Rd., St. George's GE 03, tel. 809/297–8067).

Be sure to pack proper golf attire—long pants (no jeans) or Bermuda shorts (no cutoffs) are required for men. Lessons, available at all courses, usually cost $20 for a half hour, and club rentals range between $10 and $18. Caddies are a thing of the past, except at the Mid Ocean Club. Below are reviews and ratings of all eight of Bermuda's golf courses. The ratings, devised and administered by the United States Golf Association (USGA), "represent the expected score of an expert amateur golfer based upon yardage and other obstacles." For example, a par-72 course with a rating of 68 means that a scratch golfer would hit a four-under-par round—and ordinary hackers would probably score a little better, too. Ratings below are given for the blue tees (championship), white tees (men's), and red tees (women's).

**Belmont Golf & Country Club**

**Length:** 5,777 yards from the blue tees
**Par:** 70
**Rating:** blue tees, 68.9; white tees, 67.9; red tees, 69.1

Of Bermuda's eight courses, the layout of the public Belmont Golf & Country Club is perhaps the most maddening. The first two holes, straight par fours, are a false preview of what lies ahead—a series of doglegs and blind tee shots. Playing with an experienced Belmont player, who knows where to hit drives on such blind holes as the sixth, 11th, and 16th, and how best to play a dogleg hole such as the eighth, can help a newcomer trim six or more shots from a round. Despite the layout, Belmont remains one of Bermuda's easier courses, and it is ideal for inexperienced players. Belmont is an inland course and has few ocean panoramas. Instead, most holes overlook pastel houses with white roofs, a few of which have taken a beating from errant golf balls. A new irrigation system has improved the course dramatically in recent years. Fairway grass tends to be denser—and the clay soil moister—than the grass on the close-cropped, sandy fairways typical of other Bermudian courses. The rough, too, is generally deeper, snaring any wild tee shots. For this reason, and because Belmont is a short course (only one par four is more than 400 yards), it makes sense to use a three or five wood, or even a low iron, from the tee. Belmont's chief drawback, especially on the weekend, is slow play—weekend rounds of five hours or more are common.

**Highlight hole:** The par-five 11th features a severe dogleg left, with a blind tee shot—Belmont in a nutshell. A short but straight drive is the key; trying and failing to cut the corner can be disastrous. The approach to the green is straight, although a row of wispy trees on the left awaits hooked or pulled shots. *Belmont Rd., Warwick, tel. 809/296–1301. Greens fees: $30 for the public; $10 for hotel guests. Cart rentals, $25; hand carts, $4.*

**Castle Harbour Golf Club**

**Length:** 6,440 yards from the blue tees
**Par:** 71
**Rating:** blue tees, 71.3; white tees, 69.2; red tees, 69.2

The only course on Bermuda that requires players to use golf carts is the Castle Harbour Golf Club—with good reason. The only flat areas on the course, it seems, are the tees. The first tee, a crow's-nest perch by the clubhouse, offers an indication of things to come: Looking out over the fairway, with the harbor beyond, is like peering onto a golf course from a 20th-story window. Wind can make this course play especially long. Although most par fours feature good landing areas despite all the hills, holes such as the second, 16th, and 17th require players to drive over fairway rises. A wind-shortened drive can mean a long, blind shot to the green. Carrying the rise, on the other hand, can mean a relatively easy short shot, especially on the second and 17th holes. Elevated greens are a common feature of Castle Harbour. The most extreme example is the 190-yard, par-three 13th, with the green perched atop a steep, 100-foot embankment. Balls short of the green inevitably roll back down into a grassy basin between the tee and the green. On the other hand, sand traps at Castle Harbour are mercifully few and far between by Bermudian standards; 10 holes feature two or fewer bunkers around the green.

With a $60 greens fee, plus $30 for the required cart, Castle Harbour is Bermuda's most expensive course. However, the money is clearly reinvested in the course. Greens are well maintained—firm, consistently cropped, and generally faster than most Bermudian greens. The course also rewards golfers with several spectacular views, such as the hilltop panorama from the 14th tee, where blue water stretches into the distance on three sides.

**Highlight hole:** The 235-yard, par-three 18th is the most difficult finishing hole on Bermuda, especially when the wind is blowing from the northwest. On the right are jagged coral cliffs rising from the harbor; on the left are a pair of traps. When the course was revamped a few years ago, a small, flower-lined pond was added on the front right of the green, making this hard hole even harder. *Marriott's Castle Harbour Hotel, Paynters Rd., Hamilton Parish, tel. 809/293–8161 or 809/293–0795. Greens fees: $60 ($35 after 4:30 PM), plus mandatory $30 cart rental. Shoe rentals.*

**Mid Ocean Club**

**Length:** 6,547 yards from the blue tees
**Par:** 71
**Rating:** blue tees, 72; white tees, 70; red tees, 72

It isn't Bermuda's oldest course—that honor belongs to Riddell's Bay—and other Bermudian courses are equally difficult, but the elite Mid Ocean Club is generally regarded as one of the top 50 courses in the world. Quite simply, this course has charisma, embodying everything that is golf in Bermuda—tees on coral cliffs above the ocean, rolling fairways lined with palms and spice trees, doglegs around water, and windswept views. It is rich in history, too. At the dogleg fifth hole, for example, Babe Ruth is said to have splashed a dozen balls in Mangrove Lake in a futile effort to drive the green. The course rewards long, straight tee shots and deft play around the green, while penalizing—often cruelly—anything less. The fifth and ninth holes, for example, require that tee shots (from the blue tees) carry 180 yards or more over water. And while length is not a factor on two fairly short par fives, the 465-yard second and the 487-yard 11th, accuracy is: Tight doglegs ensure that any wayward tee shot ends up in trees, shrubbery, or rough. The course may have mellowed with age, however. The course lost hundreds of trees to a tornado in 1986 and was battered again by Hurricane Emily in 1987. The tight, tree-lined fairways have become more open as a result, and the rough less threatening.

**Highlight hole:** The 433-yard fifth is a par-four dogleg around Mangrove Lake. The elevated tee overlooks a hillside of flowering shrubbery and the lake, making the fairway seem impossibly far away. Big hitters can take a short cut over the lake (although the green is unreachable, despite the Babe's heroic efforts), but anyone who hits the fairway has scored a major victory. To the left of the green, a steep embankment leads into a bunker that is among the hardest in Bermuda from which to recover. *Mid Ocean Dr., off South Rd., Tucker's Town, tel. 809/293–0330. Greens fees: $60 ($30 when accompanied by a member). Nonmembers must be introduced by a hotel activities director or a club member; nonmember starting times available only on Mon., Wed., and Fri. Cart rental, $30; caddies, $20 per bag (tip not included).*

**Ocean View Golf & Country Club**

**Length:** 3,000 yards (nine holes) from the blue tees
**Par:** 35; ladies, 37
**Rating:** none

Work on the Ocean View Golf & Country Club is still in progress. Founded nearly 40 years ago as a club for blacks, the nine-hole course fell into neglect as other courses in Bermuda began admitting black players. In 1988, the Bermudian government took over management of Ocean View and committed roughly $3 million to its refurbishment. In addition to restoring the course to good playing condition and altering a few holes, the government's plans include a new clubhouse, possibly to be finished by the end of 1991. Also under consideration is the addition of a second nine holes. Although the old clubhouse is indeed a dank place, the course is better—and in far better shape—than its reputation would suggest. Several holes challenge and intrigue: The second is a tough par four that runs up and along the side of a hill; the sixth is a wind-buffeted par five, with a 40-foot coral wall on one side, and a slope leading down to the Great Sound on the other. Some holes have as many as six tees, offering players the opportunity for considerable variation. Locals crowd the course on weekends, although Ocean View is relatively empty on weekdays. That could change, however, if the course continues to improve as expected.

**Highlight hole:** The green on the 177-yard, par-three fifth hole has been cut out of a coral hillside draped with flowering vines, giving players the sensation of hitting into a grotto. Club selection can be tricky—winds off the Great Sound might seem insubstantial on the tee, but they can be much stronger over the coral wall near the green. *Off North Shore Rd., Devonshire, tel. 809/236–6758. Greens fees: $10 per 9 holes. Cart rental, $10 per 9 holes; hand carts, $4.*

**Port Royal Golf & Country Club**

**Length:** 6,425 yards from the blue tees
**Par:** 71; ladies, 72
**Rating:** blue tees, 72; white tees, 69.7; red tees, 72.5

Such golfing luminaries as Jack Nicklaus rank the Port Royal Golf & Country Club among the world's best public courses. A favorite among Bermudians as well, the course is well laid out, and the greens fees are modest. By Bermudian standards, Port Royal is also relatively flat. Although there are some hills, on the back nine in particular, the course has few of the blind shots and hillside lies that are prevalent elsewhere. Those holes that do have gradients tend to run either directly uphill or downhill. In other respects, however, Port Royal is classically Bermudian, with close-cropped fairways, numerous elevated tees and greens, and holes raked by the wind, especially the eighth and the 16th. The 16th hole, one of Bermuda's most famous, is frequently pictured in magazines. The green sits on a treeless promontory overlooking the blue waters and pink-white sands of Whale Bay, a popular boating and fishing area. When the wind is blowing hard onshore, as it frequently does, a driver may be necessary to reach the green, which is 163 yards away. One complaint often raised about Port Royal is the condition of the course, which can become chewed up by heavy usage—more than 55,000 rounds a year.

**Highlight hole:** Like the much-photographed 16th hole, the 371-yard, par-four 15th skirts the cliffs along Whale Bay. In addition to the ocean view, the remains of Whale Bay Battery, a 19th-century fortification, lie between the fairway and the bay. Only golf balls hooked wildly from the tee have any chance of a direct hit on the fort. The wind can be brutal on this hole. *Off Middle Rd., Southampton, tel. 809/234–0974. Greens fees: $22; discount rates after 4 PM. Except for groups, tee times can be arranged no more than 2 days in advance. Cart rental, $20; hand cart, $4. Shoe rentals.*

**Princess Golf Club**

**Length:** 2,684 yards from the blue tees
**Par:** 54
**Rating:** none

The Princess Golf Club unfolds on the hillside beneath the Southampton Princess. The hotel has managed to sculpt a neat little par-three course from the steep terrain, and players who opt to walk around will find their mountaineering skills and stamina severely tested. The vertical drop on the first two holes alone is at least 200 feet, and the rise on the fourth hole makes 178 yards play like 220. Kept in excellent shape by an extensive irrigation system, the course is a good warm-up for Bermuda's full-length courses, offering a legitimate test of wind and bunker play with a minimum of obstructions and hazards. Ocean views are a constant feature of the front nine, although the looming presence of the hotel does detract from the scenery.

**Highlight hole:** The green of the 174-yard 16th hole sits in a cup ringed by pink-blooming oleander bushes. Less than a mile away, the Gibb's Hill Lighthouse dominates the backdrop. *Southampton Princess, South Rd., tel. 809/238–0446. Greens fees: $20 ($16 for hotel guests). Cart rental: $16 ($14 for hotel guests). Shoe rentals.*

**Riddell's Bay Golf & Country Club**

**Length:** 5,588 yards from the blue tees
**Par:** 69; ladies, 71
**Rating:** blue tees, 67.7; white tees, 66.4; red tees, 70.6

Built in 1922, the Riddell's Bay Golf & Country Club is Bermuda's oldest course. In design, however, it more nearly approximates a Florida course—relatively flat, with wide, palm-lined fairways. You don't need to be a power hitter to score well here, although the first four holes, including a 427-yard uphill par four and a 244-yard par three, might suggest otherwise. The par fours are mostly in the 360-yard range, and the fairways are generously flat and open. Despite the course's position on a narrow peninsula between Riddell's Bay and the Great Sound, water only comes into play on holes eight through 11. With the twin threats of wind and water, these are the most typically Bermudian holes on the course, and accuracy off the tee is important. This is especially true of the par-four eighth, a 360-yard right dogleg around the water. With a tail wind, big hitters might try for the green, but playing around the dogleg on this relatively short hole is the more prudent choice. As at the Belmont course, a few tees are fronted with stone walls—an old-fashioned touch that harks back to the old courses of Great Britain. Like Mid Ocean, Riddell's is a private club that is open to the public only at certain times, but the clubbish atmosphere is much less pronounced here.

**Highlight hole:** The tees on the 340-yard, par-four 10th are set on a grass-topped quay on the harbor's edge. The fairway narrows severely after about 200 yards, and a drive hit down the right-hand side leaves a player no chance to reach the green in two. Two ponds guard the left side of a sloped and elevated green. The hole is rated only the sixth most difficult on the course, but the need for pinpoint accuracy probably makes it the hardest to par. *Riddell's Bay Rd., Warwick, tel. 809/238–1060. Greens fees: $25 ($12.50 when accompanied by a member). Cart rental, $22; hand carts, $3.*

**St. George's Golf Club**

**Length:** 4,502 yards from the blue tees
**Par:** 63 (formerly 64)
**Rating** (based on par 64): blue tees, 62.8; white tees, 61.4; red tees, 62.8

Built in 1985, St. George's Golf Club dominates a secluded headland at the northeastern end of the island. The 4,502-yard course is short, but it makes up for its lack of length with sharp teeth. No course in Bermuda is more exposed to wind, and no course has smaller greens—some are no more than 25 feet across. To make matters trickier, the greens are hard and slick from the wind and salty air. Many of the holes have commanding views of the ocean, particularly the eighth, ninth, 14th, and 15th, which run along the water's edge. Wind—especially from the north—can turn these short holes into club-selection nightmares. Don't let high scores here ruin your enjoyment of some of the finest views on the island. The scenery, the course's shortness, and the fact that it gets little play midweek, make St. George's Golf Club a good choice for couples or groups of varying ability.

**Highlight hole:** Pause to admire the view from the par-four 14th hole before you tee off. From the elevated tee area, the 326-yard hole curls around Coot Pond, an ocean-fed cove, to the green on a small, treeless peninsula. Beyond the neighboring 15th hole is old Fort St. Catherine's, and beyond that lies the sea. With a tail wind, it's tempting to hit for the green from the tee, but Coot Pond leaves no room for error. *1 Park Rd., St. George's, tel. 809/297–8067 or 809/297–8148. Greens fees: $15; $8 after 4 PM. Cart rental, $17; hand carts, $4.*

## Horseback Riding

Because most of the land on Bermuda is residential, opportunities for riding through the countryside are few. The chief exception is **South Shore Park,** between South Road and the Warwick beaches. Sandy trails, most of which are open only to riders or people on foot, wind through stands of dune grass and oleander, along beaches and over coral bluffs. Nearby is the **Spicelands Riding Centre** (Middle Rd., Warwick, tel. 809/238–8212 or 809/238–8246), the main riding facility on the island. The center's most popular trail ride is the two-hour south-shore breakfast ride, departing at 7 AM; breakfast is included in the $35 fee. Evening rides are also offered, although it's wise to confirm all rides from October through April, when low demand can force the cancellation of certain trail rides. Spicelands also offers instruction in its riding ring.

## Jogging and Running

Many of the difficulties that cyclists face—hills, traffic, and wind—also confront runners in Bermuda. The presence of pedestrian sidewalks and footpaths along roadsides, however, does make the going somewhat easier. Runners who like firm pavement will be happiest on the Railway Trail (*see* Bicycling, above) or on South Road, a popular route. For those who like running on sand, the trails through **South Shore Park** are relatively firm, while the island's beaches obviously present a much softer surface. **Horseshoe Beach** is frequented by a large number of runners, although their interest in the beach may be more social than physical, because Horseshoe Beach is where the action is. A better beach for running is ½-mile **Warwick Long Bay**, the longest uninterrupted stretch of sand on the island. By using South Shore Park trails to skirt coral bluffs, runners can create a route that connects several beaches, although trails in some places can be winding and uneven.

The big race on the island is the **Bermuda International Marathon & 10K Race,** held in mid-January. The race attracts world-class distance runners from several countries, but it is open to everyone. For information, contact the Bermuda Track & Field Association (Box DV 397, Devonshire DV BX). The association can also provide information on other races held throughout the year. Another event for fitness fanatics is the **Bermuda Triathlon** in late September. Held in Southampton, the event combines a 1-mile swim, a 15-mile cycling leg, and a 6-mile run. For information, contact the Bermuda Triathlon Association (c/o Tony Ryan, Box HM 530, Hamilton HM CX). Less competitive—and certainly less strenuous—are the 2-mile **"fun runs,"** held every Tuesday evening from April through October. Runs begin at 6 PM on Berry Hill Road near the Botanical Gardens. No entry fee is charged.

## Squash

The **Bermuda Squash Club** (Middle Rd., Devonshire, tel. 809/292–6881) makes its four courts available to nonmembers between 10 AM and 4 PM. A $7 fee per person includes racquet, ball, and towel. Soft-ball players will enjoy the two English courts (larger than U.S. courts) at the **Coral Beach & Tennis Club** (South Rd., Paget, tel. 809/236–2233). In mid-November, the Bermuda Squash Racquets Association (tel. 809/292–6881) sponsors the **Bermuda Open Squash Tournament**, in which top international players compete.

## Tennis

Bermuda has a tennis court for every 600 residents, a ratio that even the most tennis-crazed countries would find difficult to match. Many of the tennis courts are private, but the public has access to more than 80 courts in 20 locations island-wide. Courts are inexpensive and seldom full. Hourly rates rarely exceed $10, although hotels generally charge nonguests a higher rate—guests usually play for free. Bring along a few fresh cans of balls, because balls in Bermuda cost $6–$7 per can—about three times the rate in the United States. Among the surfaces used in Bermuda are Har-Tru, clay, cork, and hard composites, of which the relatively slow plexipave composite is the most prevalent. Considering Bermuda's British roots, it's surprising that there are no grass courts on the island.

Wind, heat (in summer), and humidity are the most distinguishing characteristics of Bermudian tennis. From October through March, when daytime temperatures rarely exceed 80°F, play is comfortable throughout the day. In summertime, however, the heat radiating from the court (especially hard-surface ones) can make play uncomfortable between 11 AM and 3 PM. At such times, the breezes normally considered a curse in tennis can become a cooling blessing. Early morning or evening tennis presents players with an entirely different problem, when tennis balls grow heavy with moisture from Bermuda's humid sea air, always at its wettest early and late in the day. On clay courts, the moist balls become matted with clay, making them even heavier. In strong winds, inland courts, such as the clay and all-weather courts at the **Government Tennis Stadium** (Cedar Ave. and St. John's Rd., Pembroke, tel. 809/292–0105) or the clay courts at the **Coral Beach & Tennis Club** (off South Rd., Paget, tel. 809/236–2233 or 809/236–6495) are preferable. Despite their position at the water's edge, the plexipave courts of the **Southampton Princess Hotel** (South Rd., Southampton, tel. 809/238–1005) are reasonably well shielded from the wind (especially from the north), although the breeze can be swirling and difficult. High on a bluff above the ocean, the courts at the **Sonesta Beach Hotel & Spa** (off South Rd., tel. 809/238–1005) offer players one of the more spectacular settings on the island, but the courts are exposed to summer winds from the south and southwest. Other hotels with good tennis facilities open to the public are the **Elbow Beach Hotel** (South Shore, Paget, tel. 809/236–3535), with five courts, and **Marriott's Castle Harbour Resort** (Paynters Rd., Hamilton Parish, tel. 809/293–2040), with six cork courts. All of the above facilities have some floodlit courts for night play, as do the **Pompano Tennis Club** (Port Royal Golf Club, off Middle Rd., Southampton, tel. 809/234–0222) and the **Belmont Hotel, Golf & Country Club** (Belmont Rd., Warwick, tel. 809/236–1301). An additional fee of \$2–\$5 is usually charged to play under lights. Most tennis facilities offer lessons, ranging from \$12 to \$25 for 30 minutes of instruction, and racquet rentals for \$3–\$5 per day (a few hotels lend racquets to hotel guests for free.)

# Spectator Sports

Bermuda is a great place for sports enthusiasts seeking relief from an overdose of baseball, football, and basketball—sports that mean little to Bermudians. In addition to golf and tennis, the big spectator sports here are cricket, rugby, soccer, field hockey, and yacht racing. The Bermuda Department of Tourism (*see* Government Tourist Offices in Chapter 1, Essential Information) can provide exact dates and information about all major sporting events.

**Cricket** Cricket is the big team sport in summer, and the **Cup Match Cricket Festival** is *the* event on Bermuda's summer sports calendar. Held in late July or early August at the Somerset Cricket Club (Broome St., off Somerset Rd., 809/234–0327) or the St. George's Cricket Club (Wellington Slip Rd., tel. 809/297–0374), the competition features teams from around the island.

Although cricket is taken very seriously, the event itself is a real festival, attended by thousands of colorful picnickers and party goers. Admission is free. The regular cricket season runs from April through September.

**Field Hockey** Hockey games between local teams can be seen at the National Sports Club (Middle Rd., Devonshire, tel. 809/236–6994) on Sunday from October through April. In early September, the National Sports Club is the site of the **Hockey Festival,** a tournament with teams from Bermuda, the United States, Great Britain, Holland, and Germany. Admission is free.

**Golf** Golf tournaments are held throughout the year at various courses on the island. The highlight of the golf year is the **Bermuda Open** in early October, which attracts a host of professionals and amateurs. A schedule of events is available from the Bermuda Golf Association (*see* Golf in Participant Sports, above).

**Rugby** The mid-April **Rugby Classic** is the final event in Bermuda's rugby season, which runs from September to April. Held at the National Sports Club (Middle Rd., Devonshire, tel. 809/236–6994), the competition attracts teams from Great Britain, France, New Zealand, and Australia, as well as Bermuda. Admission is $5. During the rest of the season, matches between local teams can be seen on weekends at the National Sports Club.

**Soccer** In early April, teams from countries around the Atlantic, including the United States, Canada, Great Britain, and several Caribbean nations, compete for the **Diadora Youth Soccer Cup**. Teams play in three age divisions, and games are held on fields around the island.

**Yachting** Bermuda has a worldwide reputation as a yacht-racing center. Spectators, particularly those on land, may find it difficult to follow the intricacies of a race or regatta, but the sight of the racing fleet, with brightly colored spinnakers flying, is always striking. The racing season runs from March to November. Most races are held on weekends in the Great Sound, and several classes of boats usually compete. Good vantage points for viewing races are around Spanish Point, Hamilton Harbour, and the islands northeast of Somerset. Anyone wanting to get a real sense of the action, however, should be aboard a boat near the race course.

In late June, Bermuda acts as the finish for ocean-going yachts in two major races beginning in the United States—the **Newport–Bermuda Race** and the **Annapolis–Bermuda Race**. Of the two, the Newport–Bermuda Race is considered the more prestigious, but both provide the spectacular sight of the island's harbors filled with yachts, which range in length from 30 to 100 feet. For those more interested in racing than expensive yachts, the **King Edward VII Gold Cup International Match Racing Tournament** is the event to see. Held in late October or early November in the Great Sound, the tournament features many of the world's best skippers in one-on-one races, similar to the competition style used in the America's Cup.

# 7 Dining

## Introduction

*by John DeMers*

*The former food editor for United Press International, John DeMers is the author of three cookbooks, the most recent of which is* Caribbean Cooking.

With 150 restaurants from which to choose, visitors to this tiny island will have little difficulty satisfying their cravings for everything from traditional English fare to French, Italian, Greek, Indian, and Chinese. A quest for Bermudian food, however, is likely to be as extended and elusive as the search for the Holy Grail. And if you persist, you'll discover the single greatest truth about Bermudian cuisine: There's no such thing, but everybody on the island loves it. Waiters, in particular, prove inspirational. While heaping your plate, they will wax lyrical about their mother's turtle stew, their late uncle's fish chowder, or their great aunt's codfish and potatoes. And no islander seems to remember ever tasting anything better than a mysterious concoction called hash shark or—more intelligibly—shark hash.

In moments of candor, islanders will confide that Bermudian cuisine is really a collection of dishes showing English, American, and West Indian influences. But whatever the origins of the recipes, the island's cuisine begins and ends with Bermudian ingredients—and therein lies the island's claim to a culinary identity. Seafood is extraordinary here, especially the local lobster that is best eaten during the winter. This is the spiny lobster familiar in the Caribbean, usually prepared with a minimum of seasoned stuffing, broiled, and served drizzled with butter. Menus also feature Bermuda rockfish, the flesh of which is firm and white; red snapper, often served with onions and potatoes; shark; and mussels steamed in white wine or made into a pie or fritters. Another local variety of seafood is the guinea chick. Although it sounds more like poultry, the guinea chick is a Bermudian cross, in taste and texture, between a crayfish and a prawn. This delicate shellfish is worth ordering whenever you find it; unfortunately, you won't find it often. (At press time, a ban has been placed on the harvesting of both lobsters and guinea chicks because of overfishing. It is unknown when these shellfish will be available again.) You should also try the fish chowder, laced at the table with local black rum and sherry peppers (sherry in which hot peppers have been marinated). The result is unforgettable. Conch fritters, too, are a good bet when you can find them. Unless you venture to St. David's Island on the island's East End, you may never get to taste shark hash. The best approach is to hang around the Black Horse Tavern or Dennis's Hideaway until somebody announces that the hash is ready. The passion that East Enders hold for this dish means the pot won't be full for long.

Without doubt, the most famous vegetable is the Bermuda onion, hailed by onion lovers as a more heavenly version of the sweet Vidalia onion from Georgia. It is most commonly found in onion pie and cheese and onion sandwiches, and glazed in sugar and rum. Bermuda's soil works miracles with most common vegetables. Don't be put off if your meal is accompanied by potatoes, broccoli, or even carrots. Rarely will these vegetables taste better or fresher in their natural flavors.

In addition to onion pie and mussel pie, cassava pie is a tradition dating back three centuries. Made from dough flavored with ground cassava root, this meat pie is a Christmas standard, nearly always paired with a traditional English plum pudding. Other island dishes turn up just when you despair of ever finding any. At breakfast, ask for codfish and bananas, made with the salt cod commonly known as Portuguese bacalao. Revived by soaking in water, the cod is cooked with a savory tomato sauce and usually served with boiled potatoes and sautéed bananas. Hoppin' John, a Bermudian dish that's also popular in the Carolinas, is rice cooked with chicken, beans or peas, bacon, onion, and thyme. Another traditional favorite is syllabub, a sweet treat of guava, wine, and cream served either as a liquid or a jelly.

For the most part, however, dining on the island is fairly non-Bermudian, and it's expensive: Dinner at the island's best restaurants can cost as much as $100 per person, excluding a 15% service charge. During the summer season, reservations are essential at these restaurants. Of course, if you are staying in one of the major resorts, you can usually choose from several restaurants without ever leaving the property, and most hotels and cottage colonies offer a variety of meal plans ranging from full board to Continental breakfasts (*see* Chapter 8, Lodging).

Dining in Bermuda tends to be rather formal. In the more upscale restaurants, men should wear jackets and ties, and women should be comparably attired. Credit cards are widely accepted in the major hotels and restaurants, while the small taverns and lunch spots only take cash.

Highly recommended restaurants in each price category are indicated by a star ★.

| Category | Cost* |
|---|---|
| Very Expensive | over $50 |
| Expensive | $36–$50 |
| Moderate | $20–$35 |
| Inexpensive | under $20 |

**per person, excluding drinks and service (a 15% service charge is sometimes added)*

The following credit card abbreviations are used: AE, American Express; CB, Carte Blanche; D, Discover; DC, Diners Club; MC, MasterCard; V, Visa.

## Asian

**Expensive**

**Mikado.** This fun restaurant in Marriott's Castle Harbour Hotel brings Japanese cooking to very English Bermuda. The decor is stark, using simple lines and colors to great effect. As at many Japanese-style steak houses, the enjoyment lies less in the food than in the dazzling flash of twirling knives, slapping mallets, and airborne salt and pepper shakers—it's like judo you can eat. Although à la carte dining is available, you're better off with one of the complete dinners: a shrimp or scallop appetizer with ginger sauce, miso or *tori* soup, a seafood or beef entrée selection, salad, steamed rice, *teppan-yaki* vegetables, and Japanese tea. *Castle Harbour Hotel, Tucker's Town, tel. 809/293–2040. Reservations required. Dress: neat but casual. AE, CB, DC, MC, V.*

**Moderate**

**Bombay Bicycle Club.** The culinary scene of any British colony would be woefully incomplete without a curry house. Named

## Hamilton Dining

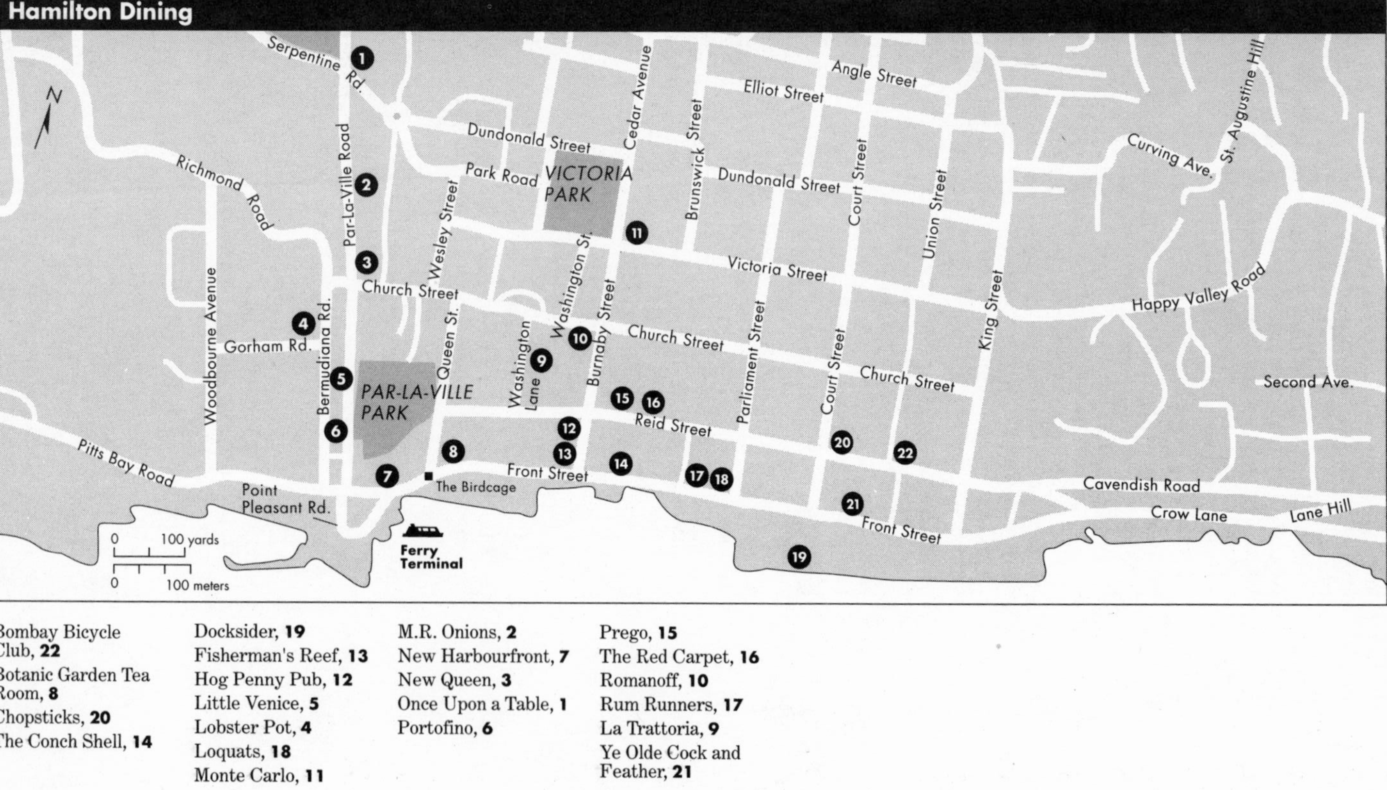


Bombay Bicycle Club, **22**
Botanic Garden Tea Room, **8**
Chopsticks, **20**
The Conch Shell, **14**
Docksider, **19**
Fisherman's Reef, **13**
Hog Penny Pub, **12**
Little Venice, **5**
Lobster Pot, **4**
Loquats, **18**
Monte Carlo, **11**
M.R. Onions, **2**
New Harbourfront, **7**
New Queen, **3**
Once Upon a Table, **1**
Portofino, **6**
Prego, **15**
The Red Carpet, **16**
Romanoff, **10**
Rum Runners, **17**
La Trattoria, **9**
Ye Olde Cock and Feather, **21**

after a private gentleman's club in the waning days of the Raj, this burgundy-hued restaurant captures the flavor of the subcontinent without becoming a caricature. All the traditional Indian favorites are offered here and prepared remarkably well. Order the *peeaz pakora* (onion fritters) and mulligatawny soup as starters, then opt for the *jhinga vindaloo* (shrimp in hot curry), *mutton saagwala* (braised lamb in creamy spinach), or anything from the clay tandoor oven. *Nan, paratha,* and *papadums* are terrific breads and snacks to accompany the meal. *Reid St., Hamilton, tel. 809/292-0048. Reservations suggested. Dress: neat but casual. AE, CB, DC, MC, V.*

**Chopsticks.** An alternative to New Queen (*see* below) at the east end of Hamilton, this Chinese restaurant features an intelligent mix of Szechuan, Hunan, and Cantonese favorites. The decor is utilitarian—red-upholstered chairs and tables—and mercifully devoid of calendars of Hong Kong's skyline. Top selections include the mandarin butterfly steak, lemon chicken Macau, and ribs in a mandarin orange sauce. For dessert, order nothing but the freshly baked pastries described as "Betty's pies." *Reid St. E, Hamilton, tel. 809/292-0791. Reservations suggested. Dress: neat but casual. AE, CB, DC, MC, V.*

**New Queen.** This Chinese restaurant is the current favorite of Bermudians, who flock here for the hot and spicy fare. The emphasis is on the food rather than the decor, but the interior is attractive, clean, and subdued. Try the Szechuan duck, steamed until tender, then pressed with black mushrooms and potato flour, deep-fried, and served with a peppery mushroom sauce. Another great choice is *wor suit* chicken—boneless chicken pressed with minced meat, lightly battered and fried, and served on a bed of vegetables. *Par-la-Ville Rd., Hamilton, tel. 809/295-4004 or 809/292-3282. Reservations suggested. Dress: neat but casual. AE, CB, DC, MC, V.*

## Bermudian

**Expensive**

**Glencoe.** The Salt Kettle ferry from Hamilton drops you off just two minutes' walk from this popular restaurant overlooking the harbor in Paget. Part of a cottage colony owned by Reggie and Margot Cooper, the restaurant offers truly stylish dining: Lunch is almost always served on the patio, and dinner is in an impressive manor house that dates back to the 1700s. The lunch menu is in English, and the dinner menu in French—a sure sign that the dining becomes fussier after sunset. Start with the *gaspacho Andaluz* (chilled vegetable soup) in summer or the fish chowder in any season. The vichyssoise is excellent at dinner, too, as are the local fish in a sauce of tomatoes, capers, and white wine, and the crispy roast duckling in a dark cherry sauce. Another dish worth considering is the chicken breast wrapped around a lobster tail, served in a red-wine sauce. *Salt Kettle, Paget, tel. 809/236-5274. Reservations required. Dress: casual at lunch, jacket and tie required at dinner. AE, CB, DC, MC, V.*

★ **Plantation.** Chris and Carol West call their trendy, clublike establishment a "truly Bermudian restaurant"; if that means the emphasis is on fresh seafood, they are absolutely right. Island wicker, flickering candles, and a glass-enclosed atrium filled with plants give the restaurant a cool, exotic look that works well with the ambitious, tropical menu. Some of the dishes can be overly exotic, however—monkfish poached with pineapple, raisins, and a host of other curry condiments, for example—

Carriage House, **2**
Gunpowder Cavern, **5**
Pub on the Square, **4**
Wharf Tavern, **1**
White Horse Tavern, **3**

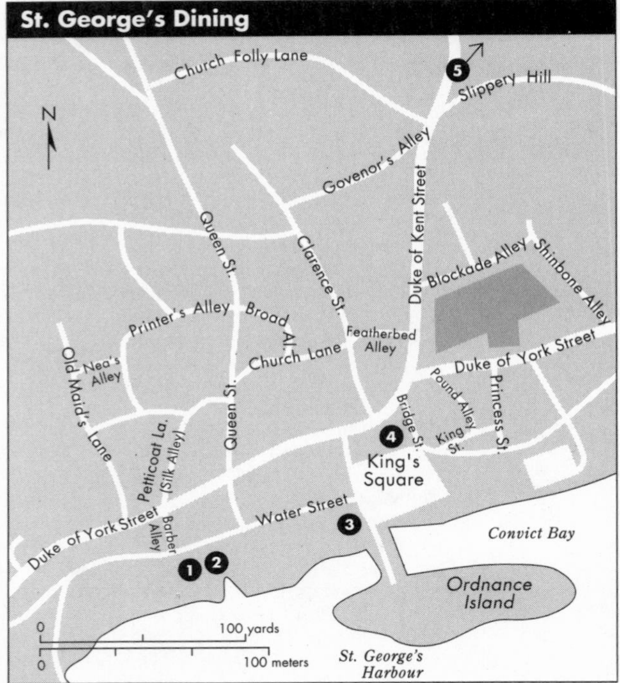


but the chef's art is in the right place. Panfried fish with prawns and coconuts offers a delightful tropical taste, as does the creative lamb loquat. *Bailey's Bay, Hamilton Parish, tel. 809/293–1188. Reservations suggested. Jacket and tie required. AE, CB, DC, MC, V.*

**Moderate**

★ **Black Horse Tavern.** Long a secret among Bermudians who flock here for the good, plentiful food, this place was finally discovered by Americans from the next-door Naval Air Station. Nothing has changed much as a result. A menacing shark, with jaws agape, still hangs on the white-plaster wall, along with an assortment of other mounted island fish. And islanders still fill the casual dining room and the six outside picnic tables to savor the culinary magic of chef Bernel Pitcher. Curried conch stew with rice is a favorite, as are Pitcher's straightforward renderings of amberjack, rockfish, shark, tuna, wahoo, and—in season—Bermuda lobster. For lunch, the fish sandwich is a taste sensation. If you want to try a Bermuda original, ask for shark hash, the chef's most popular specialty—the kitchen can never keep it in stock. *St. David's Island, tel. 809/293–9742. Reservations unnecessary. Dress: casual. No credit cards.*

**Loquats.** A popular lunch spot for businesspeople, this chic restaurant becomes far more romantic at night, serving well-prepared meals to the accompaniment of a pianist. Bright colors and eye-catching graphics will appeal to the MTV generation. The extensive menu is thoroughly international, but the best dishes have a Bermudian touch. In other words, choose the conch fritters over the Norway prawn cocktail, the fish chowder over the cucumber and watercress, and the broiled Bermuda rockfish over the so-called scampi tempura. *Front St., Hamilton, tel. 809/292–4507. Reservations suggested. Dress: neat but casual. AE, CB, DC, MC, V.*

**Inexpensive**
★ **Dennis's Hideaway.** Of all the eccentric characters who call St. David's home, Dennis Lamb may be the most eccentric. Piratical in appearance, he hunches over his pots grousing about everything from the plumbing and the government to the fate of man. The place consists of little more than a ramshackle pink building, a scattering of homemade picnic tables, and a few yapping dogs, but it serves probably Bermuda's best food. Don't come here if you're a stickler for cleanliness, however—the place is decidedly grubby. Dennis's son does most of the cooking these days, but Dennis still potters around the kitchen. If you want to make Dennis's day, order his "fish dinner with the works"—$28.50 for a feast of shark hash on toast, conch fritters, mussel stew, conch stew, fish chowder, fried fish, conch steak, shark steak, shrimp, scallops, and perhaps a bit of mussel pie. He may even include some bread-and-butter pudding for good measure. *Cash City Rd., St. David's, tel. 809/297–0044. Reservations unnecessary. Dress: casual. No credit cards.*

## British

**Expensive**
**Carriage House.** Hearty English food is the daily bread of this attractive slice of the Somers Wharf restoration. With its exposed brick walls, the interior looks rather like the exterior; try to secure a table by a window so you can watch the action on the docks. The price of dinner can add up quickly, especially if you choose something like the Bermuda Triangle—shrimp, filet mignon, and chicken breast, each prepared with its own sauce. Don't overlook the fresh Bermuda rockfish. On Sunday, a much less expensive brunch features a generous buffet of eggs, pancakes, meat and seafood entrées, pastas, salads, and desserts. There's even unlimited wine. *Somers Wharf, St. George's, tel. 809/297–1270. Reservations suggested. Jacket required at dinner. AE, CB, DC, MC, V.*

**Henry VIII.** As popular with locals as it is with tourists from the nearby Southampton resorts, this lively restaurant affects an Old England look that stops just short of "wench" waitresses and contrived Tudor styling. The food is terrific, an eclectic mix of English and Bermudian favorites. Order the mussel pie if it's offered, or opt for the lighter steamed mussels in wine. The fish chowder is wonderful, as are the very British lamb, beef, and steak and kidney pies. Save room for the dessert of bananas flamed in dark rum. *South Shore Rd., Southampton, tel. 809/238–1977. Reservations suggested. Jacket and tie required. AE, CB, DC, MC, V.*

**Moderate**
**Botanic Garden Tea Room.** One of Bermuda's most pleasant traditions is afternoon tea at Trimingham's department store in Hamilton. Like many tearooms, it has seen better days, but its faded elegance is now part of its appeal. Managed by the Fourways Inn, the tearoom also serves light lunches. A wide variety of teas, coffee, and soft drinks is available. *Front St., Hamilton, tel. 809/295–1183. Reservations unnecessary. Dress: casual. No credit cards.*

★ **Colony Pub.** A favorite meeting place for Hamilton's business and government communities, this cozy nook is an excellent

## Bermuda Dining

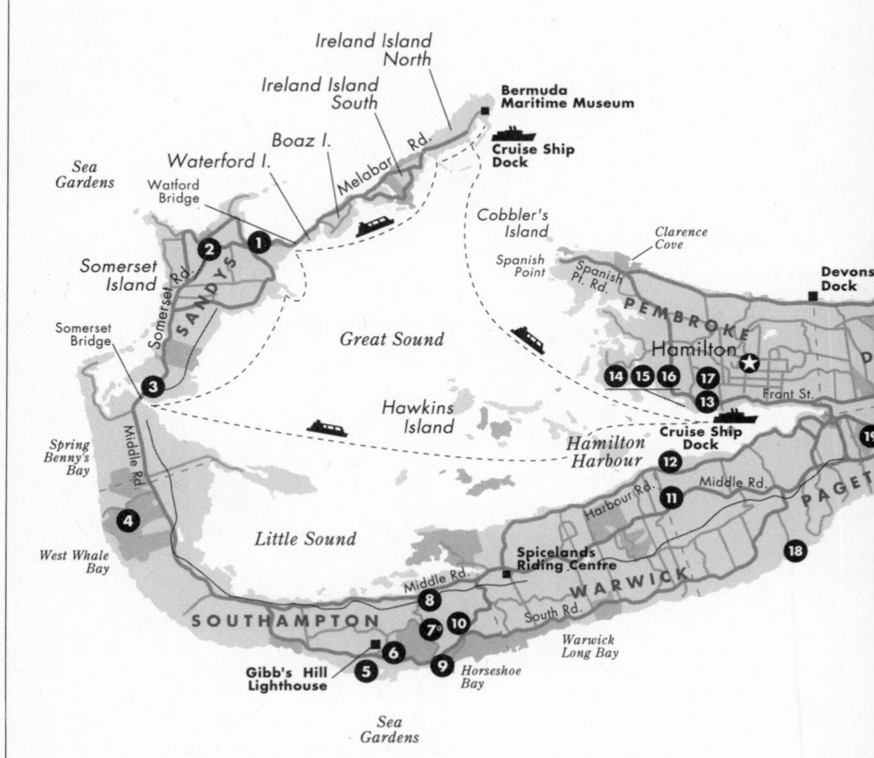


Black Horse Tavern, **27**
Blue Foam, **3**
Colony Pub, **14**
Dennis's Hideaway, **28**
Fourways Inn, **11**
Glencoe, **12**
Harley's, **16**
Henry VIII, **6**
The Inlet, **21**
Lillian's, **5**
Mikado, **26**
Newport Room, **7**
Norwood Room, **18**
Il Palio, **2**
Plantation, **24**
Port Royal Golf Club, **4**
Primavera, **17**
Somerset Country Squire, **1**
Specialty Inn, **20**
Swizzle Inn, **22**
Tavern on the Green, **19**
Tiara Room, **15**
Tio Pepe, **10**
Tom Moore's Tavern, **23**
Waterloo House, **13**
Waterlot Inn, **8**
Whaler Inn, **9**
Windsor, **25**

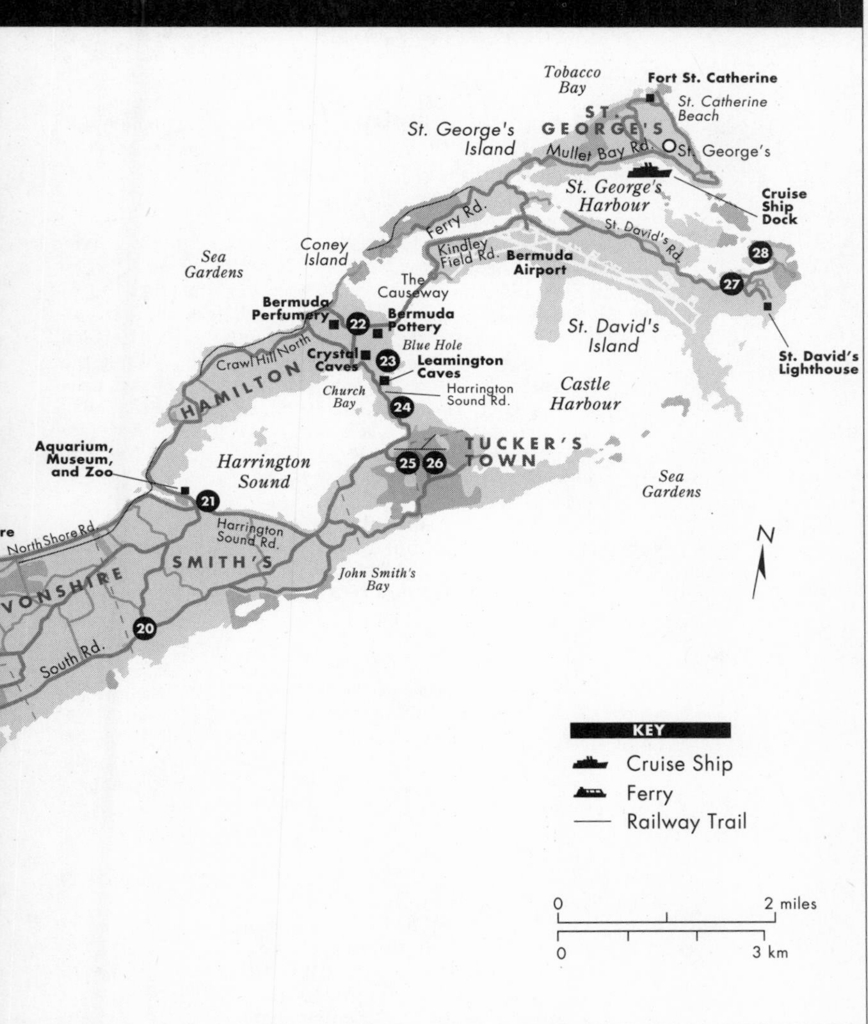

Tobacco Bay
Fort St. Catherine
St. Catherine Beach
ST. GEORGE'S
St. George's Island
Mullet Bay Rd.
St. George's
St. George's Harbour
Cruise Ship Dock
Ferry Rd.
St. David's Rd.
Sea Gardens
Coney Island
Kindley Field Rd.
Bermuda Airport
28
27
The Causeway
Bermuda Perfumery
22
Bermuda Pottery
Blue Hole
St. David's Island
Crawl Hill North
Crystal Caves
23
Leamington Caves
St. David's Lighthouse
HAMILTON
Church Bay
Harrington Sound Rd.
Castle Harbour
24
TUCKER'S TOWN
25
26
Aquarium, Museum, and Zoo
Harrington Sound
21
Sea Gardens
North Shore Rd.
Harrington Sound Rd.
SMITH'S
VONSHIRE
John Smith's Bay
N
20
South Rd.
KEY
Cruise Ship
Ferry
Railway Trail
0
2 miles
0
3 km

place for visitors to gain an understanding of how Bermuda works. Tourists are readily accepted by the lunching locals, although more as honored spectators than participants. Part of the Princess Hotel, the pub is redolent of Britain and the history of this tiny island. Rich shades of brown and green, and plenty of polished brass, give the restaurant an appealing clublike atmosphere. Food at the luncheon buffet is unpretentious but good, and the prices are very reasonable. *Princess Hotel, Hamilton, tel. 809/295–3000. Reservations unnecessary. Dress: casual. AE, CB, DC, MC, V.*

**Hog Penny Pub.** Veterans of a London pub crawl might wonder about some of the dishes offered at this atmospheric watering hole off Front Street in Hamilton—"escargots pub-style" is, after all, something of an oxymoron. Nevertheless, die-hard aficionados of British cooking (if such animals actually exist) will also be rewarded with shepherd's pie, steak and kidney pie, and bangers (sausages) and mash; there's even a small but passable sampling of curries. But look for good fun more than good food: Sunburned strangers mingle freely in this dark and smoky den, and entertainment is offered nightly. *Burnaby Hill, Hamilton, tel. 809/292–2534. Reservations suggested. Dress: casual. AE, CB, DC, MC, V.*

**Port Royal Golf Club.** This white dining room, on the 19th hole of the Port Royal Golf Club, overlooks the golf course through large plate-glass windows. Ask for a steak sandwich and English beer, although don't hesitate to order something more sophisticated from the main menu—the food is quite good. *Port Royal, Southampton, tel. 809/234–0236. Reservations suggested. Dress: casual. AE, CB, DC, MC, V. Open until dusk.*

**Pub on the Square.** After a morning wandering around St. George's, this pub on King's Square is perfect for a slaking pint of English beer. The draft beer is better than anything that comes from the kitchen, although hamburgers and fish-and-chips are reasonably prepared. Warehouse brick and plenty of dark wood give the pub a warm atmosphere. *King's Sq., St. George's, tel. 809/297–1522. Reservations unnecessary. Dress: casual. No credit cards.*

**Somerset Country Squire.** Overlooking Mangrove Bay in the West End, this typically English tavern is all dark wood and good cheer, with a great deal of malt and hops in between. The food isn't good enough to warrant a special trip across the island, but you won't be disappointed if you do stop by. Steak and kidney pie is fine, but the curried mussel pie is much better. Desserts are excellent: The hot apple pie with whipped cream approaches mythical status. *Mangrove Bay, Somerset, tel. 809/234–0105. Reservations unnecessary. Dress: casual. No credit cards.*

**Wharf Tavern.** Like most dockside restorations in Bermuda, this English-style watering hole is nondescript, with a stale atmosphere; it should be much better than it is. The mainstays are a selection of so-called Black Beard's pizzas (of which the privateer would surely disapprove) and an equally varied selection of burgers. The quality and service are typical of a pub, but the menu and prices are what you would expect in a proper restaurant. *Somers Wharf, St. George's, tel. 809/297–1515. Reservations unnecessary. Dress: casual. AE, CB, DC, MC, V (with a $25 minimum).*

**Ye Olde Cock and Feather.** One of the busiest spots along Front Street in Hamilton, this is a favorite meeting place for locals.

Patrons sit either in a room that is a cross between a British pub and a Key West–style tropical outpost or on the upstairs balcony overlooking the harbor. Food here is served pub-style, but the eclectic menu spans several cuisines and continents, from gazpacho Andaluz to steak and kidney pie and chicken Kiev. Live entertainment is featured nightly. *Front St., Hamilton, tel. 809/295–2263. Reservations suggested. Dress: casual. AE, CB, DC, MC, V.*

**Inexpensive**

**Docksider.** This Front Street hangout boasts that it has the widest selection of draft beers on the island, which says a lot about its priorities and the priorities of its young clientele. However, that's no reason to steer clear of the fish-and-chips or the hamburgers. The club sandwiches are a good bet, too, although taste just won't matter once you've drunk your way through the bar's large selection of European brews. The interior is crowded with hundreds of beer bottles, labels, and beer paraphernalia. *Front St., Hamilton, tel. 809/292–4088. Reservations unnecessary. Dress: casual. No credit cards.*

## French

**Very Expensive**

**Newport Room.** With its nautical theme, this lovely restaurant in the Southampton Princess has occupied a special place in the hearts of the island's elite for several years. French cuisine is the specialty. Glistening teak and models of previous America's Cup winners set the tone for some culinary winners, especially the grilled snapper with ratatouille and garlic quenelles (dumplings), and the venison medallions with orange sauce and fresh pasta. *South Shore Rd., Southampton, tel. 809/238–8167. Reservations suggested. Jacket and tie required. AE, CB, DC, MC, V. Dinner only.*

**Tiara Room.** After something of an identity crisis, the gourmet restaurant in Bermuda's historic Princess Hotel has rediscovered those elements of dining that make for fine cuisine and theater. Renovations in 1990 have given the restaurant a fresh look, utilizing clean lines and bright colors (particularly mauve), but the highlight remains the stunning view of Hamilton Harbour. The emphasis is on classic French cuisine and service that can be overwhelming. Whenever possible, dishes are finished tableside, often flambéed dramatically. These tableside theatrics may not be chic in Paris or New York nowadays, but they work in these surroundings. The rack of lamb carved tableside is always an excellent choice, as are the cherries Jubilee and the crepes suzette. *Princess Hotel, Hamilton, tel. 809/295–3000. Reservations suggested. Jacket and tie required. AE, CB, DC, MC, V.*

★ **Waterlot Inn.** Housed in a graceful, single-story manor house that dates back to 1670, this restaurant is a Bermudian treasure. Like most Bermudian restaurants, it has good days and bad, but it works hard to live up to its reputation and age. Chef Regis Neaud watches over the kitchen, while the dining room staff has just enough island exuberance to take the edge off their European-style training. The menu's French selections are far superior to most of the cuisine that passes for French on the island, although the chef seldom misses an opportunity to prepare dishes indigenous to Bermuda. Waterlot serves one of the best fish chowders on the island, while the Bermuda rockfish, wrapped in spinach leaves and baked in puff pastry, is spectacular. For dessert, try the chocolate domino—white chocolate mousse in a domino of dark chocolate. *Middle Rd., Southampton, tel. 809/238-0510. Reservations suggested. Jacket and tie required. AE, CB, DC, MC, V.*

**Expensive**

**Monte Carlo.** Southern French cooking is the trademark of this bright new restaurant just behind City Hall in Hamilton. Beams of old Bermuda cedar add a touch of local color, as does the unusual original artwork on the walls. There is a good selection of pizzas, but the main emphasis is on a sprightly collection of hot and cold appetizers. The carpaccio (thinly sliced raw beef served with lemon) and the stuffed mussels are superb. Favorite entrées include roast duck in mango sauce, and veal breaded with Parmesan and served with two sauces. *Victoria St., Hamilton, tel. 809/295-5453. Reservations suggested. Dress: neat but casual. AE, MC, V.*

**Waterloo House.** A private home a century ago, this restaurant/guest house on Hamilton Harbour serves Bermudian and Continental cuisine. Guests can eat either on the waterside patio adjoining the flower-shaded buildings, or in the uncluttered English dining room, where a fire is kept burning during the winter. Chef Bruno Heeb usually offers a special or two, but don't overlook such appetizers as St. Jacques ravioli and sautéed periwinkles in a pink champagne sauce. For an entrée, consider one of the stranger dishes on the island: Bermuda rockfish stuffed with oysters and wrapped in fresh salmon, with caviar sauce and an avocado rice timbale. *Pitt's Bay Rd., Pembroke, Hamilton, tel. 809/295-4480. Reservations suggested. Jacket and tie required at dinner. No credit cards.*

## International

**Very Expensive**

**Fourways Inn.** This restaurant has risen to preeminence on the island in recent years, as much for its lovely 18th-century surroundings as anything coming out of the kitchen. The decor is evocative of a wealthy plantation home, with plenty of expensive china, crystal, and silver. Order the local mussels simmered in white wine and cream, and any of the sautéed veal dishes. The Caesar salad is a good choice, too, but leave enough room for strawberry soufflé, if it's available. For a slightly different cocktail, try a Fourways Special, made with the juice from the Bermuda loquat and other fruits, and a dash of bitters. *1 Middle Rd., Paget, tel. 809/236-6517. Reservations suggested. Jacket and tie required. AE, CB, DC, MC, V.*

**Romanoff.** Elegant European meals served in a theatrical Russian setting are the specialty of this restaurant run by Anton Duzavic. A deep rich red is the restaurant's predominant color, providing a dramatic backdrop for the vodka and black caviar that Duzavic himself presents to each diner. Stick to the well-known dishes or select a seafood special from the cart that is wheeled around the tables. *Church St., Hamilton, tel. 809/295-0333. Reservations suggested. Jacket and tie required. AE, CB, DC, MC, V.*

**Expensive**

**Norwood Room.** Don't be put off that this restaurant in the Stonington Beach Hotel is run by students of the Bermuda Department of Hotel Technology. Under the supervision of their mentors, the students offer a dining experience notable for the high quality of the food and superb service. The kitchen uses local ingredients and European culinary techniques to create a whole range of bright, fresh tastes. Seafood is the best bet here, well prepared and served with excellent sauces. Enjoy a preprandial cocktail at the sunken bar overlooking the swimming pool. *South Shore Rd., tel. 809/236–5416. Reservations suggested. Jacket and tie required. AE, CB, DC, MC, V.*

**Tavern on the Green.** No connection to the famous restaurant in New York's Central Park, this stylish tavern is hidden away in Bermuda's Botanical Gardens. Tables overlook the gardens, a waterfall, and a statue of Caesar. Additional seating for 100 was recently added, and there's a small dance floor and a honeymoon retreat. The eight-page menu focuses on dishes with a Mediterranean flair, including such specialties as duck breast sautéed in a fruit sauce and garnished with kiwi, and beef sirloin served with a sauce of green peppercorns and Bermuda's own sherry peppers. *Botanical Gardens, Paget, tel. 809/236–7731. Reservations suggested. Dress: neat but casual. AE, CB, DC, MC, V.*

**Tom Moore's Tavern.** Set in an old home that dates to 1652, this restaurant overlooking Bailey's Bay clearly enjoys its colorful past. Irish poet Tom Moore visited friends here frequently during his stay on the island in 1804 and wrote several of his odes under the nearby Calabash Tree. Today, fireplaces, casement windows, and copper appointments capture a sense of the building's history. The cuisine, however, labors under none of history's baggage—it is fresh, light, and innovative. Seafood lovers should try the Treasures of St. David's Island, a marriage of local fish, flame fish, and lobster tail. *Bailey's Bay, Hamilton Parish, tel. 809/293–8020. Reservations suggested. Jacket required. AE, CB, DC, MC, V.*

**Windsor.** Overlooking Castle Harbour, this elegant dining room in Marriott's Castle Harbour Hotel features an international blend of cuisines with a strong European underpinning. Try the salmon, fettuccine Alfredo, escargot Café de Paris, or prime rib with Yorkshire pudding. Don't expect too much innovation, however; as a hotel dining room, the restaurant must hedge its culinary bets. Nevertheless, with its unhurried atmosphere, live piano music, and view of Castle Harbour, the Windsor makes for a fine night out. *Castle Harbour, Tucker's Town, tel. 809/293–2040. Reservations required. Jacket and tie required. AE, CB, DC, MC, V. Dinner only. Closed Sun. in winter.*

**Moderate**

**The Conch Shell.** This attractive, modern restaurant is the setting for an unusual mix of cuisines and ingredients, from seafood and steaks to Asian specialties—the latter are done so well that the restaurant could easily be classified as Chinese. Egg rolls, ginger beef, and lamb curry are served alongside fried seafood platters and conch fritters. *Emporium Bldg., Front St., Hamilton, tel. 809/295–6969. Reservations recommended. Dress: casual. AE, CB, DC, MC, V.*

**The Inlet.** With beautiful views over Harrington Sound, this restaurant in the Palmetto Hotel is filled with sunlight and fresh air. None of the dishes is likely to find its way into a gourmet magazine, but the quality is reasonable and guests have a wide selection from which to choose. In winter, there are good steaks and rack of lamb. *Palmetto Hotel, Flatts Village, tel. 809/293–2323. Reservations suggested. Jacket and tie required. AE, CB, DC, MC, V.*

**M. R. Onions.** The Bermudian equivalent of TGIFriday, this fun restaurant got its name from the phrase "Him are Onions," meaning "he's one of us" (Bermudians are referred to as Onions, after the sweet onion that grows on the island). Friendly service and good spirits (both from the heart and the bar) make for an enjoyable evening here. Finger foods, such as potato skins, zucchini sticks, and breaded mushrooms, are especially good, although don't hesitate to order anything from fish chowder to charbroiled fish, steaks, and barbecued ribs. A special children's menu is available until 8 PM, but children are discouraged any later than that. *Par-la-Ville Rd. N, Hamilton, tel. 809/292–5012. Reservations suggested. Dress: casual. AE, CB, DC, MC, V.*

**New Harbourfront.** Few of the restaurants along Front Street have the courage to be so inventively Mediterranean or ambitious as this thoroughly modern restaurant, where unusual architectural elements clash with a tropical decor. At lunch, try the frittata, an open-face Italian omelet, or the *fusilli pesto*, a plateful of twisted noodles in a lush basil cream. For dinner, consider the swordfish *oreganato* cooked Greek-style, or the Italian *cacciuco Mediterranee:* scampi, swordfish, salmon, and Bermuda rockfish, in a sauce of white wine and raspberry vinegar. *Front St., Hamilton, tel. 809/295–4207. Reservations recommended. Dress: casual. AE, CB, DC, MC, V.*

★ **Once Upon a Table.** Hailed by many Bermudians as the finest restaurant on Bermuda, this delightful restaurant offers elegant service in an 18th-century island home, complete with elegant china and crystal. Dinner here is theatrical—the restaurant is not unlike a theme park in its use of costumes and setting to create a sense of a bygone era. From the menu, consider rack of lamb, roast duckling, or pork, although you can also order a dinner of Bermudian specialties with 48-hours' notice. *Serpentine Rd., Hamilton, tel. 809/295–8585. Reservations recommended. Jacket and tie required. Dinner only. AE, CB, DC, MC, V.*

**Rum Runners.** This popular Front Street restaurant assumes different personalities throughout the day. It is at its most formal at dinner, when it becomes a full-service restaurant with terrific seafood and well-coached waiters. The best bets are the seafood brochette and the fish pot, both combination plates of immense proportions. Meat patrons will be amply satisfied by the mixed English grill. Lunch is far more casual, with traditional pub fare as well as sandwiches, salads, and the unavoidable array of burgers. *Front St., Hamilton, tel. 809/292–4737. Reservations suggested for dinner. Dress: casual. AE, CB, DC, MC, V.*

**Swizzle Inn.** People come to this outwardly nondescript place as much to drink as to eat. Just west of the airport near the Bermuda Perfume Factory, the inn created one of Bermuda's most hallowed drinks—the rum swizzle. Sit in the shadowy bar—plastered with business cards from all over the world—sipping one of these delightful concoctions, and watch the mopeds whiz by. If you get hungry, try a "swizzleburger." *Blue Hole Hill, Bailey's Bay, tel. 809/293–9300. Reservations unnecessary. Dress: casual. MC, V.*

**White Horse Tavern.** Set on the water's edge overlooking the harbor in St. George's, this restaurant has such a great location and atmosphere that a little more local color in the menu would work wonders. As it is, however, you can only get high-quality burgers, steaks, and a small selection of fish—nothing that sets the place apart. Still, the memorable chocolate cake makes the tavern worth a visit. *King's Sq., St. George's, tel. 809/297–*

*1838. Reservations unnecessary. Dress: casual. AE, CB, DC, MC, V.*

**Inexpensive** **Gunpowder Cavern.** A short walk from the center of St. George's, this interesting restaurant is tucked away in the ruins of Fort William. The owners stripped away the elements of years past, leaving a bare-bones look that works well with its military setting. Even the menu is lean, including such unpretentious items as peanut butter and jelly sandwiches. More substantial fare is available, such as lasagna, steak, chicken-and-chips, or chicken cordon bleu. The prices are reasonable. *Fort William, Sapper La., St. George's, tel. 809/297–0904. Reservations unnecessary. Dress: casual. No credit cards. Closed Mon.*

## Italian

**Expensive** **Little Venice.** The name of this restaurant may refer to the lovely city of canals, but the atmosphere is strictly Roman—stylish, self-confident, and urbane. Bermudians head for this trattoria when they want more from Italian cooking than pizza. Little Venice can be expensive, but the food is decent enough to command higher prices and the service is expert. In particular, try the eggplant with grilled cheese and herbs as an appetizer, or perhaps the crepes filled with ricotta and spinach. Marinated in fresh mint and simmered with scallions, wine, and fresh tomatoes, the swordfish makes an excellent main course. A special early evening dinner deal, featuring appetizer, main course, dessert, and coffee, is available for $16.75—less than most of the à la carte entrées. *Bermudiana Rd., Hamilton, tel. 809/295–3503 or 809/295–8279. Reservations suggested. Dress: neat but casual. AE, CB, DC, MC, V.*

**Moderate** **Il Palio.** A ship's spiral staircase leads upstairs from the bar to the dining room at this West End restaurant. Some of the best pizzas on the island are served here, with all the usual trimmings. Among the other offerings are a wide range of good antipasti and pasta dishes, including cannelloni and pasta primavera. The selections of veal, chicken, and beef are straightforward. *Main Rd., Somerset, tel. 809/234–1049 or 809/234–2323. Reservations suggested. Dress: casual. AE, CB, DC, MC, V.*

**Primavera.** White and burgundy dominate this pleasing Mediterranean dining room in the west end of Hamilton. Ultimately, however, it's the food that makes a visit here worthwhile. A spectacular starter is baked mushrooms in garlic butter with paprika and cream, followed by one of the house specialties: breast of duck with black peppercorns, brandy, and cream. Guests can also choose from a wide variety of consistently good pastas. *Pitt's Bay Rd., Hamilton, tel. 809/295–2167. Reservations suggested. Dress: neat but casual. AE, CB, DC, MC, V. No lunch weekends.*

**The Red Carpet.** Very popular at lunch, this tiny restaurant sports a few New York touches, such as a ravioli dish named for Frank Sinatra, but otherwise the flavor is Old World Italian. The clever use of mirrors dispels a sense of claustrophobia, while plentiful brass gives the place a stylish look. Among the culinary highlights are the veal, the Bermuda fish dishes, an incongruous beef Stroganoff, and chicken Normand (prepared with Calvados apple brandy). *Armoury Bldg., Reid St., Ham-*

*ilton, tel. 809/292–6195. Reservations suggested. Dress: neat but casual. AE, CB, DC, MC, V.*

**Inexpensive** **Portofino.** Busy for both lunch and dinner, this popular Italian restaurant, with its traditional red-check tablecloths, is really a fancy pizza parlor. A wide selection of pizza toppings is available, and customers are asked to phone 15 minutes ahead if they want their pie to go. If you're not in the mood for pizza, however, try the excellent sirloin steak with olives, capers, and tomato sauce, or the fried calamari in a delicate batter. More adventurous diners will enjoy the octopus, cooked in red sauce with olives and capers and served on a bed of rice. *Bermudiana Rd., Hamilton, tel. 809/292–2375 or 809/295–6090. Reservations suggested. Dress: casual. AE, CB, DC, MC, V. Closed for lunch weekends.*

**Prego.** Accented with brass and burgundy, this cozy restaurant on Hamilton's east side is usually very busy. There's nothing on the menu that you couldn't find at most Italian restaurants, but the prices are quite reasonable. Pizzas are a specialty, as is the excellent rendition of *penne puttanesca,* pasta with tomatoes, anchovies, capers, olives, and hot peppers. *Reid St. E, Hamilton, tel. 809/292–1279. Reservations suggested. Dress: casual. AE, CB, DC, MC, V.*

**Specialty Inn.** A favorite with locals, this south-shore restaurant is cheerful, clean, and cheap. The low prices are reflected in the fact that the restaurant is almost totally lacking in decoration. Try the fish chowder or the red-bean soup. Otherwise, all the dishes are just what you would expect of a family-style Italian restaurant, plus milk shakes and ice cream. *Collectors Hill, Smith's, tel. 809/236–3133. Reservations suggested. Dress: casual. No credit cards.*

**Tio Pepe.** You don't need to spend a lot of money for a satisfying meal at this Italian restaurant with a Mexican name. Photocopied menus and flourishes of red and green (also rather Mexican) create an easygoing atmosphere ideal for bathers returning from a day at Horseshoe Bay Beach. Try an appetizer such as spicy eggplant baked in tomato sauce and cheese, followed by a small pizza or pasta dish. *South Shore Rd., Southampton, tel. 809/239–1897 or 809/238–0572. Reservations suggested. Dress: casual. AE, DC, MC, V.*

**La Trattoria.** Tucked in a Hamilton alley, this comfortable trattoria is typical of every no-nonsense Italian restaurant with red-check tablecloths: Veal parmigiana is the staple, and tortellini is a typical starter. However, this restaurant also serves an interesting "diet" pizza, made with whole-wheat flour and topped with zucchini and tomatoes, and an antidiet Italian buffet every Thursday night from 5 PM to 10 PM; eat as much as you want for $15.75. *Washington La., Hamilton, tel. 809/292–7059 or 809/295–1877. Reservations suggested. Dress: casual. AE, CB, DC, MC, V.*

## Seafood

**Expensive** **Lillian's.** Part of the Sonesta Beach Hotel, this elegant art nouveau restaurant gains much of its character from testimonials and mementos in honor of Aunt Lillian, whose counsel appears on the menus advising diners to "be wonderful or be horrible, but for heaven's sake, don't be mediocre." Lillian's is neither mediocre nor horrible, and it is well worth a visit. Seafood is the specialty, starting with the so-called Bermuda Fish Market—two fresh fish cooked as you wish and topped with the sauce of your choice. The grilled swordfish, with its herb and spice marinade, is also excellent. *Sonesta Beach Hotel, Southampton, tel. 809/238-8122. Reservations suggested. Jacket required. AE, CB, DC, MC, V. Closed Mon.*

**Whaler Inn.** Perched above the rocks and surf at the Southampton Princess, this seafood house has one of the most dramatic settings on the island. The table d'hôte menu ($32 per person, plus a 15% gratuity) entitles you to an appetizer, a salad, a main course, dessert, and a beverage. Start with the crisp, lightly battered Bermuda rockfish and the fish chowder. Cooked the way you want, any of the selections of fresh wahoo, yellowfin tuna, barracuda, shark, or dolphinfish makes an excellent main course. *Southampton Princess Hotel, South Shore Rd., Southampton, tel. 809/238-0076. Reservations suggested. Dress: neat but casual. AE, CB, DC, MC, V.*

**Moderate**

**Blue Foam.** Don't let its location at the motel-like Somerset Bridge Hotel put you off this restaurant. Grilled, baked, sautéed, or fried, the local fish served here needs nothing more than a drizzle of lemon and butter. In summer, do your best to secure one of the tables on the terrace overlooking Ely's Harbour and the world's smallest drawbridge, or settle for the cozy, greenhouse atmosphere of the dining room. For something other than grilled food, try the seafood brochette—fish, shrimp, and scallops fried Asian-style in a light batter and served with sweet-and-sour sauce. *Somerset Bridge, Sandys, tel. 809/234-1042. Reservations required. Dress: neat but casual. AE, CB, DC, MC, V.*

**Fisherman's Reef.** Located above the Hog Penny Pub, this restaurant has a predictable nautical motif. The Reef draws a crowd of locals, who are attracted by the restaurant's high-quality seafood and steaks, for lunch and dinner. The fish chowder is excellent, as is the St. David's conch chowder. Of the wide selection of seafood entrées, the best are the Bermuda lobster, the wahoo Mangrove Bay (seasoned and broiled with slices of Bermuda onions and banana), and the dolphinfish Cardinal (panfried and coated with a rosy pink lobster sauce). *Burnaby Hill, just off Front St., Hamilton, tel. 809/292-1609. Reservations recommended. Dress: casual for lunch, neat but casual for dinner. AE, CB, DC, MC, V.*

**Harley's.** Mildly nautical in theme, this pleasant restaurant in the Princess emphasizes fresh fish and simple presentation. Best bets are the grilled grouper, snapper, and dolphinfish, or the scallops en brochette. The restaurant stopped short of placing the grill in the open as entertainment, but the muted sea and sand tones bespeak a consultant's touch. *Princess Hotel, Hamilton, tel. 809/295-3000. Reservations recommended. Dress: casual. AE, CB, DC, MC, V.*

**Lobster Pot.** Locals swear by this place, which serves local lobster in winter, excellent Maine lobster, and a host of other local shellfish and fish. In keeping with its specialty, the restaurant sports a nautical decor, including shining brass instruments and sun-bleached rope. The menu is a little too cute for its own good ("Frankie's Fish and Fun" belongs in a fast-food restaurant), but it features some of the best versions of the local standards. *Bermudiana Rd., Hamilton, tel. 809/292-6898. Reservations suggested. Dress: casual. AE, CB, DC, MC, V. Closed Sun.*

# 8 Lodging

*by Honey Naylor*

If all the accommodations available on Bermuda were reviewed here, this book would barely qualify as carry-on luggage. Visitors to this tiny island can choose from a huge array of full-service resort hotels, cottage colonies, small inns, guest houses, and housekeeping apartments. It is the beachfront cottage colonies for which Bermuda is probably most famous, however—free-standing cottages clustered around a main building housing a restaurant, a lounge, and an activities desk. Many properties, especially these cottage colonies, are sprawling affairs set in extensive grounds and connected by walkways and steps; at some of the smaller guest houses and housekeeping apartments visitors must carry their own luggage on the long walk to their rooms. Disabled visitors or anyone unwilling to climb hills may be happier at a conventional hotel with elevators and corridors.

Like everything else in Bermuda, lodging is expensive. The rates at Bermuda's luxury resorts are comparable to those at posh hotels in New York, London, and Paris. The high prices would be easier to swallow if you received first-class service in return. However, such features as 24-hour room service and same-day laundry service are rare; in most instances, you pay extra for room service when it is available. You can shave about 40% off your hotel bill by visiting Bermuda during the low or shoulder seasons, which run from October to April. Temperatures rarely dip below 60°F during this period, and the weather is ideal for tennis, golf, and shopping, although the water is a bit chilly for swimming. Low-season packages are attractively priced, and during this time a host of government-sponsored special events (many of which are free) are staged for tourists.

The greatest concentration of accommodations is along the south shore, in Paget, Warwick, and Southampton parishes, where the best beaches are located. If shopping is your bag, however, there are several hotels just a stone's throw from the main shopping area in Front Street in Hamilton, as well as a host of properties clustered around Hamilton Harbour, a five- to 10-minute ferry ride from the capital. The West End is a bit remote, but it is ideal for boaters, fishermen, and those who want to get away from it all. The East End has its share of nautical pursuits, too, but its major attraction is the charming, historic village of St. George's's. In truth, the island is so small that it's possible to see and do everything you want, regardless of where you unpack your bag.

Whether or not they are officially classified as cottage colonies, a large number of guest accommodations are in cottages—usually pink with white trim and gleaming white, tiered roofs. There are some sprawling resorts, but no high rises and no neon signs. An enormous property like the Southampton Princess is hard to miss, but many hotels and guest houses are identified only by small, inconspicuous signs or plaques. The island is noted for its lovely gardens and manicured lawns, and the grounds of almost every hotel and cottage are filled with subtropical trees, flowers, and shrubs.

A 6% tax is tacked onto all hotel bills, and a service charge is levied in lieu of tipping: Some hotels calculate the service charge as 10% of the bill, others charge a per diem dollar amount. Some of the smaller guest houses and housekeeping units have also instituted a 5% "energy surcharge." All guests are required to make a two-night deposit two to three weeks before their arrival; those accommodations that don't take credit cards for payment—and many do not—may accept them for the deposit. Virtually every hotel on the island offers at least one vacation package—frequently some kind of honeymoon special—and many of these are extraordinarily good deals. It's worth learning about the various policies and programs at the properties that interest you before booking.

Bermuda is not noted as a great family destination, and some hotels discourage parents from bringing small children. In 1990, however, three properties inaugurated family packages during high season: The Grotto Bay Beach Hotel & Tennis Club, the Sonesta Beach Hotel & Spa, and the Southampton Princess offer free room and board for children up to age 16 staying in the same room as their parents on the Modified American Plan (MAP). All packages include free, supervised day camps for children. The Elbow Beach Hotel also offers a MAP package that includes daily supervised children's activities. Many of the hotels on the island can arrange for baby-sitters, but only these four hotels offer special programs for children.

Most lodgings offer their guests a choice of meal plans, and the hotel rate varies according to the meal plan you choose. Under the American Plan (AP), breakfast, lunch, and dinner are included in the hotel rate; the Modified American Plan (MAP) offers breakfast and dinner; the Bermuda Plan (BP) includes a full breakfast but no dinner, while the Continental Plan (CP) features a breakfast of pastries, juice, and coffee. The rates quoted below are based on the European Plan (EP), which includes no meals at all. Many hotels also have a variety of "dine-around" plans that allow guests to eat at other restaurants on the island as part of their meal plan. During the low season, there is an island-wide dine-around program, in which 25 participating restaurants—including Italian, Japanese, English, and Continental establishments—offer three-course, prix fixe meals for $18.50, $23.50, and $29 per person. The Princess and the Southampton Princess offer a Royal Dine-Around program year-round, which allows guests to eat at any of the several Princess restaurants. The eight properties in the Bermuda Collection (Cambridge Beaches, Lantana, the Reefs, Horizons, Newstead, Glencoe Harbour Club, Stonington Beach, and the Pompano) have a similar arrangement, known as the Carousel Dine-Around program, as do Horizons, Newstead, and Waterloo House. Dinner is usually formal in restaurants at hotels and cottage colonies, and men are asked to wear jackets and ties; neat but casual dress is suggested for women. Many hotels will pack a picnic lunch for those guests who want to get out and about.

Cottage colonies and hotels offer entertainment at least one night a week during high season, staging everything from calypso to classical music; barbecues and dinner dances are also popular. Afternoon tea is served daily in keeping with British tradition, and a rum-swizzle party is usually held on Monday night. Featuring the Bermudian beverage of choice, these parties present a pleasant opportunity to welcome new arrivals, get acquainted—and, of course, knock back some rum. Guest houses and housekeeping apartments do not have regularly scheduled entertainment, although informal gatherings are not uncommon.

Most of the large hotels have their own water-sports facilities where guests can rent Windsurfers, Sunfish, paddle boats, and other equipment. Even the smallest property, however, can arrange sailing, snorkeling, scuba, and deep-sea fishing excursions, as well as sightseeing and harbor tours. The Coral Beach & Tennis Club and the Mid Ocean Club are posh private clubs, where an introduction by a member is necessary to gain access to their excellent beach, tennis, and golf facilities. However, many hotels have arrangements with one or the other to allow guests certain club privileges.

Highly recommended lodgings in each price category are indicated by a star ★.

| Category | Cost* |
| --- | --- |
| Very Expensive | over $200 |
| Expensive | $125–$200 |
| Moderate | $90–$125 |
| Inexpensive | under $90 |

**All prices are for a standard double room for two (EP) during high season, excluding 6% tax and 10% service charge (or equivalent).*

The following credit card abbreviations are used: AE, American Express; CB, Carte Blanche; DC, Diners Club; MC, MasterCard; V, Visa.

## Resort Hotels

**Very Expensive**

**Elbow Beach Hotel.** Set amid 34 acres of botanical gardens overlooking the superb south-shore beach for which it is named, this large sports-oriented resort is popular with tour groups and is a major venue for College Weeks events. Guests are given a map to help them sort out the myriad paths and roads that wind down the hillside to the beach, past cottages, lanais, bars, and the pool. The main building, a five-story white stone edifice perched on top of the hill, houses a dining room, a nightclub, a shopping mall, library, health club, and a game room. Two hundred guest rooms and suites are also contained in this building, and the majority of these rooms have balconies or patios with ocean views. However, 71 are tiny "landside" rooms that have no balconies and overlook rooftops. Those guests who seek peace and quiet should avoid the ground-floor rooms off the main hallway—the area sees plenty of activity and can be noisy. The remainder of the rooms and suites are in duplex cottages and multi-unit lanais set amid the gardens or by the beach. Three types of suites are available: junior suites, with one bedroom, a small sitting room, and a patio; royal suites, with one or two bedrooms, a Jacuzzi, a lounge, and a large private patio; and family suites, with two bedrooms, a lounge, and private patio. The decor throughout is contemporary, with thick carpeting, sofas and chairs upholstered in flame-stitch fabrics, and attractive framed prints. Each room has a minibar. There are cabanas and showers on the beach, and weekly scuba lessons are offered at the Sea Horse Club. A playground is provided for children, and the swimming pool has a shallow area; during July and August special children's pro-

## Lodging

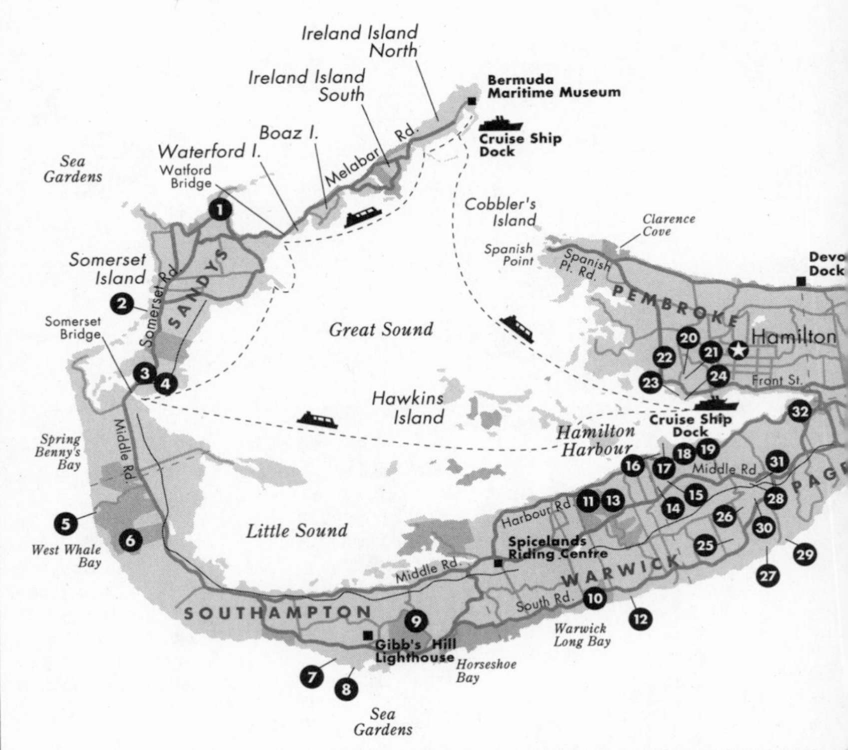


Angel's Grotto, **35**
Ariel Sands Beach Club, **33**
Barnsdale Guest Apartments, **28**
Belmont Hotel, Golf & Country Club, **13**
Cambridge Beaches, **1**
Edgehill Manor, **22**
Elbow Beach Hotel, **27**
Fourways Inn, **14**
Glencoe Harbour Club, **16**
Granaway Guest House & Cottage, **11**
Greenbank Cottages, **17**
Grotto Bay Beach Hotel & Tennis Club, **38**
Harmony Club, **31**
Hillcrest Guest House, **39**
Horizons & Cottages, **25**
Lantana Colony Club, **4**
Little Pomander Guest House, **32**
Longtail Cliffs, **10**
Loughlands Guest House & Cottage, **30**
Marley Beach Cottages, **12**

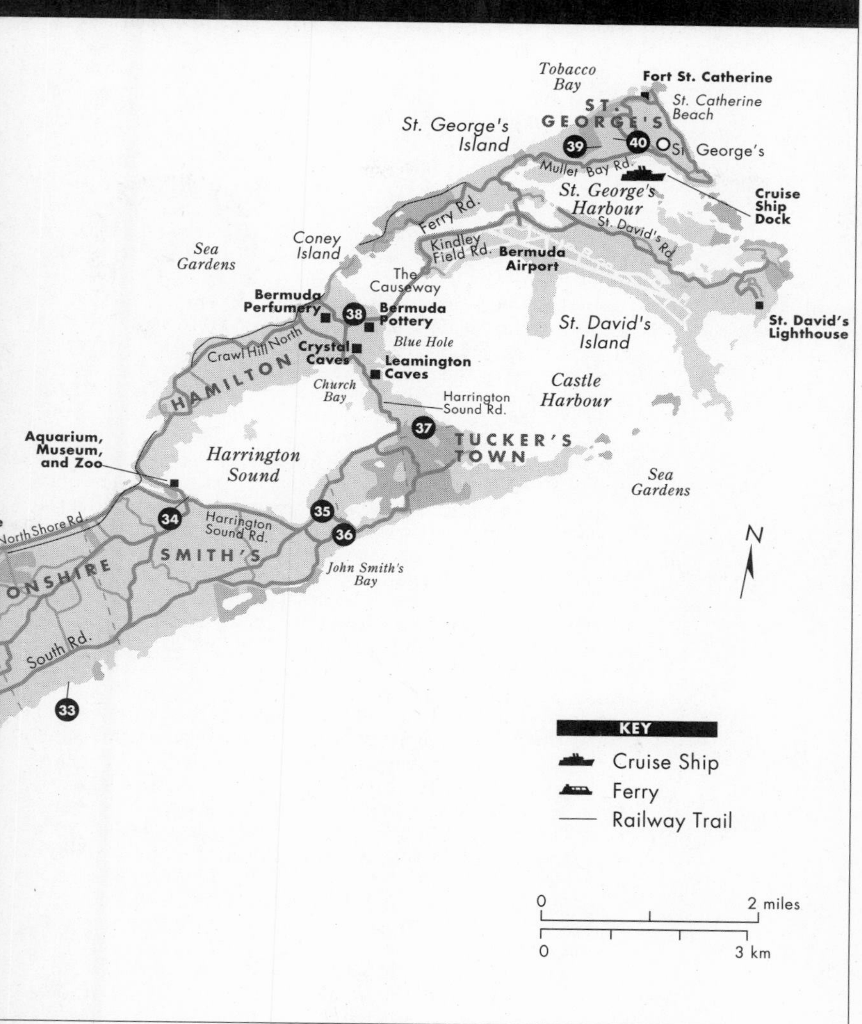


Marriott's Castle Harbour Resort, **37**
Newstead, **19**
Oxford House, **20**
Palmetto Hotel & Cottages, **34**
Pink Beach Club & Cottages, **36**
Pompano Beach Club, **5**
Pretty Penny, **15**
The Princess, **23**
The Reefs, **7**
Rosedon, **21**
The St. George's Club, **40**
Salt Kettle House, **18**
Sky Top Cottages, **26**
Somerset Bridge Hotel, **3**
Sonesta Beach Hotel & Spa, **8**
Southampton Princess, **9**
Stonington Beach Hotel, **29**
Waterloo House, **24**
Whale Bay Inn, **6**
Willowbank, **2**

grams are held. Use of the health club, with its exercise machines and whirlpool, is free, but there's a $5-per-hour fee for the tennis courts ($8 for night play) and racquet rentals cost $3. A shuttle bus is available for those guests who don't want to tackle the surrounding hills on foot, and there are taxi stands at the hotel entrance and by the beach. *Box HM 455, Hamilton HM BX, tel. 809/236–3535; in U.S., 800/223–7434; in Canada, 800/363–4080. 223 rooms, 75 suites, all with bath. Meal plans: BP, MAP. Facilities: 3 restaurants, 3 bars, nightclub, private beach, beauty salon, moped rental, heated freshwater pool, shopping mall, game room, playground, 5 tennis courts (3 lighted), water sports, health club with exercise room and whirlpool. AE, DC, MC, V.*

**Grotto Bay Beach Hotel & Tennis Club.** Only a mile from the airport, this is the smallest and least luxurious of the hotels in this price category. Set in 20 acres of gardens, it appeals to a young crowd that likes the hotel's informal atmosphere and the romantic coves and natural caves in the nearby enclosed bay. Also in the bay are a fish-feeding aquarium and two illuminated underground attractions: the Cathedral Cave for swimming, and Prospero's Cave disco for dancing beneath the stalactites. The hotel itself consists of a main building and 11 three-story pink lodges dotting a hill that slopes to the waters of Ferry Reach. The lobby is subdued, with tile floors, wicker furniture, and low ceilings; adjacent are the large dining room and lounge, where floor shows and dancing are held nightly in season. You can avoid a long hike across the hotel grounds by requesting a room in a lodge near the main building. Each lodge contains 15–30 sunny rooms featuring light woods and fabrics, private balconies, and views of the water. Most rooms have a TV, coffee maker, and hair dryer. The four suites have two bedrooms, three bathrooms, a living room, and a balcony. Regardless of the location of your room, you will be forced to do a fair amount of walking at this sprawling resort; and the lodges don't have elevators. The hotel has its own sightseeing excursion boat and offers scuba diving and snorkeling from a private deep-water dock. The beach—not the island's best by any means—is a small strip of sand just below the pool. Guests can play on the resort's four tennis courts for $5 an hour ($7 after 6 PM), and racquets can be rented for $5 an hour. There is a children's playground, and children's activities are held in season. *11 Blue Hole Hill, Hamilton Parish CR 04, tel. 809/293–8333; in U.S. (except MA), 800/225–2230; in MA, 800/982–4770. 197 rooms, 4 suites, all with bath. Meal plans: BP, EP, MAP. Facilities: restaurant, 3 bars, nightclub, disco, beach, 2 coves, 4 cork tennis courts (2 lighted), freshwater pool, gift shop, children's playground, excursion boat, water sports. No credit cards.*

**Marriott's Castle Harbour Resort.** Bordered by Harrington Sound on one side and the Castle Harbour golf course on the other, this whitewashed hilltop resort is an impressive sight from the air. If "castle" conjures up images of King Ludwig, though, forget it. This is a big, busy, modern hotel geared to groups and conventions. The original Castle, which opened in 1931, was built by the Furness Withy Steamship Line as a hotel for steamship passengers traveling between U.S. and British ports. Since 1984 Marriott has spent $60 million in renovation and expansion, and four new wings are now connected to the original building by glass-enclosed skywalks: the two-story Golf Club wing, the Bay View wing, and the two nine-story

Harbour View wings, which descend in terraces to the water. Rooms throughout the hotel are identical, featuring upholstered wing-back chairs, windows dressed in ruffled valances, and heavy drapes with matching quilted bedspreads. All rooms have minifridges, and many have balconies. Suites boast wet bars, refrigerators, and huge balconies. The resort's two beaches are miniscule, but guests have access to a private beach on the south shore and to three pools, including an Olympic-size lap pool and a cascading pool. Tennis courts are $8 an hour (plus $4 for racquet rental), but the well-equipped health club is free to guests. The big draw is the 18-hole Castle Harbour golf course; designed by Robert Trent Jones, it is one of the best courses on the island. *Box HM 841, Hamilton HM CX, tel. 809/293–2040; in U.S., 800/228–9290. 375 rooms, 27 suites, all with bath. Meal plan: EP. Facilities: 2 restaurants; 3 bars; 2 beaches; beauty/barber shop; concierge; moped rental; 3 heated freshwater pools; 6 all-weather tennis courts; 18-hole golf course; shops; same-day laundry/dry cleaning; water sports; health club with exercise room, sauna, and whirlpool. AE, DC, MC, V.*

**Sonesta Beach Hotel & Spa.** A sloping, serpentine drive leads through landscaped lawns to this hotel, the only property on the island where you can step directly from your room onto a sandy south-shore beach. Set on a low promontory fringed by coral reefs, the six-story modern building has a stunning ocean view and direct access to three superb beaches. Totally refurbished in 1989, the Sonesta caters to guests who want an action-packed vacation: A social director coordinates bingo games, theme parties, movies, water sports, and other diversions. Vacationers seeking a quiet beachfront retreat will probably be happier elsewhere—perhaps at The Reefs (*see* below), adjacent to the Sonesta. A glass-enclosed entranceway leads to the enormous, low-ceiling lobby, where large groups are, it seems, always checking in or out. Guest rooms and suites are decorated in creams, island prints, and light woods. The two natural beaches on the 25-acre property are at Cross Bay and Sinky Bay, but beach lovers should insist on a Bay Wing minisuite that opens onto a private, man-made sandy beach. The split-level minisuites feature lacquered art deco and art nouveau furnishings, hair dryers, and VCRs. Sports facilities include an indoor pool under a huge glass dome, a well-equipped health spa (extra charge), and six tennis courts ($8 an hour; $5 for racquet rental). A shuttle bus transports guests between the hotel and South Road, at the top of the hill. *Box HM 1070, Hamilton HM EX, tel. 809/238–8122; in U.S., 800/343–7170. 365 rooms, 25 suites, all with bath. Meal plan: MAP. Facilities: 3 restaurants; 2 bars; nightclub; 2 beaches; beauty salon; concierge service; moped rental; heated indoor and outdoor freshwater pools; 6 tennis courts (2 lighted); shuttle bus; health spa with steam room, saunas, whirlpool, exercise and massage rooms; shopping arcade; game rooms; children's playground; water sports. AE, DC, MC, V.*

**Expensive–Very Expensive**

**Belmont Hotel, Golf & Country Club.** Occupying 110 acres between Harbour and Middle roads, this large, gray hotel was built at the turn of the century and has a distinctly British personality. As its name suggests, it's also a sports-minded resort: Golf and tennis pros are on hand to give lessons and organize golf scrambles and tennis round-robins (hotel guests pay a $10 greens fee and $5 an hour for lighted tennis courts). A social director coordinates a range of other activities. The enormous lobby, decorated with chandeliers and fresh flowers, bustles with the golf groups that frequent the hotel. Refurbished in 1988, the rooms are average in size (bathrooms are quite small), but their large windows admit plenty of light and create a sense of spaciousness. Mahogany Queen Anne furniture is mixed with wicker, and the bedspreads and drapes sport bold floral patterns on dark backgrounds. With views over the harbor and the resort's gardens and pool—one of the largest on the island—the rooms on the fourth floor are probably the best. The Hamilton ferry stops at the Belmont Wharf; it's a long haul up the hill from the wharf to the hotel, but a shuttle bus makes the trip regularly. *Box WK 251, Warwick WK BX, tel. 809/236–3101; in U.S., 800/225–5843. 149 rooms, 1 suite, all with bath. Meal plans: BP, MAP. Facilities: 2 restaurants, bar, beauty salon, heated freshwater pool, 18-hole golf course, 3 lighted tennis courts, shops, ferry dock, water sports. AE, CB, DC, MC, V.*

**Southampton Princess.** This hotel is much larger and livelier than its older sister, The Princess (*see* below) in Hamilton. This is not the place for those seeking a quiet retreat, but it's an excellent choice for anyone who enjoys planned activities, such as theme parties, bingo, aerobics, cooking demonstrations, and tennis matches. For families, it offers the island's best children's program, including parties and baby-sitting services. The six-story, ultramodern main building, which contains all rooms and suites, dominates a hilltop near Gibb's Hill Lighthouse; the 300-year-old Waterlot Inn restaurant (*see* Chapter 7, Dining) occupies a dockside spot on the north side, and the beach club is perched above the surf at South Shore Beach. A jitney churns over hill and dale to connect them all, and a regiment of staffers is on hand to assist you if you get lost. Rooms vary in size, but they're all decorated in soft corals and light woods, and all have plenty of marble in their spacious bathrooms. Obviously, oceanfront deluxe rooms are preferable; if possible, avoid rooms on the first three floors of the west and north wings, which overlook rooftops. Some of the elegant suites feature kitchens, dishwashers, and four-poster beds. Perks in the 54-room Newport Club include private check-in/out, complimentary Continental breakfast, hair dryers, bathrobes, and a business center. Guests pay a one-time $10 fee to use the health club; the greens fee is $16, and tennis costs $8 an hour ($4 an hour for racquet rental). *Box HM 1379, Hamilton HM FX, tel. 809/238–8000; in U.S., 800/223–1818. 598 rooms, 36 suites, all with bath. Meal plan: MAP. Facilities: 6 restaurants, 4 bars, nightclub, disco, 2 beaches, beauty salon, concierge, moped rental, heated indoor and outdoor freshwater pools, dive shop, 18-hole par-54 golf course, 11 tennis courts (3 lighted), health club, croquet, boccie court, shopping arcade, water sports. AE, DC, MC, V.*

**Expensive** ★ **The Princess.** Named in honor of Princess Louise, Queen Victoria's daughter who visited the island in 1883, this large pink landmark opened in 1884 and is credited with starting Bermuda's tourist industry. Refurbished in 1989, this traditional grand hotel retains a slightly formal atmosphere, and its staff provides swift, courteous service. The walls at the entrance to the Tiara Room restaurant are covered with pictures of the politicians and royals who have visited the hotel. Ideally located on Hamilton Harbour, the hotel now caters to business and professional people, convention groups, and other visitors who want to be near downtown Hamilton. Mahogany dominates the original six-story main building, and the two three-story wings are filled with light woods and art deco touches. Plush cream-colored upholstery, bedspreads, and drapes are used throughout the hotel, and most of the rooms and suites have balconies. There are several categories of suites, and all are large and sumptuous—the penthouse suite has a Jacuzzi. The Princess Club's amenities include Continental breakfast, and showers and changing facilities for travelers with late flights who want to swim after morning check-out. In high season a ferry makes regular runs across the harbor to the Southampton Princess (*see* above), which has excellent sports facilities (none of which is free to guests). The Hamilton Princess has no beach, but there are stretches of lawn with deck chairs for relaxing and sunning. In season, glittery Vegas-style shows are presented in the Gazebo Lounge. Details of the Royal Dine-Around plan are somewhat Byzantine, but essentially there are nine Princess restaurants from which guests can choose. *Box HM 837, Hamilton HM CX, tel. 809/295–3000; in U.S., 800/223–1818; in Canada, 800/268–7176. 422 rooms, 28 suites, all with bath. Meal plans: BP, EP, MAP. Facilities: 3 restaurants; 2 bars; nightclub; beauty salon; concierge; moped rental; heated freshwater pool; saltwater pool; putting green; private dock and ferry; shopping arcade; water sports; access to Southampton Princess for golf, tennis, health and beach clubs. AE, DC, MC, V.*

## Small Hotels

**Very Expensive**

**Harmony Club.** Nestled in lovely gardens, this two-story pink-and-white hotel was built in the 1930s as a private home and extensively renovated in 1990. The hotel has a couples-only policy, but a couple can be two aunts, two friends, or any other combination—only children are not welcome. The base rate covers everything, including meals, alcohol, and even two-seater scooters. Although such a package is ideal for people who don't like to stray too far from their accommodations, food lovers might prefer to experiment with the interesting cuisine offered elsewhere on the island. The spacious reception area has warm wood paneling; and the club lounge has a big-screen TV and an assortment of games, including cards, darts, and backgammon. Upon arrival, guests find complimentary champagne in their rooms, which are luxuriously decorated with Queen Anne furnishings and feature hair dryers, bathrobes, and coffee makers. All but 12 of the rooms have a patio or balcony. The hotel is not on the water, but it's only about a five-minute scooter ride to the south-shore beaches. Guests can partake of a host of activities during high season, from informal barbecues to twice-weekly tennis clinics to formal dances. *Box PG 299, Paget PG BX, tel. 809/236–3500; in U.S., 800/225–5843. 72 rooms with bath. Meal plan: AP. Facilities: restaurant, bar, freshwater pool, whirlpool, sauna, moped rental, putting green, 2 tennis courts. AE, CB, DC, MC, V.*

**Pompano Beach Club.** Expect a friendly, personal welcome when you arrive at this informal seaside hotel, owned and operated by the American-born Lamb family. Located on the western end of the island, adjacent to the Port Royal Golf & Country Club, the hotel was a fishing club until 1950. Today, it still appeals primarily to fishermen, water-sports enthusiasts, and anyone in search of a quiet, remote getaway. The main building is a crescent-shape, split-level structure of pink and white stone, containing the main dining room, a British-style pub, and a cozy lounge with a large stone fireplace. Spread across the luxuriant hillside are cabanas, one-bedroom suites, and deluxe rooms, all with balconies and ocean views. Living rooms in the suites have Queen Anne furnishings and velvet chairs, but elsewhere the decor is tropical, featuring rattan, light woods, and glass-top tables. All guest rooms have minifridges, irons, and ironing boards; some have kitchenettes. The cabanas are the best choice, not only because the rooms are larger than in the suites, but also because guests wake in the morning to a splendid ocean view through the bedroom window (suites have an ocean view through the living room window). Perched on a hill adjacent to the main building is an attractive pool and a small conference center. There's only a small patch of beach for sunbathing, and it's not easily accessible; serious beach goers are advised to head elsewhere. The hotel's new water-sports facility offers Sunfish, Windsurfers, paddle boats, and small glass-bottom boats for rent; at low tide guests can stroll 250 yards into the ocean, in waist-deep water. Sunsets viewed from this hotel are spectacular events. *32 Pompano Beach Rd., Southampton SB 03, tel. 809/234–0222; in U.S., 800/343–4155. 51 rooms, 23 suites, all with bath. Meal plans: BP, MAP. Facilities: restaurant, bar, heated freshwater pool, Jacuzzi, water sports, conference center. No credit cards.*

★ **The Reefs.** The pink lanais of this small, casually elegant resort are set in cliffs above the beach at Christian Bay, adjacent to the Sonesta Beach Hotel & Spa (*see* above). The pace here is sedate, offering guests a restful stay in a spectacular beachfront setting. Vacationers looking for action are better off at such sports-oriented resorts as the Sonesta, Elbow Beach, or the Southampton Princess (*see* above). In the pink Bermuda cottage that serves as the clubhouse, a small registration area opens onto a spacious, comfortable lounge, where a pianist or guitarist entertains nightly. Beyond the lounge lies the main dining room, with additional seating in a tropical glass-ceiling conservatory and on a large terrace. Dinner dances are held frequently during the high season. Another restaurant is the waterside Coconuts, which is popular for casual lunches and candlelight dinners under the stars. Two guest rooms are located in the clubhouse, but the best rooms are in the lanais around the pool and on the hillside above the sandy beach. Lanais near the beach are the most expensive. Earth tones and rattan predominate in the guest rooms; bathrooms are small, with beige-marble vanities and an adjoining dressing area. All rooms have balconies and a stunning ocean view. In addition to the lanais, there are seven secluded cottages, one a three-bedroom, two-bathroom unit. Changing rooms near the beach are available for travelers with late flights who want to swim after morning check-out. The tennis courts are free to guests. *56 South Rd., Southampton, tel. 809/238–0222; in U.S., 800/223–1363; in Canada, 800/268–0424. 49 rooms, 7 cottage suites, all with bath. Meal plans: BP, MAP. Facilities: 2 restaurants, 2 bars, beach, moped rental, heated freshwater pool, 2 tennis courts, water sports. No credit cards.*

**Stonington Beach Hotel.** A training ground for students of the Bermuda Department of Hotel Technology, this south-shore hotel has one of the friendliest, hardest-working staffs on the island. Like students everywhere, they make mistakes, but if you have a little patience and a sense of humor your stay here should be most enjoyable. The place has a warm, gracious atmosphere; the formal restaurant is excellent; and the beach at the bottom of the hill rivals any on the island. However, the hotel is terribly overpriced—it's one of the most expensive properties on the south shore—and simply does not offer the kind of amenities guests expect for the money. In size and style guest rooms can be compared with those in an upscale Holiday Inn. Set in two-story terraced lodges leading to the beach, each room features a balcony with an ocean view. The furnishings are modern, and the decor includes heavy drapes and quilted bedspreads in matching fabrics; a minibar is tucked into the small dressing area adjacent to the bathroom. The small hotel lobby gains much of its character from its beamed ceiling and large windows with graceful fanlights. The adjoining library features Regency furnishings, bookshelves, a fireplace, and TV. Weekly champagne receptions are held during the high season, and classical music is played in the attractive Norwood Dining Room. Use of the tennis courts is free. *Box HM 523, Hamilton HM CX, tel. 809/236–5416; in U.S., 800/223–1588; in Canada, 800/268–0424. 64 rooms with bath. Meal plans: BP, MAP. Facilities: restaurant, bar, beach, moped rental, heated freshwater pool, 2 tennis courts, library, game room, gift shop, water sports. No credit cards.*

**Expensive–Very Expensive**

**Glencoe Harbour Club.** Located in a manor house dating to the 1700s, this quiet, secluded inn on Salt Kettle Bay is a favorite of boaters. It is not a beachfront hotel, however: A tiny man-made beach offers deep-water swimming, sailing, and windsurfing, but for other beach activities guests must head to the Coral Beach & Tennis Club, where they are welcome. The lobby is small and unprepossessing, but a few steps away is a cozy wood-paneled lounge with a fireplace and nautical decor. Dining (and dancing in season) is in a chic room with velvet chairs, candlelight, and crisp napery. The waterside terrace is open for meals and frequent barbecues during high season. Rooms are in the main house (Number 10 has its original fireplace and Old World charm) or across the road in two-story pink-stone buildings with rambling decks. The individually decorated rooms have cathedral ceilings and elegant wicker furniture with bold plaid or flame-stitch fabrics. All rooms have balconies or patios, but the best rooms are those with a view of the harbor; the least expensive rooms overlook the garden. TVs can be rented. *Box PG 297, Paget PG BX, tel. 809/236–5274; in U.S., 800/468–1500; in Canada, 416/622–8813; in U.K., 071/730–7144. 33 rooms, 7 suites, all with bath. Meal plans: BP, MAP. Facilities: 2 restaurants, 2 bars, 2 heated freshwater pools, man-made beach. AE, MC, V.*

**Newstead.** This renovated manor house could accommodate only 12 people when it opened in 1923. Since then the elegant harborside hotel has expanded considerably, with brick steps and walkways now leading to several poolside units and cottages. Set amid tall trees and a profusion of flowering shrubs and plants, the main house and cottages are typically Bermudian—in fact, some of the cottages were originally private residences. The spacious drawing room boasts handsome wing chairs, traditional furnishings, fresh flowers, and a fireplace, and the less-formal lounge has large windows overlooking the harbor. A harpist entertains during dinner. The large guest rooms feature polished mahogany campaign chests with brass drawer-pulls, framed prints, and fresh flowers; sliding glass doors open onto a balcony. The units are oddly designed—the front door opens into the large dressing area adjoining the bathroom—but there is ample vanity space, as well as a coffee maker, trouser press, hair dryer, and heated towel rack. Radios and TVs can be rented. The hotel has no beach, but a private dock is available for deep-water swimming in the harbor, and guests have use of the facilities at the Coral Beach & Tennis Club, on the south shore, about 10 minutes away by cab. Men's and women's changing rooms by the pool allow guests to go straight from swimming to the Hamilton ferry at Hodsdon's Landing. Tennis costs $3.50 an hour, and tennis whites are mandatory. *Box PG 196, Paget PG BX, tel. 809/236–6060; in U.S., 800/468–4111. 47 rooms, 3 suites, all with bath. Meal plans: BP, MAP. Facilities: restaurant, bar, freshwater pool, private dock for deep-water swimming, men's and women's saunas, putting green, 2 tennis courts. No credit cards.*

★ **Waterloo House.** About a three-minute walk from the Hamilton ferry and the Front Street shops, this quiet retreat is so secluded you can easily pass by without noticing it. A pink archway and steps leading to the flower-filled patio from Pitts Bay Road were later additions to a house that predates 1815, when it was renamed in honor of the defeat of Napoleon. The white-column house faces the harbor, and a spacious harborside terrace filled with umbrellas and tables is used for outdoor dining and entertainment. The stately lounge is furnished traditionally, with oil paintings, wing chairs, and a large fireplace. The majority of the rooms are in the main house; others are in pink two-story stone buildings beside the pool and patio. The quietest rooms are on the second floor of the main house. Matching fabrics are used in the rooms' quilted bedspreads, dust ruffles, draperies, and valances. Bathrooms are large, and most have double vanities. TVs can be rented. Guests on MAP have dine-around privileges at Horizons & Cottages (*see* below) and Newstead (*see* above); the short golf course at Horizons is also open to guests. *Box HM 333, Hamilton HM BX, tel. 809/295–4480; in U.S., 800/468–4100. 28 rooms, 6 suites, all with bath. Meal plans: BP, MAP. Facilities: restaurant, bar, heated freshwater pool. No credit cards.*

**Expensive**

**Palmetto Hotel & Cottages.** Set amid tall shade trees on the banks of Harrington Sound, this casually elegant property was once a private home. The main building is a sprawling two-story pink-and-white structure typical of Bermuda. Adjoining the small reception area is the Ha'Penny, a very British pub, where tea is served in the afternoon. Twenty-four rooms are located in the main building, but the 16 rooms in cottages on the banks of the sound are the most luxurious. Most rooms have balconies with a good view of the water. The hotel's beach is small, but a complimentary shuttle ferries guests to a south-shore beach. In addition, guests can swim or snorkel off the hotel's private dock; windsurfing lessons are available. *Box FL 54, Flatts FL BX, tel. 809/293–2323; in U.S., 800/982–0026. 42 rooms with bath. Meal plans: BP, EP, MAP. Facilities: restaurant, bar, beach, private dock, saltwater pool. No credit cards.*

★ **Rosedon.** Notable for its spacious veranda and white iron furniture, this stately Bermuda manor attracts an older crowd—mostly of women—that appreciates the hotel's ambience, service, and proximity to Front Street shops. Some of the four rooms in the main house have leaded-glass doors and other Old

World touches; all other rooms are in two-story buildings arranged around a large pool in the back garden. Rooms are rather dark, despite their white wicker furniture and bright prints and wallpaper. Each has a minifridge, a coffee maker, and a small dining table. There is no restaurant, but breakfast, sandwiches, and light meals are served either in your room or under umbrellas by the pool. Afternoon tea is served in the large lounges in the main house, where a TV and an honor bar are also located. The hotel has no beach of its own, but use of the beach and tennis courts at the Elbow Beach Hotel (*see* above) is free; transportation is provided for the 15–20 minute drive. *Box HM 290, Hamilton HM AX, tel. 809/295–1640; in U.S., 800/225–5567. 43 rooms with bath. Meal plans: BP, EP. Facilities: 2 lounges, heated freshwater pool, complimentary shuttle to beach, same-day laundry service. No credit cards.*

**Somerset Bridge Hotel.** About a three-minute walk from the Somerset Bridge ferry landing and within walking distance of Scaur Hill Fort, this three-story building resembles the kind of motels found on U.S. turnpikes. Its position on pretty Ely's Harbour makes it ideal for water-sports enthusiasts and those who want to explore the West End. The hotel has no charm, however, and no appeal whatsoever for anyone primarily interested in Hamilton's shops or the south-shore beaches. It's also overpriced. All of the apartments have kitchenettes and utensils, and most have Murphy beds, which leave little room for moving about when they're pulled down. This is the home of the Blue Foam (*see* Chapter 7, Dining), a good place to eat when you're ambling around this part of the island. *Box SB 149, Sandys SB BX, tel. 809/234–1042; in U.S., 800/468–5501. 24 apartments with bath. Meal plans: CP, EP, MAP. Facilities: restaurant, bar, small beach, freshwater pool, Jacuzzi. AE, MC, V.*

**Moderate–Expensive**

**Willowbank.** On a high promontory overlooking Ely's Harbour, this former home is essentially a Christian religious retreat. Morning devotionals are held in a lounge, for those who wish to attend, and grace is said before meals, which are announced by an ancient ship's bell and are served family-style. There is no proselytizing, however, and no pressure to participate in religious activities. The hotel is simply a serene alternative to the glitzy resorts; anyone who likes plenty of action will not be happy here. With their cedar paneling and fireplaces, the two large lounges in the main building are the focal point for quiet conversations, TV viewing, and afternoon tea; there are also a restaurant and library. Guests may have liquor in their rooms, but there is no bar. Located in one-story white cottages, the guest rooms are large and simply furnished—they have neither phones nor TVs. Rooms with an ocean or harbor view are the most desirable and expensive. No service charge is added to the bill and tipping is not expected, but the staff is friendly and helpful nonetheless. *Box MA 296, Sandys MA BX, tel. 809/234–1616. 58 rooms with bath; 2 double rooms share bath. Meal plan: MAP. Facilities: restaurant, 2 lounges, 2 small beaches, heated freshwater pool. No credit cards.*

## Cottage Colonies

**Very Expensive**
★

**Cambridge Beaches.** Within walking distance of Somerset Village in the West End (*see* Chapter 3, Exploring Bermuda), this outstanding resort occupies a beautifully landscaped peninsula edged with private coves and six pink-sand beaches. The original cottage colony (it opened in 1958), it remains a favorite among British and Saudi royalty, as well as a host of commoners. Many guests return year after year, attracted by the elegant style, superior water-sports facilities, and those unsurpassed pink-sand beaches. Registration is in a Bermuda-style clubhouse with large, elegantly furnished lounges. Candlelight dining and dancing take place in the lower-level restaurant and on the terrace, which has a splendid view of Mangrove Bay. A wide range of accommodations is offered—the entire peninsula is dotted with cottages—and prices vary considerably. Pegem is a 300-year-old, two-bedroom Bermuda cottage with a cedar-beam ceiling, English antiques, a den, and a sunporch. On the other end of the spectrum is Windswept, a two-unit cottage near the pool, that features one of the smallest, least expensive units in the colony. The decor differs from cottage to cottage, but antiques and fireplaces are common throughout; 30 cottages have Jacuzzis. Don't fret about being far from Front Street: A shopping launch makes twice-weekly trips from the resort's private dock. Ferry tokens are complimentary, as are the use of tennis courts, racquets, and balls. *Somerset MA 02, tel. 809/234–0331; in U.S., 800/468–7300. 61 rooms, 17 suites, all with bath. Meal plan: MAP. Facilities: restaurant, 2 bars, 6 beaches, heated saltwater pool, private marina, ferry, 3 tennis courts, putting green, water sports. No credit cards.*

**Fourways Inn.** About a five-minute ride from the ferry landing and the south-shore beaches, this luxury hotel has a sedate, formal ambience. Look elsewhere if you want exciting nightlife or if you plan to bring the kids—children under 16 are discouraged at the inn, and nothing here would interest them anyway. The architecture is typically Bermudian: The main building is a one-time family home that dates from 1727; the five cottages, set in a profusion of greenery and flowers, each contain a poolside suite and a deluxe upper-floor room. Marble floors and marble bathrooms are common throughout, and plenty of flowers give the rooms a bright freshness. In addition, each room has a balcony or terrace, a stocked minibar, a bar/kitchenette, and large closets paneled with full-length mirrors. Amenities in the suites include hair dryers, bath phones, bathrobes, and slippers. Guests receive a complimentary bottle of champagne on arrival, and homemade pastries and the morning paper are delivered daily to the door. The hotel serves a sumptuous Sunday brunch. *Box PG 294, Paget, PG BX, tel. 809/236–6517; in U.S., 800/962–7654. 5 rooms, 5 suites, all with bath. Meal plan: CP. Facilities: restaurant, bar, freshwater pool. AE, DC, MC, V.*

★ **Horizons & Cottages.** Oriental rugs, polished wood floors, cathedral ceilings, and knee-high open fireplaces are elegant reminders of the 18th century, when the main house in this resort was a private home. Today, the cottage colony maintains a formal atmosphere that appeals to an older crowd. Horizons Restaurant is a chic place for intimate candlelight dining; in pleasant weather, tables are set on the terrace. Monday-night rum swizzling is done downstairs in a wood-panel pub, where Austrian-born manager Wilhelm Sack makes every effort to see that guests (many of whom are European) are introduced. Guest cottages dot the terraced lawns, and each cottage has a distinct personality and decor: Most have two or three rooms and a large common room with a fireplace, library, and shelves of board games. Some of the spacious guest rooms feature white wicker furnishings, and others have an Old European flavor. Most cottages also have a kitchen, where a maid prepares breakfast before bringing it to your room. The hotel has no beach of its own, but guests may use the facilities of the Coral Beach & Tennis Club, within walking distance along South Road. Tennis courts cost $3.50 per hour and the greens fee for the short nine-hole golf course is also $3.50. *Box PG 198, Paget, PG BX, tel. 809/236–0048; in U.S., 800/468–0022. 45 rooms, 5 suites, all with bath. Meal plans: BP, MAP (combination also available). Facilities: restaurant, bar, heated freshwater pool, 3 tennis courts, 9-hole golf course, 18-hole putting green. No credit cards.*

**Lantana Colony Club.** A short walk from the Somerset Bridge ferry landing in the West End, this cottage colony is known for its lavish gardens and impressive (if sometimes bizarre) objets d'art. Several life-size sculptures by Desmond Fountain are dotted through the grounds, including a delightful rendering of a woman seated on a bench reading a newspaper. The solarium dining area in the main house is dazzling, with hanging plants and wall brackets of frosted Bohemian glass grapes. Rooms and suites come in a variety of sizes and configurations: lanais, split-levels, garden cottages, and "family houses" with two bedrooms, two bathrooms, and a living/dining room. Many guest rooms have parquet or tile floors and beamed ceilings and all have private balconies or patios. Lunch is a featured attraction here, something to bear in mind when you're tooling around the West End. *Box SB 90, Somerset Bridge SB BX, tel. 809/234–0141; in U.S., 800/468–3733. 56 suites, 6 cottages, all with bath. Meal plans: BP, MAP. Facilities: 2 restaurants, 2 bars, beach, freshwater pool, private dock, 2 tennis courts, putting green, croquet lawn, shuffleboard, water sports. No credit cards.*

**Pink Beach Club & Cottages.** With its two pretty pink beaches, this secluded, relaxing colony is a favorite of international celebrities. The location is a bit remote, however, and might not appeal to those who want to be near the shops of Front Street or the swinging resorts. Built as a private home in 1947, the main house has a clubby ambience derived from its dark-wood paneling, large fireplace, and beamed ceilings. Paved paths lace the attractively landscaped grounds and lead to 23 pink cottages and to the beaches. Each cottage contains four units, ranging from single rooms to two-bedroom suites with two bathrooms and twin terraces. Each spacious unit has wall-to-wall carpeting, wood paneling, and sliding glass doors that open onto a balcony or terrace. Extensive use is made of marble, complemented by white rattan furniture and light woods in some rooms, and by dark woods and velvet upholstery in others. The best accommodations are, of course, those near the beach. Breakfast is prepared by a maid and served in your room. Use of the tennis courts is free. *Box HM 1017, Hamilton HM DX, tel. 809/293–1666; in U.S., 800/372–1323. 14 rooms, 67 suites, all with bath. Meal plan: MAP. Facilities: restaurant, bar, 2 beaches, saltwater pool, 2 tennis courts, water sports. MC, V.*

**The St. George's Club.** Within walking distance of King's Square in St. George's, this ultramodern time-share property adjoins an 18-hole golf course designed by Robert Trent Jones. The sleek, three-story main building contains the office, activities desk, a game room, a restaurant, a pub, and the Club Shop, where you can buy everything from champagne to suntan lotion. In two-story white cottages sprinkled over 18 acres, the individually decorated apartments are huge and filled with sunlight. In some, stark white walls are offset by bright accent pieces and fabrics in muted colors. In others, sweeping bold designs draw upon the entire spectrum of colors. Each apartment has a full kitchen with dishwasher, fine china, and crystal. Bathrooms are large and lined with marble; some feature double Jacuzzis in dramatic settings. *Box GE 92, St. George's GE BX, tel. 809/297–1200. 61 suites with bath. Meal plan: EP. Facilities: restaurant, bar, 3 freshwater pools (1 heated), 18-hole golf course, putting green, tennis court, convenience store. AE, DC, MC, V.*

**Expensive–Very Expensive**

**Ariel Sands Beach Club.** This most informal of the cottage colonies surrounds Cox's Bay in Devonshire Parish, not far from the Edmund Gibbons Nature Reserve. The beach here is large and sandy, and a graceful statue of Ariel perches on a rock in the sea. The one-story white-limestone clubhouse, designed in Bermudian cottage style, contains the dining room and a lounge. A grand piano, a fireplace, and Oriental rugs give the resort an air of distinction. The large patio is ideal for outdoor dining, dancing, and barbecues in season. Two- to six-unit white cottages are set in the sloping, tree-shaded grounds. Guest rooms are small and furnished with white or natural rattan and island prints. Shakespeare's Dream has two bedrooms, one of which has a single bed. Rooms in the lowest price bracket have no ocean view. Tennis is free to guests. *Box HM 334, Hamilton HM BX, tel. 809/236–1010; in U.S., 800/468–6610. 48 rooms with bath. Meal plans: BP, MAP. Facilities: restaurant, bar, beach, freshwater pool, saltwater lagoon, 3 tennis courts (2 lighted), putting green, water sports. AE, MC, V.*

## Housekeeping Cottages and Apartments

**Expensive–Very Expensive**

**Marley Beach Cottages.** Scenes from the films *Chapter Two* and *The Deep* were filmed here, and it's easy to see why—the setting is breathtaking. Near Astwood Park on the south shore, the resort sits high on a cliff overlooking a lovely beach and dramatic reefs; a long path leads down to the sand and the sea. If you plan to stay here, pack light—there are a lot of steep steps, and you may have to carry your own luggage. The price is also steep, considering that you have to prepare your own meals. Each cottage contains a suite and a studio apartment, which can be rented separately or together, by families or friends. This is not a good place for children, and there's little to occupy them except the pool and the beach. The rooms are individually decorated, but all have large rooms, superb ocean views, private porches or patios, and fully equipped kitchens. Heaven's Above, the deluxe suite, is a spacious affair with two wood-burning fireplaces, tile floors, upholstered rattan furniture, and ample kitchen facilities. TVs can be rented, and groceries delivered. *Box PG 278, Paget PG BX, tel. 809/236–1143 (ext. 42); 809/236–8910; in U.S., 800/541–7426. 7 suites, 6 studios, all with bath. Meal plan: EP. Facilities: private beach, heated freshwater pool, whirlpool. No credit cards.*

**Expensive**
★

**Longtail Cliffs.** Don't be put off by the small office and the concrete parking lot that serves as the front yard of this motel-like establishment. Although it may not have the personality or splendid beach views of Marley Beach Cottages (*see* above), its relatively flat setting makes it much more suitable for elderly people or anyone who doesn't want to do a lot of climbing. Housed in a modern, two-story building, guest apartments are large, light, and airy, with balconies and ocean views. Each has two bedrooms and two spacious bathrooms decorated with brightly colored tiles. A small but well-equipped kitchen features a microwave oven, an iron, and an ironing board. Italian-tile floors grace the living areas and are accented by scatter rugs and high-quality white wicker furniture. Many units have beamed ceilings and some have fireplaces. There's a coin-operated laundry and a gas barbecue grill for cookouts. Despite its location on the south shore, the complex does not have a beach, although Horseshoe Bay is not far away. *Box HM 836, Hamilton HM CX, tel. 809/236–2864; 809/236–2822; in U.S., 800/541–7426. 14 apartments with bath. Meal plan: EP. Facilities: freshwater pool. No credit cards.*

**Moderate–Expensive**

**Angel's Grotto.** Some 30 years ago this was a swinging nightclub and one of the hottest spots on the island. Now, it's a quiet residential apartment house close to Devil's Hole Aquarium on the south shore of Harrington Sound. Don't come here if you want to spend a lot of time in Hamilton or on the beach—it's a long way from the best south-shore beaches. None of the one- or two-bedroom efficiencies (each with full kitchen facilities) is glamorous, but all are well-maintained by owner Daisy Hart and her efficient staff. Most of the guests are couples; the secluded Honeymoon Cottage is particularly appealing to those who want privacy. A large patio is ideal for cocktails in the evening, and there is also a barbecue. Deep-water swimming is possible in Harrington Sound. *Box HS 62, Smith's HS BX, tel. daytime, 809/295–6437; evening, 809/293–1986; in U.S., 800/541–7426. 7 apartments with bath. Meal plan: EP. Facilities: swimming in Harrington Sound. MC, V.*

**Moderate**
★

**Pretty Penny.** A three-minute walk from the ferry dock at Darrell's Wharf and 10 minutes by scooter from the south-shore beaches, this upscale lodging has one of the friendliest, most helpful staffs on the island. A two-story cottage next to a small shaded pool serves as the office and home of manager Ewan Kirkpatrick and his family. The grounds are small and offer no good views, but guest cottages are surrounded by trees and shrubs. Each room is brightened by a colorful tile floor and has a dining area and private patio. A small kitchen area features a microwave oven, refrigerator, and cupboards well-stocked with china, cooking utensils, and cutlery. TVs can be rented. If you want absolute privacy ask for the Play Penny, which is tucked away by itself. Across the street from the main house are a couple of quaint cottages that were being renovated at press time. Owner Steve Martin throws frequent cocktail parties so guests can get acquainted. *Box PG 137, Paget PG BX, tel. 809/236–1194; in U.S., 800/541–7426. 9 apartments with shower bath. Meal plan: EP. Facilities: freshwater pool. MC, V.*

**Inexpensive–Moderate**

**Barnsdale Guest Apartments.** Budget travelers who want to be near the south-shore beaches would do well to consider the small apartments in this two-story white cottage. The setting may not be spectacular, and the amenities are less than luxurious, but the units are clean and neat. Apartments with sofa beds can sleep four, but the four people must be able to get along well—the quarters are close. Kitchenettes have sufficient utensils to prepare light meals, and each has an iron and ironing board. Apartment Number 5 is a charmer—a somewhat larger, light, airy room decorated with colorful prints—but it's next to the pool area, which can become noisy. Long-distance calls can be made from a phone kiosk at the side of the house. *Box DV 628, Devonshire DV BX, tel. 809/236–0164; in U.S., 800/514–7426. 5 apartments with bath. Meal plan: EP. Facilities: freshwater pool. AE, MC, V.*

★ **Sky Top Cottages.** This establishment is aptly named—guests will be happy to have a scooter or taxi to climb the high hill on which the cottages sit. The ascent is worthwhile, though, because the views of the ocean from here are spectacular. Neat sloping lawns, paved walks bordered by geraniums, and a nearby citrus grove provide a pleasant setting for studio and one-bedroom apartments that are only five minutes by scooter from Elbow Beach. Although the furnishings are basic, the individually decorated units do have character. The friendly owners, Marion Stubbs and Susan Harvey, have decorated the rooms with attractive prints and carefully coordinated colors, and the property is well-maintained. Studio apartments have full kitchens and shower baths; one-bedroom apartments have limited kitchen facilities and full baths. Frangipani is furnished in white wicker and rattan and has an eat-in kitchen, a king-size bed, and a sofa bed. Honeysuckle is a three-level apartment with a sitting room, kitchen, dining room, and a bedroom and bathroom upstairs; each room is small but decorated in bright colors. A barbecue grill is available for guests' use. *Box PG 227, Paget PG BX, tel. 809/236–7984; in U.K., 071/242–9964. 11 apartments with bath. Meal plan: EP. No facilities. MC, V.*

**Inexpensive**

**Greenbank Cottages.** Located on a quiet dead end two minutes' walk from the Salt Kettle ferry landing, these one-story green cottages nestle among tall trees beside Hamilton Harbour. This is not a grand hotel—it's small and family-owned—but guests can count on plenty of personal attention from the Ashton family. In the 200-year-old main house, the guests' lounge has Oriental rugs, hardwood floors, a TV, and a grand piano; a billiards room is across the hall. There are two guest rooms in the main house; all other units are self-contained, with private entrances and shaded verandas. Most units have fully equipped kitchenettes for preparing light meals. The waterside cottages are the best choice, especially The Pink One—the view of the harbor from the dining table in the kitchen is lovely. Some simply furnished rooms are not air-conditioned, and none has a phone. There is no beach, but there is a private dock suitable for deep-water swimming, and Salt Kettle Boat Rentals is located on the property. *Box PG 201, Paget PG BX, tel. 809/236–3615; in U.S., 800/541–7426. 2 rooms and 7 apartments, all with bath. Meal plans: CP, EP. Facilities: private dock for deep-water swimming, billiards room. MC, V.*

**Whale Bay Inn.** Golfers approaching the 14th hole of the Port Royal course are sometimes baffled to find golf balls other than their own dotting the green. Little do they know that it's a mere chip shot from the front lawn of this new inn, and some guests can't resist the challenge to play through. Vacationers who want to be near good beaches or Hamilton's shops are better served elsewhere, however. The friendly Metschnabel family owns, operates, and lives on the premises of this small, attractive property in the remote West End. The ocean is visible beyond beds of flowers and the rolling lawn that surrounds the Bermuda-style pink building. At the bottom of the hill, a tiny patch of pink beach is tucked under the rugged cliff; it's pretty and private, but you'll have to do a fair amount of climbing to reach it. The decor of the guest rooms is contemporary, relying on rattan and muted prints. All five ground-floor units have a bedroom, a separate sitting room, and a private entrance. The two end units have larger bathrooms and are better-suited to families. Small, modern kitchens are equipped with microwave ovens, two-burner stoves, small refrigerators, cutlery, dinnerware, and cooking utensils. Groceries can be delivered from nearby markets. *Box SN 544, Southampton SN BX, tel. 809/238–0469; in U.S., 800/541–7426. 5 apartments with bath. Meal plan: EP. No facilities. No credit cards.*

## Guest Houses

**Moderate** **Edgehill Manor.** Atop a high hill surrounded by gardens and shrubs, this large colonial house is within easy walking distance of downtown Hamilton. Anyone wanting to spend a lot of time on the beach should stay elsewhere, however—the best south-shore beaches are 15–20 minutes away by scooter. The staff is friendly and helpful, and guests are guaranteed plenty of personal attention. In the morning, feast on home-baked muffins and scones in the cheery breakfast room, which is decorated with white iron chairs, glass-top tables, and vivid wallpaper. The individually decorated guest rooms feature French provincial furniture, colorful quilted bedspreads, large windows, and terraces. If you want air-conditioning be sure to request it—the four upstairs rooms have ceiling fans only. A large poolside room has a kitchen and is suitable for families. Anyone traveling alone on a tight budget should ask for the small ground-level room that offers a kitchen and private terrace. *Box HM 1048, Hamilton HM EX, tel. 809/295–7124. 9 rooms with bath. Meal plan: CP. Facilities: freshwater pool. No credit cards.*

**Granaway Guest House & Cottage.** In the 18th and 19th centuries, this 1734 manor house on Hamilton Harbour was used as a storehouse for pirate's booty. Surrounded by mounds of shrubbery, the house is a bit hard to find even today. A pay phone, a coffee maker, and disposable cups (guests can help themselves to coffee), set the tone for the poky entrance hall. The Continental breakfast, served in the garden with antique silver and Herend china, is far more pleasant. The large Pink Room, in the main house, has a king-size bed, white wicker furniture, and soft prints. The Strawberry Room was once the kitchen of the main house. The old hearth remains, and the room is now decorated with a patchwork quilt and scarred cedar beams; the walls and rafters are adorned with ceramic strawberries and other gifts from repeat guests. The Cottage, formerly the slave quarters, has a fully equipped modern kitchen, a phone, hand-painted tile floors, and its own entrance and lawn. The other guest rooms are nondescript. There is no beach—south-shore beaches are 10–15 minutes away by scooter—but the waterside patio can be used for deep-water swimming and snorkeling. In the evening, guests gather on the patio for cocktails. *Box WK 533, Warwick WK BX, tel. 809/236–1805; in U.S., 800/541–7426. 4 rooms, 1 cottage, all with bath. Meal plans: CP, EP. Facilities: waterside patio, TVs provided on request. MC, V.*

★ **Oxford House.** This is the closest you can get to downtown Hamilton without pitching a tent. The two-story establishment is popular with older people and is an excellent choice for shoppers. It is family-owned and operated, and guests receive friendly, personal attention. Just off the small entrance hall a fireplace and colorful floral tablecloths lend warmth to the breakfast room, where guests sample scones, English muffins, fresh fruit, and cereal in the morning; tea is served here in the afternoon. The rooms (doubles, triples, and quads) are bright and airy and are decorated with white rattan and bold fabrics. Two of the rooms have shower baths only. A small bookcase in the upstairs hall is crammed with paperbacks and serves as a library for guests. *Box HM 374, Hamilton HM BX, tel. 809/295–1503; in U.S., 800/548–7758. 12 rooms with bath. Meal plan: CP. No facilities. No credit cards.*

**Inexpensive–Moderate**

**Loughlands Guest House & Cottage.** Built in 1920, this stately white mansion sits on a green hill above South Road, a mere 5-minute ride by scooter from the best beaches. The house contains an eclectic collection of fine antiques and flea-market bric-a-brac. China figurines grace the mantelpiece in the formal parlor; grandfather clocks stand in corners; and handsome breakfronts display Wedgwood and cut glass. There are an Empire chaise longue, an elegant pink-satin prie-dieu, and a refrigerator for guests' use in the upstairs hallway. A Continental breakfast of cereals, fresh fruit, croissants, and coffee is served in the enormous, well-appointed dining room. The guest rooms are not nearly as interesting as the public rooms, however. No two are alike—there are singles, doubles, triples, and quads—but the furnishings are functional at best. Some rooms are unattractively adorned with large overstuffed chairs and chenille spreads. There are additional rooms in a large cottage near the main house. *79 South Rd., Paget PG 03, tel. 809/236–1253. 19 rooms with bath, 6 with shared bath. Meal plans: CP, EP. Facilities: freshwater pool, tennis court. No credit cards.*

**Inexpensive**

**Hillcrest Guest House.** Set back from Nea's Alley in St. George's, behind a gate and gardens, this green double-gallery house dates to the 18th century. It's been a guest house since 1961, but owner Mrs. Trew Robinson says her father took in shipwrecked sailors in 1914, when this was a private home. Today, Mrs. Robinson offers personal attention and helpful advice to budget travelers. The upstairs and downstairs lounges are spacious and homey, decorated with Oriental rugs, treasured family pictures, and heirlooms. Although they are spotlessly clean, guest rooms lack the charm of the public rooms—they are Spartan, drab, and haphazardly decorated. No meals are served, but guests can keep refreshments in the refrigerator. The house is far from Hamilton and the best beaches. *Box GE 96, St. George's GE BX, tel. 809/297–1630. 10 rooms with bath. No facilities. No credit cards.*

★ **Little Pomander Guest House.** A little jewel in a quiet residential area near Hamilton Harbour, this is a find for budget travelers seeking accommodations near Hamilton. The house was professionally decorated with a keen eye for detail—nothing here is out of place. Soft colors, fresh flowers, and tastefully arranged sofas and chairs make the living room spacious and airy. Guest rooms are decorated in French provincial style: Plump pastel-colored comforters cover the beds; the shams, dust ruffles, drapes, headboards, and shower curtains are made of matching fabrics. Continental breakfast is served family-style in a sunny room where tables are set with china in a blue-and-white floral design. Guests may use the microwave oven and refrigerator, as well as a barbecue grill in the backyard. There's also a soda machine. *Box HM 384, Hamilton HM BX, tel. 809/236–7635; in U.S., 800/541–7426. 5 rooms with bath. Meal plan: CP. No facilities. No credit cards.*

★ **Salt Kettle House.** Set behind a screen of palm trees on Hamilton Harbour, this small secluded guest house attracts plenty of repeat visitors and is popular with boating enthusiasts. Just to the left of the entrance is a cozy lounge with a fireplace where guests gather for cocktails (BYOB) and conversation. A hearty English breakfast is served family-style in the adjacent dining room. Two guest rooms are located in the main house, and an adjoining apartment features a double bedroom, bathroom, living room, and kitchen. The best accommodations are in the waterside cottages, which have shaded patios and lounge chairs. Two of the cottages have a bed/sitting room and a kitchen. The Starboard, which accommodates four people, is a two-bedroom, two-bathroom unit with a living room, fireplace, and kitchen. Guest rooms overall are small, however, and are arranged haphazardly. The tiny kitchens have adequate utensils for preparing light meals. Only a few of the units are air-conditioned—some have heaters only. *10 Salt Kettle Rd., Paget PG 01, tel. 809/236–0407. 6 rooms with bath. Meal plan: BP. Facilities: deep-water swimming, lounge. No credit cards.*

# 9 The Arts and Nightlife

# The Arts

*by Honey Naylor*

Available in all hotels and tourist information centers, *This Week in Bermuda, Preview Bermuda,* and *Bermuda Weekly,* are free publications that list what's happening around the island. *The Bermudian* ($4) is a glossy monthly magazine that also carries a calendar of events. The Bermuda Channel (Channel 4), a local television station, broadcasts a wealth of information about sightseeing, restaurants, cultural events, and nightlife on the island. Tourist-related information can also be heard on an AM radio station, VSB-1160, between 7 AM and 12:30 PM. The island is so small, however, that virtually everyone knows what's going on—taxi drivers, in particular, have a good idea of what's hot and what's not. In truth, the arts scene in Bermuda is not extensive, and many of the events and performing groups listed below operate on a casual or part-time basis. **City Hall Theatre** (City Hall, Church St., Hamilton) is the major venue for a number of top-quality cultural events each year, although performances and productions are sometimes staged elsewhere on the island. Contact the **Box Office** (Visitors Service Bureau, tel. 809/295–1727) for reservations and information about all cultural events on the island. MasterCard and Visa are accepted.

In January and February the **Bermuda Festival** brings internationally renowned artists to the island for a series of performances. The two-month program includes classical and jazz concerts and theatrical performances. The 1991 festival includes appearances by classical and jazz trumpeter Wynton Marsalis, author James Thurber, the Dance Theatre of Harlem, the Royal Shakespeare Company, and the Flying Karamazov Brothers. Most of the performances take place in City Hall, although some are held in major hotels. Ticket prices range from $17 to $25 ($12 for students). For information and reservations, contact Bermuda Festivals, Ltd. (Box HM 297, Hamilton HM AX, tel. 809/295–1291) or the Bermuda Department of Tourism (*see* Government Tourist Offices in Chapter 1, Essential Information).

## Concerts

**The Bermuda Philharmonic Society** presents several programs throughout the year, including classical music concerts by the full Philharmonic and by soloists. Students of the Menuhin Foundation, established in Bermuda by virtuoso violinist Yehudi Menuhin, sometimes perform with the orchestra. On February 16–17, the Philharmonic will perform *The Creation* by Joseph Haydn. Concerts take place either in City Hall Theatre (*see* above) or the Cathedral of the Most Holy Trinity in Hamilton (*see* Chapter 3, Exploring Bermuda).

**The Gilbert & Sullivan Society of Bermuda** mounts a musical production each year, usually in October. In addition to Gilbert and Sullivan operettas, the group occasionally does Broadway shows.

## Dance

The **Gombey Dancers,** a Bermudian dance group, perform each week as part of the off-season (mid-November–March 31) fes-

## The Arts and Nightlife

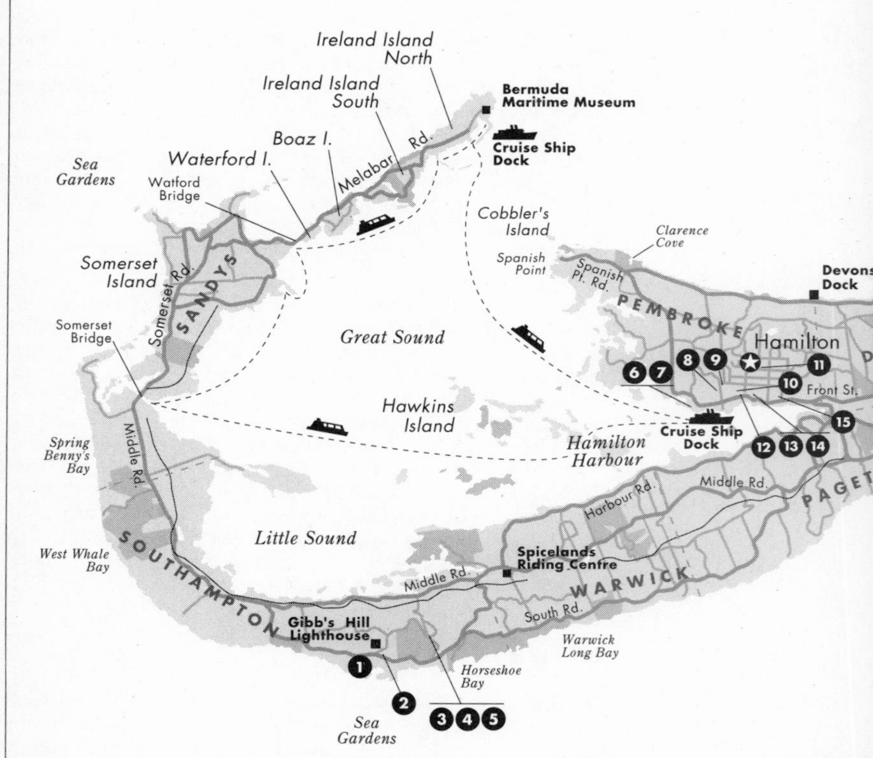


Blossoms Bar, **19**
Casey's, **9**
City Hall Theatre, **11**
The Clayhouse Inn, **16**
The Club, **8**
Colony Pub, **15**
Empire Room, **5**
Gazebo Lounge, **6**
Henry VIII, **2**
Hog Penny Pub, **12**
Lillian's, **1**
Load of Mischief Pub, **10**
Neptune Lounge, **3**
The Oasis, **14**
Prospero's Cave, **18**
Ram's Head Inn, **7**
Swizzle Inn, **17**
Touch Club, **4**
Wharf Tavern, **20**
Yuk Yuk's, **13**

Tobacco Bay
Fort St. Catherine
St. Catherine Beach
ST. GEORGE'S
St. George's Island
20
St. George's
St. George's Harbour
Cruise Ship Dock
Ferry Rd.
St. David's Rd.
Sea Gardens
Coney Island
17
18
The Causeway
Kindley Field Rd.
Bermuda Airport
Bermuda Perfumery
Bermuda Pottery
Blue Hole
St. David's Island
St. David's Lighthouse
Crawl Hill North
Crystal Caves
Leamington Caves
HAMILTON
Church Bay
Harrington Sound Rd.
Castle Harbour
19
TUCKER'S TOWN
Aquarium, Museum, and Zoo
Harrington Sound
Sea Gardens
North Shore Rd.
16
Harrington Sound Rd.
SMITH'S
John Smith's Bay
N
ONSHIRE
South Rd.
KEY
Cruise Ship
Ferry
Railway Trail
0
2 miles
0
3 km

tivities. Gombey (pronounced "gum-bay") dancing is a blend of African, West Indian, and American Indian influences. The Gombey tradition in Bermuda dates to the mid-18th century, when costumed slaves celebrated Christmas by singing and marching through the streets. The masked male dancers move to the accompaniment of skin-covered drums, called gombeys, and the shrill whistle commands of the captain of the troupe. The ritualistic, often frenetic movements of the dancers, the staccato drum accompaniment, and the whistle commands are passed from generation to generation. Dancers wear colorful costumes that include tall headdresses decorated with peacock feathers and tiny mirrors. On all major holidays the Gombeys dance through the streets, attracting large crowds of followers. It's traditional to toss coins at the feet of the dancers.

**The Bermuda Civic Ballet** performs classical ballets at various venues during the year. Internationally known artists sometimes appear as guests.

### Movies

Bermuda has three cinemas showing first-run movies—two are in Hamilton and the third is in the West End. Check the listings in the *Royal Gazette* for movies and show times.

**Neptune Cinema** (The Cooperage, Dockyard, tel. 809/238–9432 or 809/234–1709) is a 250-seat cinema that shows feature films at night. During the day, it runs *The Attack on Washington,* a multimedia account of Bermuda's role in the sacking of Washington, DC, during the War of 1812.

**The Little Theatre** (Queen St., Hamilton, tel. 809/292–2135) is a 173-seat theater across the street from Casey's Bar. Show times are usually 2:15, 7:15, and 9:30 daily.

**Liberty Theatre** (corner Union and Victoria Sts., Hamilton, tel. 809/292–7296) is a 270-seat cinema located in an unsavory section of Hamilton. The area is safe during the day, but visitors should avoid it after dark. Show times are usually at 2:15, 7:15, and 9:30.

### Theater

Bermuda is the only place outside the United States where **Harvard University's Hasty Pudding Theatricals** are performed. For almost 30 years, the satirical troupe has performed on the island during Bermuda College Weeks (March–April). Produced by the estimable Elsbeth Gibson, an American-born actress/producer who lives in Bermuda, each show incorporates political and social themes and issues of the past year. The Hasty Pudding Theatricals are staged in the City Hall Theatre (*see* above); ticket prices are about $17.

## Nightlife

During high season all hotels and cottage colonies feature entertainment—barbecues, steel bands, dinner dancing, and other diversions. Otherwise, the island's nightlife is fairly subdued; there are no casinos and only a few nightclubs and discos. Much of the action occurs in the pubs and lounges, which range from hotel bars to local hangouts. Some places close during the off-season, so check *This Week in Bermuda* and *Preview Bermuda* (*see* above) for the latest information about what's happening each night. As a general rule, men should wear a jacket and tie to clubs; for ladies the dress code is smart but casual. Pubs and discos begin to fill up around 9:30 or 10.

The music scene is dominated by local acts and bands playing the island's hotel and pub circuits. Occasionally, outside performers are billed, particularly during the Bermuda Festival (*see* above). The island superstar is **Gene Steede,** a guitarist, singer, and comedian who has been described as Tony Bennett, Harry Belafonte, and Johnny Carson rolled into one. Steede and his trio often headline the local shows at the two Princess hotels (*see* Cabaret, below). Among the other popular entertainers to watch for are the **Talbot Brothers,** calypso singers and instrumentalists, the **Bermuda All-Star Steel Band,** the **Coca-Cola Steel Band,** and the **Bermuda Strollers.** You can catch **Mike Meredith,** a popular folk singer/political satirist, at the Hog Penny, Henry VIII (*see* below), and other pubs on the entertainment circuit. **Electronic Symphony** is a glitzy show band that performs an eclectic selection of pop, country, gospel, rock, and island music. **Jimmy O'Connor** heads a band that plays Kenny Rogers and Neil Diamond tunes, as well as island music and '50s hits. The **Shinbone Alley Cats** play Dixieland jazz, and the flamboyant trio of **Tino and Friends** plays a mix of classics and standards. **Sharx** is a rock band; the **Travellers** straddle country and rock music.

Around 3 AM, when the bars and discos close, head for the **Ice Queen** (Middle Rd., Paget, tel. 809/236–3136). This place is like a drive-in movie without the movie—the parking lot is jammed with cars and mopeds. The main attraction is the $2.50 burgers, which are probably the best on the island. You don't sit down here—there's just a take-out window where you line up to place your order—but it's *the* place to be after hours.

## Bars and Lounges

Almost anyone will tell you that **Casey's** (Queen St., across from the Little Theatre, Hamilton, tel. 809/295–9549) is the best bar on the island. It's not fancy, nor is it touristy by any means. It's just a bar—a narrow room with a juke box and a few tables—but the place packs them in, especially on Friday night. It's open 10–10 every day except Sunday. **Blossoms Bar** (Marriott's Castle Harbour Resort, Paynters Rd., Hamilton Parish, tel. 809/293–2040) is a popular meeting place for young professionals, as is the **Colony Pub** (The Princess, Pitts Bay Rd., Hamilton, tel. 809/295–3000), where the lights are low and the piano music is soft and soothing. **Henry VIII** (South Shore Rd., Southampton, tel. 809/238–1977) is a wild and popular place with a devoted following of locals of all ages, who like its piano player, its sing-alongs, and its British ambience. The **Hog Penny Pub** (Burnaby St., between Front and Reid Sts., Hamilton, tel. 809/292–2534) has a nightly lineup of local talent, and the **Load of Mischief Pub** at Rum Runners (60 Front St., Hamilton, tel. 809/292–4737) hosts local bands nightly, attracting a crowd of young locals and tourists. In the Bailey's Bay area, the **Swizzle Inn** (Middle Rd., Hamilton Parish, tel. 809/293–1854) is strictly for the young, with a dart board, a juke box that plays soft and hard rock, and business cards from all over the world tacked on the walls, ceilings, and doors. The yachting crowd gathers at the **Wharf Tavern** (Somers Wharf, St. George's, tel. 809/297–1515) for rum swizzling and nautical talk. **Lillian's** (Sonesta Beach Hotel & Spa, off South Rd., Southampton, tel. 809/238–8122) is a chic, art nouveau restaurant where a sedate crowd dances to the music of a trio.

## The Club Scene

**Cabaret** There are Las Vegas–style tourist shows at the Hamilton Princess and Southampton Princess hotels during high season. The **Gazebo Lounge** (The Princess, Pitts Bay Rd., Hamilton, tel. 809/295–3000), a 280-seat nightclub, and the 750-seat **Empire Room** (Southampton Princess, South Rd., Southampton, tel. 809/238–8000) feature two shows nightly from mid-April to mid-November. Local entertainers perform at the 9:30 show, and the glitz-and-glitter international show takes the stage at 10:45. At both places, a $29 cover charge includes two drinks and the two shows.

**Calypso** The **Clayhouse Inn** (North Shore Rd., Devonshire, tel. 809/292–3193) is a dark dive that packs in locals and tourists for a rowdy show involving limbo dancers, calypso singers, fire eaters, steel bands, and an occasional top-name entertainer. The pace picks up around 9:30. A $12.50 cover charge includes one drink. The ambience is considerably more sophisticated at the **Neptune Lounge** (Southampton Princess, South Rd., Southampton, tel. 809/238–8000), a posh establishment with a small dance floor, large-screen TV, and live calypso music nightly until 1 AM during high season.

**Comedy** On the international comedy circuit, **Yuk Yuk's** (Emporium Bldg., Front St., Hamilton, tel. 809/295–9857) is in the Bambu Lounge of The Oasis disco (*see* below). The $15 charge covers the show and admission to the disco. A package deal for $39.95 (plus tips) includes a three-course dinner at the Conch Shell (*see* Chapter 7, Dining), admission to the show, and dancing.

## Discos

**The Club** (Bermudiana Rd., Hamilton, tel. 809/295–6693) is a ritzy room with red velvet, brass, and mirrors, that attracts an older professional crowd. Open for dancing every night from 10 PM to 3 AM, the disco also hosts Club Hour, on Friday from 5 PM to 7 PM. The $8 admission fee is waived if you have dinner at The Harbourfront, La Trattoria, Tavern on the Green, or Little Venice beneath the disco (*see* Chapter 7, Dining). **The Oasis** (Emporium Bldg., Front St., Hamilton, tel. 809/292–4978 or 809/292–3379) is a hot spot for a slightly younger crowd that gladly pays the $8 cover charge. Another trendy place where the young come to show off the latest fashions is the **Touch Club** (Southampton Princess, South Rd., Southampton, tel. 809/238–8000), a clubby disco decorated with glass bricks and leather. The $10, two-drink-minimum charge is waived during the off-season; dancing is from 9 PM to 1 AM. At **Prospero's Cave** (Grotto Bay Beach Hotel & Tennis Club, 11 Blue Hole Hill, Hamilton Parish, tel. 809/293–8333), you can dance from 9 PM to 1 AM beneath the stalactites in a huge underground cave. A DJ spins the disks for a young crowd.

# Index

# Personal Itinerary

**Departure** *Date*

*Time*

**Transportation**

**Arrival** *Date* *Time*

**Departure** *Date* *Time*

**Transportation**

**Accommodations**

**Arrival** *Date* *Time*

**Departure** *Date* *Time*

**Transportation**

**Accommodations**

**Arrival** *Date* *Time*

**Departure** *Date* *Time*

**Transportation**

**Accommodations**

*Personal Itinerary*

**Arrival** *Date* *Time*

**Departure** *Date* *Time*

**Transportation**

**Accommodations**

**Arrival** *Date* *Time*

**Departure** *Date* *Time*

**Transportation**

**Accommodations**

**Arrival** *Date* *Time*

**Departure** *Date* *Time*

**Transportation**

**Accommodations**

**Arrival** *Date* *Time*

**Departure** *Date* *Time*

**Transportation**

**Accommodations**

*Personal Itinerary*

**Arrival** *Date* *Time*

**Departure** *Date* *Time*

**Transportation**

**Accommodations**

**Arrival** *Date* *Time*

**Departure** *Date* *Time*

**Transportation**

**Accommodations**

**Arrival** *Date* *Time*

**Departure** *Date* *Time*

**Transportation**

**Accommodations**

**Arrival** *Date* *Time*

**Departure** *Date* *Time*

**Transportation**

**Accommodations**

*Addresses*

*Name*

*Address*

*Telephone*

*Name*

*Address*

*Telephone*

*Name*

*Address*

*Telephone*

*Name*

*Address*

*Telephone*

*Name*

*Address*

*Telephone*

*Name*

*Address*

*Telephone*

*Name*

*Address*

*Telephone*

*Name*

*Address*

*Telephone*

*Name*

*Address*

*Telephone*

*Name*

*Address*

*Telephone*

*Name*

*Address*

*Telephone*

*Name*

*Address*

*Telephone*

*Name*

*Address*

*Telephone*

*Name*

*Address*

*Telephone*

*Name*

*Address*

*Telephone*

*Name*

*Address*

*Telephone*

# Fodor's Travel Guides

## U.S. Guides

Alaska
Arizona
Boston
California
Cape Cod
The Carolinas & the Georgia Coast
The Chesapeake Region
Chicago
Colorado
Disney World & the Orlando Area
Florida
Hawaii
Las Vegas
Los Angeles
Maui
Miami & the Keys
New England
New Mexico
New Orleans
New York City
New York City (Pocket Guide)
Pacific North Coast
Philadelphia & the Pennsylvania Dutch Country
Puerto Rico (Pocket Guide)
The Rockies
San Diego
San Francisco
San Francisco (Pocket Guide)
The South
Texas
USA
The Upper Great Lakes Region
Vacations in New York State
Vacations on the Jersey Shore
Virgin Islands
Virginia & Maryland
Waikiki
Washington, D.C.

## Foreign Guides

Acapulco
Amsterdam
Australia
Austria
The Bahamas
The Bahamas (Pocket Guide)
Baja & the Pacific Coast Resorts
Barbados
Belgium & Luxembourg
Bermuda
Brazil
Budget Europe
Canada
Canada's Atlantic Provinces
Cancun, Cozumel, Yucatan Peninsula
Caribbean
Central America
China
Eastern Europe
Egypt
Europe
Europe's Great Cities
France
Germany
Great Britain
Greece
The Himalayan Countries
Holland
Hong Kong
India
Ireland
Israel
Italy
Italy 's Great Cities
Jamaica
Japan
Kenya, Tanzania, Seychelles
Korea
Lisbon
London
London Companion
London (Pocket Guide)
Madrid & Barcelona
Mexico
Mexico City
Montreal & Quebec City
Morocco
Munich
New Zealand
Paris
Paris (Pocket Guide)
Portugal
Rio de Janeiro
Rome
Saint Martin/ Sint Maarten
Scandinavia
Scandinavian Cities
Scotland
Singapore
South America
South Pacific
Southeast Asia
Soviet Union
Spain
Sweden
Switzerland
Sydney
Thailand
Tokyo
Toronto
Turkey
Vienna & the Danube Valley
Yugoslavia

## Wall Street Journal Guides to Business Travel

Europe
International Cities
The Pacific Rim
USA & Canada

## Special-Interest Guides

Cruises and Ports of Call
Healthy Escapes
Fodor's Flashmaps New York
Fodor's Flashmaps Washington, D.C.
Shopping in Europe
Skiing in North America
Smart Shopper's Guide to London
Sunday in New York
Touring Europe